D1084634

WITHDRAWN

Perspectives in Sociology

HERMAN R. LANTZ, GENERAL EDITOR

ADVISORY EDITORS

ALVIN W. GOULDNER, *Washington University*

ROBERT A. NISBET, *Columbia University*

MELVIN M. TUMIN, *Princeton University*

JERRY GASTON, *Southern Illinois University*

Ransom Kidnapping
in America / 1874–1974

The Creation of a Capital Crime

Ernest Kahlar Alix

SOUTHERN ILLINOIS UNIVERSITY PRESS

CARBONDALE AND EDWARDSVILLE

F E F F E R & S I M O N S , I N C .

LONDON AND AMSTERDAM

DELTA COLLEGE
LEARNING RESOURCES CENTER

SEP - 1978

HV 6598 .A54 1978

Alix, Ernest Kahlar.

Ransom kidnapping in
  America, 1874-1974

Copyright © 1978 by Southern Illinois University Press
All rights reserved
Printed in the United States of America
Designed by Guy Fleming

Grateful acknowledgment is made for permission to
quote from the New York Times: © 1874–1974 by
The New York Times Company. Reprinted by
permission.

Library of Congress Cataloging in Publication Data

Alix, Ernest Kahlar.
Ransom kidnapping in America, 1874–1974.

(Perspectives in sociology)
Includes bibliographical references and index.
1. Kidnapping—United States—History.
2. Ransom—United States—History. 3. Criminal law—United States—History.
I. Title. II. Series.
HV6598.A54 364.1'54'0973 78-1985
ISBN 0-8093-0849-5

To the memory of

DEAN EGGERT GIERE *of North Central College*

Contents

Preface

THE FIRST RANSOM KIDNAPPING IN AMERICA, as we know it today, apparently occurred in 1874. In the ensuing one hundred years, ransom kidnapping evolved from a shocking, but modestly punished, act into a capital crime in forty-five states and under federal law. Only murder was a capital crime in more American jurisdictions. Some of the most sensational episodes in the annals of American crime involved ransom kidnapping: the ransom slaying of Robert Franks by Leopold and Loeb in 1924, the Lindbergh case in 1932, and the Hearst case in 1974. In spite of these circumstances, the crime and the creation of the laws have never been subjected to scholarly research. This book reports the findings of a sociological investigation aimed at remedying the deficiency.

The method of study had to be appropriate for an exploratory investigation: an investigation concerned with describing a previously unstudied phenomenon as much as with analyzing it. The method had to be suitable for studying the operation of a social process over an extended period of time. Finally, the method had to yield data which might reveal not only actions taken by officials and the public in response to the crime but also their beliefs about ransomings and about law creation as a crime control strategy. A sociohistorical method (a method of study in which historical data are analyzed from a sociological perspective) was selected as best meeting these requirements.

The initial plan of study was to use official crime rate data on ransom kidnapping to provide a numerical overview of the American experience with the crime, supplemented by newspaper accounts of ransom cases. The plan had to be revised when it was discovered that suitable official crime statistics on ransom kidnapping were not available. Kidnapping in any form is not included among the major offense categories covered in the FBI's *Uniform Crime Reports*, the main source of national crime statistics. Written inquiries to the Department of Justice and to the Law Enforcement Assistance Administration concerning the availability of unpublished kidnapping statistics brought replies that they were not available in any form from any federal agency.

Contrary to the replies from the agencies contacted, national kidnapping statistics, based upon admissions to the federal judicial system, have been furnished by the Federal Bureau of Prisons since 1933. However, these official statistics make no distinction among the fifteen forms which the crime can take. Since ransom kidnapping could not be isolated, the Federal Bureau of Prison statistics could not serve as an index of the crime for our purposes.

Annual reports to Congress from the Office of the U.S. Attorney General and the Office of the Director of the FBI provided another available but unsuitable source of national kidnapping statistics. These figures not only lacked continuity from one year to the next, but their reliability was highly suspect. One writer, for example, has noted the discrepancies in the kidnapping figures reported by one federal office as compared with the figures reported by the other.[1] Other writers maintain that the FBI did not bother to keep accurate kidnapping records "perhaps lest the facts injure the legend."[2] The comment of a leading student of capital punishment summed up the situation: "[E]xcept for disconnected bits of information which have appeared from time to time in hearings before Congress and in the reports of the U.S. Attorney General, we have no reliable information on the extent of this capital crime at all."[3]

The *New York Times* became the primary source of data on the crime and on reactions to it, including law creation. From its initial appearance in 1851 under another banner, the *Times* has furnished a remarkable index of the material contained in the newspaper. Except for 1860, and the period of June 1905 through December 1913, the continuity of the *New York Times Index* has been uninterrupted.[4] No other single source of historical data on American society is comparable as to its breadth, detail, or continuity. The *Index* and the material contained in the newspaper itself provided a detailed chronology of ransomings,[5] offenders and victims, and reactions to the crime. Material contained in other newspapers throughout the country was searched to the limits of the microfilmed archives available to the writer.[6] In addition, the *Times* reprinted articles and editorials from other newspapers on the occasion of sensational ransomings and significant reactions.

The *Times Index* also served as the chronological key for locating official government documents and proceedings. Data of this sort more readily were available for the federal than for state jurisdictions. All relevant documents and proceedings listed in the federal *Monthly Catalog of Government Publications* from 1874 through 1974 were searched. In addition, searches were made of the *Congressional Record, Reports of the U.S. Attorney General*, and the published proceedings of legislative committees and subcommittees. The chronology provided by the *Times Index* also facilitated searching of federal and state appellate court reporters.

Newspaper data are of questionable reliability and validity for many types of sociological research. As noted by one writer, sociologists "are especially wary about information reported in the newspapers because of the well-deserved reputation the press have for inaccuracy and selective reporting."[7] For a societal reaction perspective (a perspective which focuses on official and public reactions to crime as well as on crime itself), however, "selective reporting" itself is crucial data. Newspapers are the main source of detailed information about crime for most members of the social audience. It is upon the basis of this information, biased as it may be, that evaluations are made and actions taken.

The accuracy of newspaper reports nevertheless had to be scrutinized as to the facts of reported ransomings, the characteristics of the offenders and the victims, and as to the specific reactions generated. This was accomplished in the present study to the extent that given newspaper reports could be cross-checked against reports in other newspapers and against official documents and court records.

A major advantage of using the *New York Times* as a data

source is that it has been used extensively in sociohistorical research. Much is known about the nature of the selectivity and bias in the paper's reporting in general and about its reporting of crime and social unrest in particular.[8] In any case, as noted recently by an investigator who has utilized the *Times* as a primary data source, there are no universal standards for judging the sociological validity of data: "There are only standards of validity for given purposes."[9] For the purposes of this study, newspaper data are valid.

The crime data consist of all ransom kidnappings occurring in whole or in part within the United States, and reported in the *New York Times* from 1851 through 1974. The reactions studied are those that occurred in response to the ransom kidnappings, and as reported in the *Times* for the same period.

The crime data constitute indexes of the *reported incidence* of kidnapping and of ransom kidnapping in America. While we are confident that the indexes reflect major fluctuations in the actual incidence of kidnappings, the indexes clearly are biased in some respects, more so for the other types of kidnapping than for ransom kidnapping. The crime data are biased geographically; more kidnappings of all types which occurred in areas closest to New York City are reflected in the reported incidence figures than cases occurring in other parts of the country. The geographical bias is evident particularly for child stealing and domestic relations kidnappings. Because of the more sensational, and therefore more newsworthy, character of ransom kidnapping, however, the reported incidence figures for this variety of the crime are less subject to geographical bias. The same situation characterizes that portion of the reaction data gleaned from newspapers.

The law-creation data, as to the nature of the laws and the date of their creation, are complete on both the federal and state levels. The completeness of the data as to the circumstances surrounding the creation of the laws varies from jurisdiction to jurisdiction. We are confident, however, that the data on the circumstances surrounding the creation of the federal laws and the capital laws of the states are representative.

With no previous study available to serve as a comprehensive model, the mechanics of data collection, organization, and analysis involved much trial and error. Eventually a systematic procedure was developed for supplying every reference in the *New York Times* to kidnappings of all types from 1851 through 1974. Each newspaper account was read in its entirety, and information from the accounts was abstracted according to the format detailed in the Preface notes.[10] After the data in the *Times* were exhausted, the chronology provided by the *Times Index* concerning the events of each case and each reaction was used to search the other data sources described earlier. The procedure yielded a wealth of data on the crime, victims, offenders, official and public reactions, and law creation. During the six years required to complete the project, several persons exhibited incredible patience and understanding. Foremost among them were Kathleen and Christopher Alix, who tolerated a husband and father whose physical presence most times belied his mental absence.

Academic colleagues also extended themselves unreasonably. Appreciation is extended to the Graduate School of Southern Illinois University-Carbondale for summer research support, to Roger Beyler, former Dean of the College of Liberal Arts, and to Lon Shelby, present Dean. Special appreciation is extended to Charles Snyder, former Chairman of the Department of Sociology, and to Jerry Gaston, who succeeded him. Since the project was carried out without governmental or foundation research funds, their encouragement and unfailing support were vital.

Herman Lantz has served as mentor, friend, and colleague for fifteen years. From him I gained an appreciation for social history as an exciting method of study long before it became fashionable in the field. It is especially gratifying to have the opportunity to acknowledge his contributions in the present context.

Several present and former graduate students jeopordized their good eyesight for pay and for a first-hand survey of one hundred years of American history via microfilmed newspaper files: Gary Thompson, Max Schlueter, Randy Shelden, Young Hee Han, Marty Schultz, Jim Graham, Richard Liu, Mike Eley, and Nancy Balzadeh.

I wish to express my appreciation to Beverly Morber. In addition to her already-taxing secretarial duties in the department, she managed to type the original and each of several revisions of the manuscript. Finally, I wish to thank Teresa White for her personal enthusiasm and skilled copy-editing.

ERNEST KAHLAR ALIX

Carbondale, Illinois
August 1977

Introduction

A Sociological and Historical Perspective

ANY SCHOLARLY INVESTIGATION is guided by the particular perspective employed by the investigator. In this book, a societal reaction perspective was chosen as uniquely appropriate for viewing crime and law creation as interdependent components of man's efforts to maintain social order.

"Societal reaction" is a social process, a process in which individuals "alter their behavior in response to the suspicion that a deviant act has occurred or may occur." [1] A societal reaction perspective is characterized by its emphasis "on the nature of social rules . . . and the . . . reaction aimed at individuals who contravene such rules." [2]

When applied to crime, a societal reaction perspective emphasizes that crime, rather than being an inherent quality of an act, is a label given by some members of a society to behavior engaged in by other members, behavior which the labelers evaluate as threatening. Applied to law creation, the perspective views legislation as a product of a social process in which designated members of a society create formal rules (laws) threatening potential rule breakers with punishment. Law creating, then, is viewed as a dynamic social activity engaged in by persons who exhibit the full range of human strengths and weaknesses. Such a view contrasts sharply with the more traditional view of the legislative process as the terribly solemn activity of august solons, possessing awesome powers of rationality and uniquely qualified to assess and to act in the common good.

While the commission of any threatening act can initiate societal reaction, careful attention must be paid to the implications of specific acts for the societal reaction process initiated.

For ransom kidnapping, this task is complicated by the wide range of behaviors commonly labeled *kidnapping*.

Legal definitions of kidnapping traditionally have embraced "a wide and ill-defined range of behavior."[3] The legal basis of kidnapping is the taking or detention of a person against his will and without lawful authority. Closely associated with the crime of kidnapping is the separate crime of abduction, which also involves the unlawful taking of a person. In abduction, however, the illegality arises not from the lack of consent by the victim but from unlawful interference with a family relationship, such as taking a child from its parents without lawful authority even if the child consented.[4] Historically, the label "kidnapping" has been applied to a variety of unlawful takings ranging from manstealing, under colonial law, to the contemporary practice of a divorced parent taking their offspring from the spouse in violation of a custody decree. Using a combination of legal definitions, a typology proposed by two other writers,[5] and the unlawful takings of human beings commonly labeled kidnapping by the media, fifteen types of kidnapping were identified:

1) White Slavery: women kidnapped for commercial prostitution; 2) Hostage Situation: victim taken to facilitate the escape or protection of an offender during the commission of another crime; 3) Child Stealing: child taken from parent or lawful guardian without authority for reasons not covered in other types of kidnapping; 4) Domestic Relations Kidnapping: child taken by divorced or separated parent, or agent of parent, in violation of a custody decree; or unlawful taking of an adult family member to gain an advantage, usually financial; 5) Kidnapping for Rape or Other Sexual Assault: victim taken for sexual purpose other than commercial prostitution; 6) Kidnapping for Murder or other Nonsexual Assault: victim taken for purposes of murder or physical assault in order to coerce some action on part of victim or associates; 7) Kidnapping for Robbery: victim taken for purpose of being unlawfully deprived of property other than by payment of ransom; 8) Romantic Kidnapping: usually an abduction in which a minor voluntarily accompanies an offender against the wishes of a parent or

guardian for such purposes as elopement; 9) Ransom Skyjacking: skyjacking in which the primary motivation is ransom and sometimes a political motivation as well; 10) Ransom Kidnapping Hoax: a situation in which a ransom kidnapping is alleged to cover a variety of acts, such as extorting money from one's own family or associates, homicide, and runaways by minors; 11) Plot or Abortive Ransom Kidnapping: a ransom kidnapping plot uncovered prior to the taking of the victim, or an actual attempt aborted before a ransom demand is made; 12) Ransom Threat for Extortion: a situation in which ransom kidnapping is threatened to extort money; 13) Developmental Ransom Kidnapping: a ransoming which evolves out of another crime already in process, such as an adjunct to an armed robbery; 14) Classic Ransom Kidnapping: a situation in which the exclusive or primary motivation is the collection of ransom, the victim is taken and sequestered, the ransom demand is made, the ransom is collected or not collected, the victim is or is not released unharmed, and the offender does or does not escape with the ransom; 15) Miscellaneous Kidnappings: rare cases involving the unlawful taking of persons not falling within another category.

Of the fifteen categories of kidnapping contained in the typology, this study concentrated on Classic Ransom Kidnapping, primarily because it possesses unique qualities as to its potential for generating societal reaction.

Classic ransom kidnapping is the most visible among the types of unlawful takings. For most members of the population, the visibility of a crime is proportional to the amount of attention given to it by the mass media. Since classic ransom kidnapping usually requires a considerable amount of time to run its course, as compared to the other types, the opportunity for media coverage as the crime transpires is maximized, to say nothing of the publicity given to the legal aftermath.

Classic ransom kidnapping is condemned more uniformly than the other types of kidnapping and most other types of heinous crime. Little sympathy usually is extended to the offender, and it is difficult to attribute partial responsibility to the victim. Even rape and murder can elicit sympathetic reaction to the offender if it is felt that the victims were partially responsible for their plight. The rape of a prostitute or hitchhiker and the murder of a member of the underworld are examples.

To the extent that societal reaction to crime is affected by the social identity of victims and offenders, classic ransom kidnapping is unique in yet another respect. Wealthy and prominent members of the society are more likely to be victimized by ransom kidnapping than by any of the other types of unlawful takings. If the more wealthy and prominent members of society get uniformly better service from the criminal justice system than less wealthy and prominent members, as contended by radical critics of the system, then classic ransom kidnapping possesses different implications for law creating than the other types.

Efforts to maintain order in society involve several social control mechanisms in addition to the criminal law; among them, however, criminal law is crucial. Resorting to legal punishment threats, including death, to coerce conformity to social rules in many respects represents a last-ditch effort to maintain order in the face of a perceived crime control crisis. The perspective employed in this study emphasizes a number of features of the reactive social control process which spawns criminal laws.

A distinction proposed by a leading student of social control between "normative" and "actual" reactions to a suspected deviant act facilitates the refinement of the process into two phases. A normative reactions phase, in which the social audience evaluates the behavior in question, is followed by an actual reactions phase, in which the social audience takes action upon the basis of their evaluations.[6] Underlying normative reactions are beliefs held by members of the social audience about the type of reaction called for. Of particular significance to law creation as societal reaction are beliefs about the ability of legal punishment threats to deter potential violators. Indeed, it has been contended that this belief is a " 'primary and essential postulate' of almost all criminal justice systems." [7]

Societal reaction to deviance can be refined further if it is recognized that both normative and actual reactions have a dual focus: the act that has occurred and other actors who may repeat it. Normative reactions focused on the act are concerned with whether it is threatening enough to warrant any concrete action to prevent its recurrence and, if so, what action. Creating laws in the hope that fear of suffering the threatened punishment will deter potential repeaters is only one possible crime control strategy. A variety of other informal and formal strategies instead may be deemed adequate: calling upon the population to exercise moral constraint and thereby police themselves, or urging stricter enforcement of existing laws that could be extended to cover the act in question.

It is the normative reactions focusing on the actor, however, to which a belief in the deterrent efficacy of criminal laws is central. The extent to which such a belief is operative during normative reactions may be critical in explaining why the actual reactions take the form of law creation. In other words, while normative reactions focused on the heinousness of the act may explain why any concrete action at all is taken by reactors, normative reactions focused on the deterrability of potential offenders may explain specifically legislative reactions.

To this point in the description of the perspective, the "social audience" has been treated as a nebulous group of witnesses to an act, who may or may not react to it. Exactly who are these potential reactors, and where are they located in society? Knowing this information might help explain not only the sources of societal reaction to crime but also the nature of the reactions. The failure of sociologists to provide such information recently has been cited as a basic deficiency of the perspective.[8]

A variety of schemes was available for conceptualizing the societal locations of reactions to crime.[9] We drew upon several of them to conceptualize six reactive sectors: the mass media sector, the general public sector, the political sector, the law enforcement sector, the judicial sector, and the legislative sector.

Mass media sector. This reactive sector is comprised of the mass communications media, such as the press, radio, and television. The mass media are the main sources of public information about crime and laws. In addition to simple news reporting, members of the sector provide editorials and commentaries containing normative evaluations of crime and laws. The normative evaluations reflect beliefs held by members of the sector about the heinousness of deviant acts and about the deterrability of potential offenders by legal punishment threats. As one writer has observed: "A conception of crime is presented in the mass media. That conception, diffused throughout society, becomes the basis for the public's view of reality." [10]

General public sector. In this sector are located members of the social audience who do not occupy positions in any of the other sectors. The beliefs held by these potential reactors and the actions they take, support, or resist are crucial to the law-creating process. Public opinion carries weight with criminal justice policy makers, including legislators and jurists. The effect of public opinion on the latter was demonstrated recently in the 1976 *Gregg* decision of the U.S. Supreme Court. In the face of scientific evidence on deterrence judged inconclusive by the justices, the public's belief that the death penalty does deter potential murderers was decisive in the Court's upholding the constitutionality of certain capital murder laws. As written in the majority opinion of the Court: "In this posture of the case [the scientific evidence being inconclusive], it would be neither a proper or wise exercise of the power of judicial review to refuse to accept the reasonable conclusions of Congress and 35 state legislatures that there are indeed certain circumstances in which the death penalty is the more efficacious deterrent of crime." [11]

Political sector. In this sector, the normative and actual reactions of political officials and members of political bureaucracies at the local, state, and federal levels are of central interest. Political officials can exert considerable control over crime control policies and actions, as was revealed in the aftermath of Watergate. In addition, a range of political bureaucracies not directly involved in the criminal justice system can influence the workings of the system. The amount of such influence, however, and the specific ways in which it operates have not been appreciated adequately by sociologists of crime and law. The authors of a recent book on radical criminology wrote, for example: "[F]ew criminologists have been able to deal with the ways in which political initiatives that give rise to (or abolish) legislation, that define sanctionable behavior in society or ensure the enforcement of that legislation, are intimately bound with the structure of the political economy of the state." [12]

Law enforcement sector.   In this sector are located potential reactors charged directly with crime control in the society. They include the police, prosecutors, prison officials, and other members of crime control bureaucracies on the local, state, and federal levels. Reactions from members of this sector, or lack of reactions, frequently are at the heart of crime control controversies. Their beliefs about criminality and its control carry great weight with reactors in other sectors, as do their normative and actual reactions based upon such beliefs.

Judicial sector.   The judicial sector is treated apart from the law enforcement sector because of the strategic role of courts in the creation of law, as demonstrated by the *Gregg* decision. The exercise of judicial discretion in sentencing is an important actual reaction in its own right. In addition, sentencing decisions generate reactions from reactors located in the other sectors. Some members of the social audience applaud given decisions, others are outraged.

Legislative sector.   In this sector, at both the state and federal levels, are located the reactors most directly and publically implicated in the creation of law. The laws created and the rationales offered for them are rich sources of beliefs about law creation as a mechanism of social control. The legislative sector, while influenced by reactions from other sectors, is the focal point of the reaction context in which behaviors are labeled crimes and punishment threats are posed to prevent others from repeating them.

Crime and law creation are viewed as interdependent components of a social control process which operates over time. In broadest outline, we propose that the process operates in the following manner. The occurrence of a nonconforming act generates normative reactions by members of the social audience. Depending upon the quality and scope of the normative reactions, a variety of actual reactions may follow, one of which is law creation.

Early in the reaction process, a variety of normative reactions is possible. Consensus could develop among members of all reactive sectors that the threat posed by the nonconforming act is serious enough to warrant the creation of law as a crime control strategy. The consensus could be that nonlegislative crime control measures will suffice. Alternatively, the act could be evaluated as not sufficiently threatening to warrant any concrete action. The lack of consensus within or among sectors as to the most appropriate action could prevent any action from being taken. However, consensus within one reactive sector could be sufficient to initiate concrete action despite the lack of support or even active resistence from reactors located in other sectors.

If a need for legislation is supported, the attention of the reactors would turn to the severity of the legal punishment to be threatened. Reactors who believe that the death penalty, for example, does deter potential offenders would be expected to base their recommendations on this belief. Reactors not sharing the belief would be expected to refuse to support or to resist such a recommendation. Alternatively, beliefs about the deterrent efficacy of the death penalty may play little or no role in the recommendations of other reactors; instead, they may believe that a death penalty is warranted solely on grounds of retribution or societal protection.

Later in the process, normative reactions will be manifested in concrete actions taken by members of the social audience. Actions taken by members located in the legislative sector obviously are central for law creation; however, the legislative sector exists in interdependence with the other reactive sectors. Its members are influenced and, in turn, influence reactions in the mass media, general public, political, law enforcement, and judicial sectors.

It is unlikely that initial law-creation efforts would take the form of capital threats. It is more likely that noncapital threats would constitute the early crime control strategy. When it is perceived that existing threats are not having the intended crime control effect, however, and if it is believed that more severe threats will deter potential offenders, then the level of severity is likely to be elevated. Successive cycles of the reactive social control process (repetitions of the act—normative reactions—actual reactions) may culminate in the creation of capital laws.

Other than a few brief descriptions and analyses of ransoming during selected periods, little has been written about the crime in historical perspective. Writing on ransom kidnappers has consisted of necessarily tentative efforts to place them in typologies of offenses and offenders.[13] The victims of ransom kidnapping have been neither described nor analyzed in any systematic way.

A photojournalistic survey of sensational ransom kidnappings in America and abroad was published in the wake of the Hearst case in 1974. While not intended by its authors to be a scholarly analysis, it constituted the only previous effort to view the crime in broad historical perspective.[14] The authors suggested that the American experience with the crime began in 1874 (a claim supported by our investigation) and that only isolated cases appeared until the 1920s when ransom kidnapping became a weapon of warring Prohibition gangsters. The crime then reached its peak incidence during the depression of the 1930s, virtually disappeared during the next forty years, and reappeared dramatically in the 1970s, according to the authors.

Two brief scholarly analyses examined the crime as it existed in brief earlier periods. One writer noted that during the Prohibition era of the 1920s ransom kidnapping became a profession among organized criminals.[15] Initially, kidnapping was merely a means of disposing of rivals by seizing them, "taking them for a ride," and murdering them. According to the writer, the gangsters "soon discovered that they could profit by kidnapping another racketeer and holding him for ransom. This worked so successfully that they turned to kidnapping law-abiding citizens for purposes of ransom."[16] The second brief account focused on ransomings perpetrated by the infamous desperado gangs of the Midwest during the 1930s, such as "Machine Gun" Kelly, Alvin Karpis, and the "Ma" Barker gang. The writer concluded that this style of ransom kidnapping was but a brief and geographically confined episode lasting less than a decade.[17]

Together with the typology of kidnapping developed by two

other sociologists (referred to above, see also n. 5), a typology based largely upon fictionalized accounts of famous ransomings, these contributions constituted the total of sociological and quasi-sociological knowledge about ransom kidnapping in America. It is obvious that even in terms of merely describing the American experience with the crime, let alone explaining it, little had been accomplished.

Of the limited amount of writing that has been done on ransom kidnapping laws, the bulk of it pertains to the content of the federal laws. The writers agree that ransom kidnapping has been one of the most severely punished crimes in America. They also agree that laws have been vague in defining the crime,[18] and that they have varied so widely from jurisdiction to jurisdiction that generalization is difficult.[19]

The creation of ransom kidnapping laws, even of the federal laws, has been virtually unstudied. When casual references to the creation of the federal laws were scrutinized, it was clear that the writers did not agree even as to when the laws were created. Some alleged that the crime was made a capital offense in 1932.[20] Another implied that ransom kidnapping first became a federal crime in 1932 and simultaneously was made a capital offense.[21] That carrying hostages or kidnapping victims from one state to another was made a federal offense in 1934 was another version.[22] Another scholar had written only that the crime became a capital offense in more than "two dozen states during the 1930s after the death of the kidnapped Lindbergh baby." [23]

The questions to be addressed in our investigation were obvious: When did ransom kidnapping become a federal crime? When did it become a federal capital crime? Did the two crime control actions occur simultaneously? Did state legislators merely mimic their federal counterparts? From a societal reaction perspective, the historical timing of the legislation is crucial. Formally labeling an act a crime and providing a noncapital punishment threat toward deterring potential offenders suggest one kind of normative reaction. Subsequently elevating the crime to capital status suggests a different kind. The creation of a capital law as the initial crime control strategy, however, suggests a normative reaction of a quite different quality.

Although writers disagreed on the dating of specific legislative reactions, they agreed that the creation of capital ransom laws in American jurisdictions was primarily, if not exclusively, the result of outraged emotions provoked by the Lindbergh case of March 1932. It is a fact that the federal ransom legislation became known as the "Lindbergh Laws." However, have scholars and the general public alike been led astray by this fact concerning the creation of the laws? Was the Lindbergh case by itself sufficient to generate federal and state legislation that made ransom kidnapping a crime, a capital crime, or both? If so, why? This was not the country's first ransom kidnapping. Finally, if ransom kidnapping laws in America, capital or noncapital, were not merely products of the emotional aftermath of the Lindbergh case, what other forces could have been involved in their creation?

To determine what factors could have been involved in the creation of ranson kidnapping legislation, we had to search the sociological literature on the creation of criminal laws in general. Prior to the 1960s, there had been only a handful of sociological studies of the creation of specific criminal laws. Among the major efforts was a study of the creation of the law of theft in fifteenth-century England,[24] the diffusion of sexual psychopath laws in America in the 1940s,[25] the study of the development of criminal laws in England between the fifth and seventeenth centuries,[26] and studies of the creation of federal drug laws in America.[27] More recently, increased interest in criminal law creation had resulted in additional studies of the creation of drug laws,[28] a study of the vagrancy laws in sixteenth-century England,[29] an analysis of the witchcraft laws in colonial America,[30] studies of the creation of Prohibition legislation,[31] analyses of the development and changes in delinquency legislation,[32] and an analysis of revisions in prostitution statutes.[33]

Two things characterize the types of law-creation studies that have been conducted by sociologists: first, the creation of only a relatively few types of criminal law has been studied; and second, few of the laws studied focused on what commonly are considered to be the more serious crimes. Sociologists have concentrated on laws least likely to be backed by consensus among the social audience that the acts in question should be crimes—marijuana, prostitution, vagrancy, alcohol offenses. The creation of laws more likely to have consensual backing, such as those against robbery, burglary, homicide, and rape, had received little attention.

Most of the studies have concluded that conflict- or interest-group forces played a greater role in the creation of the laws than consensus forces; this hardly is surprising considering the laws studied. As noted by one writer: "[T]he recent tendency to concentrate upon relatively marginal and frequently controversial areas of criminality has probably fostered neglect of the consensus which may still prevail in more central regions of the criminal law. Added to the accumulating evidence of crime's prevalence and of its pervasiveness throughout the social structure, this tendency has encouraged us in viewing the law as bereft of any very substantial foundation in social agreement." [34]

Sociological speculation about the social origin of criminal law generally has favored one or another "model" of law creation. The models distribute themselves roughly along a theoretical-ideological continuum bounded by a consensus view of society on one end and a conflict view on the other: "With respect to the sociology of criminal law the two models make quite different fundamental assumptions: the conflict model emphasizes the role of conflicts between social classes and interest groups as the moving force behind the creation and implementation of criminal laws; the consensus model emphasizes the shared interests of everyone in society and the consensus (either articulated or unarticulated) over fundamental values which this shared interest creates." [35]

Some writers have been concerned with championing, on ideological grounds, various models of law creation as characterizing criminal law creation in general. Other writers have maintained the view that the various models differ merely in the relative emphasis given to law creation as a product of society-wide or special interests, and that it becomes an empirical question as to whether the creation of a particular criminal law can best be attributed to consensus model or conflict model forces. [36]

Models favoring a consensus view differ among themselves as to the scope of the interests being protected by the creation of criminal laws. Some of them contend that the interests are those which all reasonable men agree must be protected if society is to continue.[37] The central thrust of this type of model is illustrated in the following excerpt: "The state of criminal law continues to be as it should—a decisive reflection of the social conscience of a society. What kind of conduct an organized community considers, at a given time, sufficiently condemnable to impose official sanctions, impairing the life, liberty, or property, of the offender, is a barometer of the moral and social thinking of a community." [38]

Until recently, consensus models of the type expressed in the above excerpt have dominated sociological thinking about law creation. However, they have had little support from empirical research, in part at least because of the neglect by sociologists to study laws most likely to involve consensus forces. Some empirical support had been provided by a study of the diffusion of sexual psychopath laws across America in the 1940s.[39] The investigator concluded, however, that even though nationwide alarm over spectacular sex crimes involving children was an important force in the creation of the laws, another force consisted of the narrow, vested interests of the psychiatric profession in viewing offenders as emotionally "sick" and in need of involuntary incarceration for treatment. Recent findings by sociologists on the significant amount of consensus among the public as to the relative seriousness of various criminal acts provide additional support.[40]

Another variety of law-creation model emphasizes the morally indignant reaction of some segment of the social audience, usually the middle classes, to behaviors perceived by members of this segment as threatening to the general welfare.[41] Being more morally vigilant and courageous than the masses, these "moral entrepreneurs" act on behalf of the general populace. Altruism, rather than self-interest, is claimed by the reactors as their sole motivation.

Empirical support for middle-class morality as a force in law creation has been demonstrated by sociologists in the creation of Colonial witchcraft laws,[42] Prohibition laws in America,[43] drug laws,[44] and especially in the creation of legal prohibitions against such "victimless crimes" as prostitution, gambling, and homosexuality.[45]

As we move toward models favoring the view that laws are created to protect selfish vested interests, rather than altruistic widespread interests, we enter the realm of conflict-based models. Although differing over what the conflict is about, the stakes involved, and whether criminal law is created for the benefit of pluralistic interest groups or for the benefit of a ruling elite, conflict-based models agree that conflict forces outweigh consensus forces in the law creation process. At least three varieties of conflict models exist: those that emphasize the role of bureaucratic interests in law creation, those that see law creation as a product of competition among many interest groups, and those "that emphasize the inherent conflicts between those who rule and those who are ruled and which see the criminal law as incorporating rules for enforcing the interests and ideologies of the ruling classes." [46]

Models stressing bureaucratic interests as a force in crime control emphasize that criminal laws can be created to further the "empire-building" desires of law enforcement bureaucracies. Law creation can be used as a means of acquiring new functions for an agency, to take over other agencies or some of their functions, to justify increased budgets, and to gain greater agency autonomy.[47] A proponent of this model contends that escalations in the investment of resources and energies by law enforcement bureaucracies to control a certain form of behavior can lead to legal change in order to explain or justify the agency's activities.[48] Empirical support for this model has come from research on the influence of the Federal Bureau of Narcotics on the creation of laws regulating the sale and possession of drugs.[49]

Conflict-based models which see law creation as the product of competition among various interest groups reflect even more cynicism toward the criminal law. In addition, such models tend to place more emphasis upon the influence of economic interests on law creation. In some models of this type, criminal legislation is viewed as the prize in a contest played by the interest groups.[50] The contestants may change, depending upon the specific interests involved, and it may appear that the winners are not always the same, but the winners tend to have one thing in common—they tend to be wealthier than the losers. Members of the general public are viewed as mere spectators to the contest or, more cynically, as merely being told of the final score without having been aware that a contest took place. Although there may be a modicum of compromise involved in the creation of some criminal laws, a proponent of this model maintains that "more likely than not, criminal laws mark the victory of some groups over others. . . . Some interests never find access to the lawmaking process. Other interests are overwhelmed in it, not compromised." [51]

The most extreme conflict-based models of law creation are Marxist. The game analogy used earlier to describe the interest-group models is not at all applicable to these models. A game implies that all of the contestants have some chance of winning; Marxist models imply "no contest." Criminal law is seen as the tool of a wealthy and powerful ruling elite (the capitalists) used to exploit the less wealthy, less powerful majority (the proletariat) in capitalist societies.[52] What distinguishes Marxist views of law creation from other conflict-oriented models is "that it is one overwhelming more or less cohesive elite, which is synonymous with the ruling class with no other interest above the continuance of its own capitalistic existence, which entirely determines the content and operation of the law." [53]

A leading proponent of the Marxist model views the criminal law as "the coercive instrument of the state, used by the state and its ruling class to maintain the existing social and economic order." [54] He points to the events of the Watergate scandal as merely a minor instance of the use of the legal system as a repressive instrument to secure the survival of capitalism in America.[55] As to how the law is used by the capitalist ruling elite to further its own ends, he contends that the ruling class operates through the mass media to shape public opinion and through the state, composed of such institutions as the government, the police, and the judiciary. By controlling these institutions directly, or indirectly through control of the leaders of the institutions, the ruling elite controls the creation and administration of criminal law.[56] Empirical support for the ruling-elite model of law creation has come from, among others, a study of the creation of the English laws of theft[57] and from a study of the creation of vagrancy laws in England.[58]

Despite persuasive arguments by proponents of each of the law-creation models reviewed, many sociologists would agree that it is not a matter of which type of model best explains criminal law creation in general, but which type of model best explains the creation of particular criminal laws or particular types of criminal law. The prevailing opinion is that consensus-based models should better explain the creation of laws dealing with such crimes as murder, assault, and rape. Conflict-based models should better explain the creation of laws against such behaviors as alcohol offenses, gambling, prostitution, and drug use. It also is agreed among many sociologists that the creation of most laws probably involves elements of both consensus and conflict with a predominance of one or the other. In light of these opinions, it was clear which type of model we should have found to better explain the creation of ransom kidnapping laws. Among the writers surveyed, however, only one specifically mentioned kidnapping among the crimes on which "rough consensus" exists that the state should impose legal sanctions.[59]

Our examination of previous sociological knowledge and speculation on law creation suggested two conclusions: first, the models differed markedly in the relative attention they devoted to normative and actual reaction and to the role of specific reactive sectors in each; second, the models differed as to the historical dynamics of law creation implied by each. Together, these two conclusions suggest a third: none of the proposed models probably is adequate to deal fully with the creation of criminal law when viewed as societal reaction.

The relative emphasis given by the models to normative and actual reactions centers on the element of consensus. This element is central both to consensus and conflict models of law creation. Even Marxist models imply that the ruling elite must create at least a "false reality" of consensus among the ruled; otherwise, there would be little need in the models for so much emphasis on the manipulation of public opinion by the elite. Yet, the element of consensus also points to two critical differences between consensus and conflict models.

Consensus models assume that if actual reactions take the form of law creation, then the normative reactions must have been characterized by a substantial amount of support for the action. Based upon this assumption, consensus models pay little attention to normative reactions. Instead, they concentrate on actual reactions and expect them to take the form of elected representatives effecting the consensus via legislation, deliberately and openly.

Conflict models do not take for granted the existence of censensus as a precondition for law creation. Instead, they consider it highly problematic and pay a good deal of attention to how consensus was created and orchestrated during normative reactions. Since it is assumed that the powerful elites need only a modicum of consensual support, once the attainment of the threshhold is explained, subsequent actual reactions are taken for granted. The assumption is that vested interests are realized rather automatically in the creation of laws protecting them. Hence, there is little reason to pay much attention to the actual reactions involved in the law-creation process.

A second important difference among the models in regard to consensus centers on a belief in the deterrent efficacy of legal punishment threats. Sociological thinking about law creation has treated consensus almost exclusively in reference to a belief that an act is sufficiently threatening to warrant legislative action as a crime control strategy. Consensus models assume that such a belief becomes diffused, more or less naturally, if the act is perceived as a threat to widely held interests or values. Conflict models assume that the belief has to be created.

Neither type of model has considered the potential utility of looking also at actor-focused beliefs in the deterrent efficacy of legal punishment threats. If this is done, then it becomes clear that consensus could involve both act-focused threat beliefs and actor-focused deterrent beliefs. The society-wide consensus emphasized by consensus models could mean that one, the other, or both types of beliefs are widespread among the social audience. The conspiratorial efforts to create consensus, emphasized by conflict models, could involve efforts to create one, the other, or both types of beliefs. A conclusion that any particular criminal law was created predominantly by consensus or conflict forces must take into consideration both types of beliefs.

The relative emphasis given by various models to each of the reactive sectors was very evident. Conflict-model proponents have given closer attention to a greater range of sectors than have consensus-model proponents. Once again, this situation is the result, at least in part, of the greater amount of attention given to conflict than to consensus forces in law creation. Also involved, however, is the closer attention paid by conflict-model proponents to the mucking about by interest groups, moral entrepreneurs, and economic elites in law creation. Major attention has been paid by at least one proponent of conflict-based models to each of the six reactive sectors. Among the sectors, most attention has been devoted to the law enforcement sector and, in roughly descending order of attention, to the judicial, legislative, mass media, political, and general public sectors.

Consensus-model proponents have concentrated primarily only on the general public, legislative, and mass media sectors. The political sector has been neglected, apparently because of the assumption that the reactions of members in this sector merely reflect and effect the consensual will of the majority. Also neglected have been the law enforcement and judicial sectors, apparently for much the same reason.

Proponents of both types of models, quite naturally, have concentrated on those particular reactive sectors to which their respective models have directed them. While natural, the practice has provided an uneven, if not biased, view of who does what, for what reasons, and with what results, in the creation of criminal laws.

The paucity of sociological knowledge and even speculation about the crime of ransom kidnapping and about the creation of the ransom laws raises a wealth of questions to be asked of the historical data presented in the following chapters. While the reader cannot be expected to keep all of the questions in mind, one should at least remember the following:

—Exactly what has been the American experience with ransom kidnapping from 1874 through 1974?

—Exactly when were ransom laws, particularly the capital ransom laws, created?

—What role did the Lindbergh case of March 1932 play in the creation of ransom kidnapping laws in America?

—Is the sociological literature correct in its speculation that consensus forces rather than conflict forces should be found to prevail in the creation of laws against such crimes as ransom kidnapping?

Ransom Kidnapping in America

1

Ransom Kidnapping in the Nineteenth and Early Twentieth Centuries: 1874 - 1919

THE *New York Times Index* initially categorized all criminal activities under the general heading of "crime." The headings of "child stealing" and "abduction" began to appear in the middle 1850s. In 1858, the *Index* carried its first case under the heading "kidnapping." All of the cases reported, however, occurred outside of the United States. It was not until 1866, that the first American abduction case was reported, and American cases of child stealing and kidnapping did not appear until 1868. Throughout the 1860s, reports of child stealing, abduction, and kidnapping averaged about one case a year. With the exception of isolated reports from the San Francisco area of "kidnappings for sea," the cases reported were from the New York-New Jersey area.

In the early 1870s, the number of reported unlawful takings of human beings increased sharply. Nineteen abduction cases were reported, ranging from New York, to Missouri, to Mississippi. Under the heading of "kidnapping," five cases involving the stealing of adults appeared, along with eleven cases of child stealing. One of the 1874 cases initially reported as a child stealing turned out to be what seems to have been America's first modern ransom kidnapping.

The Ransom Kidnapping of Charles Ross

The first report of the Ross case appeared on the front page of the *Times* of 5 July 1874. Datelined Philadelphia, the report was brief: "The abduction of a child from his home in Germantown on the 1st of July, continues to excite much interest and anxiety here. . . . His name is Charles B. Ross. . . . His father, Christian K. Ross, . . . has offered a reward of $300 for his recovery, or information which shall lead thereto. The facts of the case are these: Charlie, the above-mentioned boy, with his brother aged six, were induced to enter a buggy with two men. . . . They were driven about some two hours in the northern part of the city, when the oldest boy was put out of the carriage and the other carried off, since which time he has not been heard from."

The *Times* report failed to mention that on the day following the abduction, Christian Ross had received a letter demanding $20,000 for the return of his son under threat of death to the victim if the ransom was not paid. The *Times* carried daily reports on the case, and the editorials reflected the stunned disbelief with which the case was viewed. An editorial comment of July 9, for example, expressed the difficulty the writer was having in believing that what had transpired actually concerned a Philadelphia child-stealer in the United States rather than a novelist's portrayal of Greek brigandage.

A circular containing a description of the victim was distributed by the Philadelphia police throughout the country, but to no avail. Editorials in the *Times* reflected the alarm which the case was beginning to generate.

The Philadelphia kidnapping still remains an unresolved, dreadful fact—one suggestive of exceedingly unpleasant reflections, which, from their very unpleasantness, should receive thoughtful consideration. A boy is taken away in open day by two men, who are keeping him from his family for the purpose of extorting money. The child is probably in no danger of life or limb, for his kidnappers have offered to restore him for twenty thousand dollars, and he must be in their eyes too valuable a piece of property to be put in any needless peril. There seems to be no new clue to the detection of the kidnappers. . . . The father is said to be prepared to pay the ransom demand—and anybody who calls this an act of weakness had better try to imagine what he would do himself if his own child were in the hands of these unknown scoundrels.

Must it, then, be accepted as true that any of us are liable to have our children stolen from the public streets and in open day? It is extremely unlikely that the child of any reader of this article will be stolen from him; but this Philadelphia business shows that any of us is liable to such a loss; for what may be done in one instance, and in one place, may be done in another instance and in another place. It seems that the crime can be committed with a considerable chance of impunity, and there are creatures ready and able to commit it upon sufficient inducement—that is prospect of gain. And the prospect of gain is, it must be confessed, very fair. In case of a stolen child, whose restoration is offered for a sum of money, how few parents, if the sum were within their reach, would hesitate to pay it? How few men would have the firmness—say rather the stoicism—to resist the pleadings of their own hearts, enforced by the cry of a frantic mother bereaved of her child? The history of brigandage from the remotest ages tells us how few. . . . Kidnapping is sometimes resorted to in Europe, but of course it is one of the rarest means adopted; and as money is the only object of the kidnappers, . . . none but the wealthy are exposed to such attempts at extortions; and they are they who can most easily protect their children against all chance of such exposure. . . . Of perils by night we are careful enough, with our combination locks, burglar-alarms, and private watchmen; but that there are perils by day which also demand our serious attention this Philadelphia business is striking evidence. (14 July 1874, p. 4)

On July 21, a New York Police inspector received word from an informant that William Mosher and Joseph Douglass were the abductors. Both men were well known to the police of New York and New Jersey. Mosher had a long criminal record dating back to an arrest for armed robbery in 1857. In more recent years, he had turned to burglary, and it was during this phase of his career that he had taken on Douglass as a partner. At the time of the Ross abduction, both Mosher and

Douglass were escapees from a local jail where they had been awaiting trial on burglary charges.

New York City police detectives were ordered to find the two suspects, and when Christian K. Ross agreed to defray their expenses incurred on the case, the manhunt began. The practice of gaining the services of detectives, both private as well as public, not only by paying their out-of-jurisdiction expenses but by offering rewards was a common practice. Such an inducement was made in the Ross case, when, on July 22, the mayor and city fathers of Philadelphia offered $20,000 for information leading to the return of the victim and the apprehension and conviction of the abductors.

Despite the lack of newsworthy developments, the case was kept before the public through editorials and newspaper articles on the general subject of child stealing. In addition to providing historical information, the articles revealed that child stealing during this period was widespread, cases having been reported from New York, Massachusetts, Pennsylvania, Missouri, and Louisiana.

When no progress in the case had been made by August, public alarm turned to panic. The *Times* reported a near lynching of gypsies in Pennsylvania, who had in their possession a child thought to be Charles Ross. Harassment of parents with young children resembling the Ross child was reported from Vermont; Washington, D.C.; Illinois; and Nebraska. As frustration over lack of progress in the case mounted, rumors began to circulate that the victim's family somehow were implicated in the kidnapping.

Reports from around the country continued to come in that Charles had been found. Eventually, such reports would number in the hundreds. Christian Ross made all possible efforts to investigate the reports by mail or by personally traveling throughout the East to look at boys put forward as his son. The strain began to tell both financially and physically, aggravated by the persistent rumors that somehow Christian Ross was involved in the crime. Among the hundreds of letters of sympathy being received by the family, were letters from cranks, adding to the ordeal of the parents. A brand of gallows humor began to plague the family as well; a ventriloquist caused a near riot at a Philadelphia freight depot when he applied his talent to trick employees that the pleas of help apparently coming from a trunk were from Charles Ross.

In November 1874, the monotony of constant reports of the victim having been located in Connecticut, Ontario, West Virginia, and Illinois was relieved by a report of new ransom kidnappings. Although the press and authorities had been predicting that such cases would be incited by the Ross case, none had materialized. News articles described the kidnapping exploits of bandit gangs operating in Missouri, Arkansas, the Indian Territory, and along the Texas border. It was reported that these gangs, active since the end of the Civil War, recently had added the ransom kidnapping of children to their usual pursuits of robbing stagecoaches and trains and sacking towns. The media attributed the activities to the Ross case.

The events of December 14 vaulted the Ross case back into the national limelight. In an abortive attempt to burglarize a home on Long Island, New York, Mosher and Douglass were shot. Mosher was killed instantly. Douglass, mortally wounded, lived just long enough to tell authorities that he and Mosher had kidnapped Charles Ross. He died before revealing the fate of the boy.

The news of the Long Island episode was spread across all seven columns of the front page of the *Times* on December 15. Front-page headlines proclaimed: "Crime and Its Explanation," "The Charley Ross Mystery Cleared Up," "His Kidnappers Shot Dead While Committing Another Felony," "A Dying Desperado's Confession." Discovery of the victim was believed imminent, and the fate of Mosher and Douglass was hailed as a classic deterrent example to other ransomers. However, 1874 came to a close with no further progress in determining the fate of the boy.

With most people satisfied that Mosher and Douglass were the kidnappers, attention focused exclusively on the fate of the victim. Christian Ross offered a $5,000 reward for the return of the victim within ten days, no questions asked. The case was kept before the public in early 1875 with continuous reports of children believed to be the victim. The volume of the reports prompted the *Times* to comment: "It seems a poor State that fails to furnish a strong child who answers in every respect the description of Charlie Ross" (4 Jan. 1875, p. 1).

The hundreds of lost children mistakenly thought to be Charles Ross were used by the media and authorities to dramatize the need for sterner measures to curtail the crime of child stealing. A *Times* editorial of 18 June 1875 concluded: "It is time . . . that the people generally should evince a warmer interest in the necessity for putting a stop to the repetition of crimes of this particular kind. Child-stealing is an offense which should be productive of something more than a little temporary public indignation. If it cannot be stopped in any other way, a severe example should be made of those who indulge in it. If this cannot be done under existing laws, new laws should be enacted for the purpose. Young children cannot be expected to protect themselves against the machinations of bad men and women; but they have a right to all the protection which the law can give, and society, too, may justly claim some proper defense against a crime that which there are few, if any, that are more atrocious. The public cannot afford to treat it with indifference, for it is one of those things about which the exercise of too much patience itself becomes a crime" (p. 4).

The only judicial action to result from the Ross case took place in the summer and fall of 1875. William Westervelt, a brother-in-law of Mosher, was charged with helping to steal the victim, to conceal him, and with writing the $20,000 ransom letter. Press coverage of the trial was intense. Learning the fate of the victim was believed to be imminent; again the optimism proved unfounded. Westervelt steadfastly denied his involvement, despite highly publicized personal pleas from the Rosses for information on the fate of their son. A jury convicted Westervelt of conspiracy to kidnap, conspiracy to extort money by threatening letter, and conspiracy to defraud the child of its liberty. He was sentenced to seven year's imprisonment and fined the sum of $1.

During the remainder of 1875 and throughout 1876, Christian Ross continued to investigate reports that his son had been located in New York, Michigan, Pennsylvania, Connecticut, Vermont, and even in England. The situation took a pitious turn in May 1877 when it was reported that Christian Ross was in Bridgeport, Connecticut, to consult with P. T. Barnum, the circus impressario, who would make a personal offer of $10,000 for the recovery of the boy. Barnum had made the same offer earlier, but Christian Ross had turned him down. The reward was announced in a circular, carrying the signatures of P. T. Barnum and C. K. Ross, printed in newspapers throughout the country.

In February 1878, after having examined a boy sent to him from Baltimore, Christian Ross was quoted as saying: "This makes 573 boys I have been called to see, or have been written about, and my hundreds of failures to identify each waif as my own has [*sic*] taught me to entertain no sanguine hope. I suppose I shall continue going to see boys till I die, but I don't expect to find Charlie in any of them" (6 Feb. 1878, p. 1).

On the fourth anniversary of the crime, the *New York Times* launched a subscription fund, requesting a 25-cent contribution from readers to help defray the expenses of the Ross family in their continuing search for their son. Frequent listings of the contributors, each contributing between $1 and $15, appeared in the *Times*. By the end of the month, the subscription amounted to just under $50, but in a letter to the *Times*, Ross respectfully declined to accept the proceeds from any public subscription. As an alternative, he urged that the public buy his recently published book, *The Father's Story of Charley Ross*, at $1.50 per copy, mailed.

With no developments in the Ross case, media coverage was limited to recollection of the event on its yearly anniversary. Throughout 1882, Christian Ross continued his search, traveling as far west as St. Louis. A variation was added to the practice of authorities finding lost boys for Ross's inspection, when a Portland, Maine, youth put himself forward as Charles Ross. A *Times* editorial predicted correctly that he would be the first in a long line of teen-age pretenders. A news item in the *Times* of 7 November 1883 read: "Among the individuals staring at the spotted man, the tattooed girl, the albino, the Mulberry

Street Wonder, and the other curiosities in the Windsor Museum, at No. 105 Bowery, yesterday afternoon, was a mild-mannered youth of apparently 20 years of age, who wore a slight mustache, was attired in a suit of brown, and wore a glass diamond about the size of a doorknob at the end of a fob chain that dangled from his vest pocket. He will be on exhibition himself today, and if his stories are true, he is a unique curiosity, for he claims to be the long lost Charlie Ross" (p. 2).

The Ross case continued to be mentioned, usually on its anniversary, during the remainder of the 1880s, and would be revitalized repeatedly in later decades. Mrs. Ross died in 1912, predeceased by her husband in 1897. Until the day of her death, Mrs. Ross retained a lingering hope that she might find out what became of her son, but no trace ever was found.

Ransom Kidnapping in the "Gay Nineties"

When the decade of the 1890s dawned, there had not been a verified case of ransom kidnapping reported in the *Times* since the Ross case, sixteen years earlier. Child stealing, however, especially in the New York City area, continued to be well publicized. The nationwide alarm of the 1870s, however, was not in evidence.

On 20 March 1891, a second major case of ransom kidnapping was reported. The victim was a wealthy bachelor from Detroit. A ransom of $15,000 was demanded for his safe return, but the plot was frustrated by the refusal of the victim's banker to withdraw the amount from his account. Despite dire threats of harm to the victim if authorities were notified, they were notified and the crime was well publicized. Apparently as a combined result of the banker's obstinacy and the publicity, the victim was released unharmed the following evening.

In March 1892, a third ransom kidnapping was reported, this one from Longridge, New York, a hamlet on the New York-Connecticut border. As in the previous cases, the attempt to extort ransom for the return of Ward Waterbury, eight-year-old son of a well-to-do farmer, was unsuccessful. Despite a demand for $6,000, the victim was returned unharmed before any ransom was paid. Upon his safe return, a *Times* editorial expressed relief that the Waterbury case did not turn out to be another Ross case and called for exemplary punishment of the offenders.

The offenders turned out to be the nephew of the victim's father, and two accomplices, all in their early twenties. They had initially planned to kidnap the son of a wealthy Greenwich family, but later abandoned the plan as too risky and substituted the Waterbury boy as their victim. They wanted the money, they said, to start a "dive" in Greenwich, Connecticut, and that they got the idea from dime novels from which they learned about the Charles Ross case. One month after their arrest, all three offenders pleaded guilty; two were sentenced to four year's imprisonment, and the other to two years.

In August 1897, a ransom case was reported from Albany, New York, the same city in which a ransom hoax in 1881 had left a residue of cynicism about alleged ransom kidnappings. John Conway, five-year-old son of a train dispatcher for the New York Central Railroad, was abducted while playing with a young friend in front of his home. Two hours later, a messenger delivered a letter to the victim's father. The letter stated that unless $3,000 was delivered to the abductors at a stated time and place, and the utmost secrecy was maintained, the child "would be killed the same as Charlie Ross." [1] The press immediately emphasized that the case had been incited by the Ross case, not only because of the ransom note but because historical sketches of the Ross kidnapping recently had been publicized on the occasion of the death of Christian K. Ross.

That evening, the rendezvous for handing over the ransom was surrounded by Albany police, detectives, and reporters but the kidnappers did not appear. The next day, hundreds of people thronged the street on which the victim lived, expecting news of the abductors. An Albany newspaper offered a reward for the return of the victim and the arrest and conviction of the kidnappers, and the whole police force and hundreds of citizens of Albany pursued the search for the victim throughout the night.

Three days following the kidnapping, Albany authorities and reporters, acting on the information of an informant, rescued the victim from a wooded area behind a local schoolhouse. A short time later, a brother-in-law of the victim's father was arrested in Albany. The local press reported that although the victim was unharmed, the abductors had planned to kill him, as the pursuit became hot, but did not have the chance. As the suspect was being taken to police headquarters, the passage of the patrol wagon was obstructed by a crowd of citizens threatening to lynch him. Later in the day, his arraignment had to be postponed when a menacing crowd gathered around the courthouse. When a second suspect was arrested in Schenectady the next day, his train was met by an angry mob at the Albany station.

The day following the arrests, contending rumors about the case began circulating in Albany. Because of the action of the Albany newspaper offering a reward in the case, and because of the role of reporters from the paper in the rescue of the victim and in the apprehension of the suspects, many citizens believed the abduction was a hoax perpetrated by the newspaper to increase circulation. The contending viewpoint was that the kidnapping of the Conway boy was but the first in a wholesale series of ransom kidnappings of children in the vicinity, planned by a notorious gang of criminals based in New York City. The alleged plot was to take the children in the same manner as the Conway boy had been taken, and if the ransom demands were not met, to quietly dispose of the victims.

The Albany contest of realities was transported to New York City via the press. One New York City newspaper came out in favor of the wholesale kidnapping version. The *Times* countered with an editorial which charged its competitor with yellow journalism of the most dangerous type, capable of inciting potential ransomers and of causing panic among the public. Subsequent developments revealed that the Conway case actually fell somewhere between the two contending versions of reality.

As the police in several states were searching for a New York City attorney reputed to have been the chief plotter in the abduction, an Albany grand jury indicted the two Albany suspects. Both pleaded guilty to kidnapping charges and received sentences of fourteen years, four months. The maximum sentence under New York law was fifteen years, but it was the custom of the court to give sentences so the term would expire in the summer months. Nine days following his arrest in Riley, Kansas, the third defendant pleaded guilty to kidnapping and was sentenced to the maximum term of fifteen years at hard labor.

Ransom kidnapping in the nineteenth century ended on the same note on which it had begun in 1874—with a major case, this time in New York City itself. The case involved the abduction, by her nurse, of a twenty-month-old child, and served as a point of convergence for reactions generated by the infrequent, yet sensational, ransom kidnappings and reactions to the less sensational, but constant, child stealings.

About a week after the nurse had begun working for the Clarke family, she and her charge disappeared. On the afternoon of the disappearance, a letter was delivered to Clarke, warning him not to notify the police or the press, under threat of death to his daughter. The matter was not kept quiet. The *Times* of 23 May 1899 reported the abduction two days after the letter was received. A front-page story contained the leader, "Recalls the Charley Ross Case." It reviewed the Ross case, as well as the Conway kidnapping, described as a "later case that stirred the country and bid fair to rival the Ross case." In addition, the story contained the text of the ransom letter.

Three days after the abduction, it was reported that no progress had been made in the case, although the entire available New York City police force was working on it. The public was following the case closely. A news item in the *Times* reported: "No case of recent occurrence in this city has aroused so much interest as the kidnapping of Baby Clarke. Mothers living in the neighborhood, and others living at a distance, are constantly sending servants to the house to inquire if the little one has been found. As in the Charley Ross case, a sympathetic chord in the community has been touched, and there is evidence that unless the police soon make a discovery the other city officials beside the police will be asked to use vigorous methods to have the mystery unraveled" (24 May 1899, p. 1).

Public interest in the case continued to build. Each mail delivery brought the Clarke family dozens of letters from sympathizers, cranks, and even practitioners of the occult offering their services. Visitors to the house were so numerous that the family had to place a man at the door to answer inquiries and to thank sympathizers. Two New York City newspapers, the *World* and the *Journal,* offered rewards of $1,000 and $2,000, respectively, to stir the vigilance of the public. The rewards revived in the minds of some a rumor that the kidnapping was a plot of sensational journalism.

Ten days of fruitless searching came to an end with an announcement on the front page of the *Times* on June 2: "Marion Clarke Found at Last." Two residents of a rural New York hamlet had recognized the victim from her portrait carried in the newspapers, when a woman brought her into the local general store. Local authorities arrested the woman and her husband, with the baby in their possession, at a farmhouse in the vicinity. New York police were notified, and Clarke and detectives boarded a train for Garnerville.

The suspects were George and Addie Barrow. He was the twenty-eight-year-old son of a prominent Little Rock, Arkansas, family, who had been forced to leave Little Rock after numerous scrapes with the law. His wife, Addie, had been employed in a New York printing office. Bella Anderson, the nurse, was arrested later on the same day and confessed to her role in the kidnapping.

Upon hearing that the baby had been rescued, residents of the surrounding area flocked to Garnerville to see Marion. The *Times* reported that a crowd of 2,000 saw the baby and her father off for New York City aboard a one-coach train provided especially for the occasion. Wildly cheering crowds greeted the train all along its route, and a crowd estimated at 5,000 well-wishers was waiting at the Clarke home. In addition, the *Times* reported the following public reaction: "During the second act of 'The Man in the Moon,' at the New York Theatre last night, comedian Sam Bernard stepped down to the footlights and told the audience that Marion Clarke had been found. The audience broke into a demonstration such as has not been witnessed since the days of the war" (2 June 1899, p. 2).

In the nurse's confession, she admitted that she and Addie Barrow took the baby from its carriage according to a prearranged plot. She stated that the Barrows had conceived the plan of kidnapping children all over the country and holding them for modest ransoms. Her role in the kidnappings, a role which she claimed was forced upon her, was to seek employment as a nurse to small children, and when such employment was obtained, to notify the Barrows who were to take care of the ransom negotiations. The Clarkes were the third family with which she had sought employment. According to the nurse, the kidnapping of the Clarke child was a hasty trial-run of their plan, since she and the Barrows knew that Clarke was not a wealthy man. In fact, after much haggling among themselves, they had decided to ask only a $300 ransom, for that is all they expected Clarke to be able to pay.

On June 15, the trial of George Barrow began, with Bella Anderson appearing for the prosecution. Barrow was found guilty by a jury, after one and one-half hours of deliberation, sentenced to fourteen years, ten months at hard labor in Sing Sing, and taken to prison, all on June 16. On the same day, Bella Anderson was sentenced to four years. On the day following these proceedings, a *Times* editorial complimented the New York County district attorney for the convictions of George Barrow and Bella Anderson and implied that such speedy justice was not the norm in criminal prosecutions of the day. The trial of Addie Barrow began and ended on June 26. She pleaded guilty and was sentenced to twelve years and ten months. In pronouncing sentence, the judge stated: "The defendant stands here confessed guilty of one of the most abhorrent crimes known to modern civilization—a crime which strikes at the very foundation of society, and in the prevention of which every law-abiding individual has a vital interest. The defendant has committed a crime which shows her to be utterly devoid of the finer and gentler feelings which are the distinguishing virtues of her sex. By her act of consummate villainy, even though induced by another, she has spread fear and distrust throughout the length and breadth of this land. It is due to the fathers and mothers and children of this land that the punishment which the defendant shall receive should not only make it impossible for her to repeat this crime, but that it shall serve as a warning to other mercenaries who may be tempted thus to traffic in human flesh and blood" (27 June 1899, p. 14).

The Eddie Cudahy Case: The First Successful Ransom Kidnapping

Ransom kidnapping in the twentieth century debuted by providing two elements missing from the cases of the nineteenth century—very wealthy victims and success. The Cudahy case in Omaha, in 1900, contained both elements. E. A. Cudahy, father of the victim, was a millionaire meat-packer, one of the giants in the industry. The ransom demanded and collected was $25,000 in gold.

On the evening of 18 December 1900, when fifteen-year-old Eddie Cudahy failed to return home from an errand, the police were notified. Shortly after nine o'clock the next morning, a man on horseback rode past the Cudahy home and threw a letter into the front yard. The letter informed Cudahy that his son had been abducted and would be returned for a ransom of $25,000 in gold. The letter also contained detailed instructions for the delivery of the ransom. Throughout the day, the entire police and detective forces of Omaha, together with fifty of Cudahy's employees, searched the city. Cudahy announced that he would pay a substantial reward, with no questions asked, for the return of his son, committed the substantial capital of the Cudahy Packing Company to the recovery of Eddie, and wired for a force of Pinkerton detectives from Chicago. The first day of the case ended with the receipt of a second letter from the kidnappers. It stated: "If you give us the money the child will be returned as safe as when you last saw him, but if you refuse, we will put acid in his eyes and blind him, then we will immediately kidnap another millionaire's child that we have spotted and demand $100,000 and we will get it, for he will see the condition of your child and realize the fact that we mean business and will not be monkeyed with or captured. . . . This letter and every part of it must be returned with the money, and any attempt at capture will be the saddest thing you have ever done. If you remember, some twenty years ago Charley Ross was kidnapped in New York City [*sic*] and $20,000 ransom was asked . . . Ross died of a broken heart." [2]

Early on the morning of December 20, the victim was returned unharmed, after being held for thirty-six hours. E. A. Cudahy had delivered the $25,000 in gold, as instructed, on the previous evening. In response to questions about why the police did not attempt to capture the kidnappers at the ransom site, the Omaha police chief stated that they could have, but Cudahy had insisted that the police do nothing that would threaten the safe return of his son.

To stimulate the efforts of public and private detectives, Cudahy announced that he would pay a $25,000 reward for the apprehension of the kidnappers. His offering the reward after having paid the ransom, however, drew criticism from readers of the *Times*. One letter to the editor expressed the opinion that, rather than paying the reward, Cudahy should have broadcast to the nation that he was willing to commit his entire fortune to capturing the abductors and, if Eddie were harmed, to seeing to it that "the most terrible punishment for men to suffer in this world" (23 Dec. 1900, p. 6) was inflicted upon them. What Cudahy actually did, according to the writer, was to invite the ransom kidnapping of other children, now that criminals realized they could get away with it.

While the Omaha police pursued their quarry, legal authorities were confronted by a quandary over what they could do with the ransomers if they were apprehended. None of the criminal statutes of Nebraska covered the case. The state had a kidnapping statute which carried a penitentiary sentence of from two to seven years, but it only applied to kidnapping with the intention of carrying the victim out of the state. Another statute provided a penitentiary sentence for child stealing, but it referred only to the stealing of children under ten years of age. Some authorities suggested that the state's blackmail statute might be applied, but using a kidnap victim as a means of extorting blackmail would strain the legislative intent of the statute. The authorities concluded that the only charge which could be brought successfully was that of false imprisonment. False imprisonment, however, was merely a misdemeanor and carried a fine and jail sentence of less than one year as a maximum penalty. The publication in the *Times* of this state of affairs drew another response from a reader:

To THE EDITOR OF THE *New York Times:*

In reading the account in this morning's paper of the kidnapping of young Cudahy I learned, with some astonishment, that there seems to be no law under which the perpetrators of this dastardly deed would be adequately punished. If that is so, parents may, indeed, tremble, and we shall soon hear of similar outrages, for there are so many brutes who would resort to such means to extort a large sum of money when they find they can commit such a crime with impunity. To kidnap a child is one of the worst crimes one can imagine, and the mental anguish of the afflicted parents must be frightful.

There should be a law throughout the United States putting the penalty of capital punishment on the crime of kidnapping; for anyone who would deliberately blind or maim a child, as the kidnappers of young Cudahy threatened to do, would as readily commit a murder, and the sooner we are rid of such a one the better it will be for the community. Only the penalty of capital punishment, I feel, will serve to prevent crime, and the knowledge of such a law will again give parents the feeling of security which has been so rudely shaken by this Omaha outrage. (23 Dec. 1900, p. 6)

Nebraska's legal plight was noted with alarm not only by readers of the *Times* but also by legislators throughout the nation. Lawmakers from several states expressed their opinions on what action should be taken. It was reported that Iowa's kidnapping experience had been limited to divorced parents taking their own children against the order of the court, for which the existing penalty of five years' imprisonment or a $1,000 fine, or both, was adequate. Now, however, "with the inauguration of the kidnapping practice to extort money from the parents for the return of the child, it is found that the Iowa statutes do not provide punishment to fit the crime." [3] The report concluded on the note that the next legislature probably would amend the law, making the punishment for ransom kidnapping death or at least a life sentence at hard labor.

Wisconsin's kidnapping legislation dated from 1849 and did not speak to ransom kidnapping. A state senator announced his intention to introduce at the next session a measure providing life imprisonment as the punishment. Life would constitute the maximum punishment available in Wisconsin, which had abolished capital punishment for all offenses in 1853. From North Dakota, a member of the state legislature stated: "The State of North Dakota provides only a penitentiary sentence ranging from one to ten years as a punishment for kidnapping at the discretion of the judge. I favor the death penalty for the offense. There is no punishment too severe for such crimes." [4] From Wyoming, it was reported that feeling against kidnapping was strong there, and although the matter had not taken definite form, a bill might be submitted in the next legislative session making hanging the penalty for ransom kidnapping.

South Dakota found itself confronted with an even greater problem than Nebraska. In South Dakota, kidnapping in any form was not a crime. A report from Sioux Falls stated that the legislature would be asked to remedy the situation at its January session. It was not clear whether the crime would be made a capital one or not, but strong sentiment was reported among the lawmakers in favor of hanging.

As a direct reaction to the Cudahy case, a number of state legislatures took formal action. In South Dakota, Alabama, Indiana, and Oklahoma, all in 1901, and in Iowa and Connecticut in 1902, ransom kidnapping laws were created; life imprisonment was set as the maximum penalty. In 1901, the legislatures of Illinois, Missouri, Nebraska, Tennessee, and Delaware created their initial ransom kidnapping legislation and threatened death as the maximum penalty. Also in 1901, Congress enacted legislation to protect the residents of the District of Columbia from being forcibly carried out of the district. More of an abduction statute than a ransom kidnapping statute, imprisonment of not less than one nor more than seven years, plus a fine, was provided as the general penalty. For victims under sixteen years of age, however, the penalty was not more than twenty years and a possible fine.

The first editorial response of the *Times* to the Cudahy case initiated what was to become an enduring editorial theme: the private responsibility of a parent to his children versus his public responsibility as a citizen to protect the children of other parents. The same theme eventually would be expressed in numerous legislative and judicial debates about capital ransom legislation.

Within a week following the ransoming, suspicion had fallen on Pat Crowe, a former employee of Cudahy. After having been fired ten years earlier, Crowe reportedly had turned to train robbery as a pursuit. A nationwide manhunt for Crowe produced reports of his having been sighted from Chicago to Boston.

In February 1901, Cudahy received one of a series of letters from Crowe. In the letter, Crowe maintained that he was innocent, that he would return to Omaha someday and prove his innocence, and that he already would have done so but was afraid of being lynched. Another letter, this one unsigned, stated that the kidnappers were willing to return $20,000 of the $25,000 ransom upon Cudahy's assurance that they would not be punished. Cudahy stated that he had no intention of letting up in his hunt for the abductors. A short time later, the Omaha police arrested James Callahan and charged him with complicity in the kidnapping, following the victim's identification of Callahan as one of the abductors.

Callahan's four-day trial began in April. Because of the peculiar legal situation faced by the prosecution, the state attempted to try Callahan for robbery. The defense countered with the argument, which they succeeded in getting Cudahy to support on the stand, that he gave the abductors the $25,000 of his own free will with no expectation that it ever would be returned. In addition, the defense contended that Eddie was able to identify Callahan only after having been coached by the police and presented a witness who claimed Callahan was with him at the time of the kidnapping. After deliberating overnight, the jury returned a verdict of not guilty.

A report in the *Times* began: "The verdict was an evident surprise to the Court, and Judge Baker expressed his disgust in emphatic terms" (28 Apr. 1901, p. 1). The report continued: "Judge Baker studied the wording of the verdict for several minutes in silence, as if he doubted the evidence of his ears. Then, addressing the jury, he rebuked them in most vigorous terms. 'If Callahan had made his own choice of a jury,' the Court said, 'he could not have selected twelve men who would have served him more faithfully. If the State for its part had made the selection, I know of no men it could have named who could have been less careful of its interests. The jury is discharged without the compliments of the Court and the prisoner is likewise turned loose as to this trial, I presume to continue the criminal practices in which you have failed to check him. I do not know what motive actuated you in reaching this decision, but I hope none of you will ever appear again in this jury box.' "

The Omaha police chief freely expressed his suspicions of what motivated the jury's decision: "From the information I have secured as to the sentiments of the jury, I believe that its decision was based largely on the theory that the victim of the affair was a wealthy man, and as such is able to suffer. Two of the jurors, I am informed, expressed their opinion that no kidnapping had occurred, and they had taken their oath as jurors with this conviction in their minds" (ibid.). Callahan subsequently was tried on a charge that he had committed perjury in his first trial. This time, it took a jury thirty-six hours to find him not guilty.

Little more was heard of the Cudahy case until October 1901 when Crowe resumed correspondence with Cudahy, the Omaha police, and the national press. The audacity of Crowe bemused some observers, but enraged others. In his letters, Crowe offered to surrender: if rewards for his capture were withdrawn; if he was not locked up before trial; and if bail was set at a maximum of $500, since that was all that he could afford. Crowe also informed the press that, since the Cudahy affair, he had been in South America and South Africa. With this bit of chitchat, nothing would be heard from or about Crowe for five years. In the interim, the country remained free from major ransom kidnappings.

In July 1905, a development occurred which appeared to have only an oblique relationship to the Cudahy case. Datelined Chicago, a news item described the latest trust-busting triumphs of President Theodore Roosevelt against the meat-packing industry. Among seventeen men recently indicted by a federal grand jury for antitrust violations, was Edward A. Cudahy.

On 5 October 1905, Pat Crowe was arrested in Butte, Montana. Before leaving for Omaha to stand trial, Crowe freely told of a scheme to kidnap John D. Rockefeller and hold him for $2 million ransom. As reported in the *Times:* "After the Cudahy affair in Omaha, said Crowe, he and his partner fled to Chicago, where they hid. They found it easy to avoid arrest, and the Cudahy kidnapping had been so easy that they decided to go after bigger game, and Rockefeller was decided upon" (6 Oct. 1905, p. 1). According to Crowe, the plan had proceeded to the point of renting a house in which to hold Rockefeller and obtaining a horse and buggy to abduct him. At this point, however, Crowe's partner backed out and the plot had to be abandoned.

Crowe's trial took place in February 1906 and was covered in detail by the media. The trial lasted two weeks. At its conclusion, a jury found Crowe not guilty of extorting $25,000 in connection with the Cudahy kidnapping. Thus ended the first reported ransom kidnapping in the twentieth century, and the first successful one.

The Muth Case: Philadelphia Again

In 1906, national attention returned to the eastern seaboard, where, with the exception of the Cudahy case, the major kidnappings for ransom had been concentrated since the Ross case in 1874. Attention returned specifically to Philadelphia, where in June, Freddie Muth, seven-year-old son of a Philadelphia jeweler, was kidnapped for ransom.

School authorities released the boy to a messenger claiming to have been sent by the boy's mother. This ruse was to be employed again and again over the years. The next day, the parents received a special delivery letter threatening to kill the child unless a ransom of $500 was paid. The police began a search of the city and arrested, questioned, and released a number of suspects. A first in ransom kidnapping cases was represented by an announcement that United States postal authorities were working on the case trying to locate the writer of the letters. This marked the first involvement of the federal government in ransom kidnappings, as far as we could determine.

The victim was located by authorities six days later, in the company of John Keene. The *Times,* in a front-page story, reported: "The news of the capture had reached the center of the city, and when the prisoner and the boy arrived at the City Hall an angry crowd had gathered. Keene, white with fear, trembled so that he could scarcely walk, and begged the detectives not to let the crowd kill him. . . . Not since the abduction of Charlie Ross has this community been so wrought up by the commission of a crime" (19 June 1906, p. 1).

Keene, married and in his early thirties, was described as the black sheep of a respectable New York City family. He had been a bookkeeper for a bank until he was charged with absconding with between $20,000 and $30,000 of the bank's funds; the case never was prosecuted. After the incident, he had worked as a stockbroker and most recently as a real estate agent. Keene stated that he needed the money because he owed $400 to the real estate dealer for whom he worked, had other debts, and had no means of providing for his family. Previous to kidnapping the Muth child, he admitted an unsuccessful attempt to abduct the six-year-old son of another well-to-do family.

Within twenty-four hours of his arrest, Keene was arraigned on a kidnapping charge, indicted by a grand jury, pleaded guilty, received a sentence of twenty years in solitary confinement at hard labor, and was imprisoned. As the *Times* reported: "Only two hours and thirty minutes elapsed between the time the kidnapper was taken into the court of the committing magistrate and the moment when the sentence was imposed" (20 June 1906, p. 1).

The Disappearance of Horace Marvin, Jr.

In March 1907, a case was reported from Kittshammock, Delaware. Although it never was reported whether ransom actually was involved, the case was reacted to by the press, public, and authorities as a ransom kidnapping. Of particular note in the Marvin case is that the president of the United States was among the reactors.

Dr. Horace Marvin, a wealthy and highly respected physician in Sioux City, Iowa, had recently moved his family to an isolated area in the vicinity of Dover, Delaware. Horace, Jr., his four-year-old son, disappeared from the yard of the family's farm. The family made an immediate search of the farm, and an alarm then was sent out to neighbors who joined in the search of the swampy and wooded area. Dr. Marvin feared that his son had been kidnapped for ransom, although no ransom demand had been received. The next day the Delaware state's attorney general arrived on the scene accompanied by the chief of state detectives. Delaware was prepared if the case turned out to be a ransom kidnapping; in response to the Cudahy case, the legislature had enacted a death penalty for ransom kidnapping.

The governor assured Dr. Marvin that the state would do everything possible toward running down any clue that suggested ransom kidnapping. He also announced that the State Detective Department was giving its full attention to the case, and that the police departments of Philadelphia, Baltimore, and other cities had been contacted to lend assistance. At the statehouse, the legislature passed a bill empowering the governor to offer a $2,000 reward for the recovery of the boy. The hope was expressed that the reward would be sufficient to attract the services of private investigators. Later the same day, Pinkerton detectives arrived from Baltimore.

As had been the pattern in previous cases, a description of the victim was distributed nationwide. In response, reports were received from Pennsylvania, New Jersey, New York, Iowa, and Utah that the victim had been located. All of the reports received Dr. Marvin's close attention, but all proved to be unfounded. Adding to the agony of the victim's family were a number of hoax ransom demands among the many genuine offers of condolence from writers in several states.

The involvement of the federal government in the case was first reported in a front-page story of the *Times*. The story related that two Secret Service agents had arrived on the scene, presumably on orders of President Roosevelt to extend federal assistance to Dr. Marvin. The next day, however, the chief of the Secret Service denied that his agents were in Dover in connection with the Marvin case. Two days later, it was reported that a U.S. assistant secretary of state had received a cablegram from the American consul at Portsmouth, England, informing him that authorities there had a boy who was believed to be Horace Marvin, Jr. When notified by the assistant secretary, President Theodore Roosevelt authorized extending the cooperation of the federal government to Delaware officials.

Almost at the same time as the English report, Dr. Marvin received a message from Toronto that police officials there had arrested a man with a boy who positively was the victim. These developments prompted Dr. Marvin to appeal for aid to the president in a telegram. Authorities in England then reported that the boy in Portsmouth was not Horace Marvin, Jr., but it was some consolation to the father that on the same day he received a reply from President Roosevelt.

THE WHITE HOUSE, March 23, 1907.

My Dear Mr. Marvin:

I am in receipt of your telegram of the 22d inst. Anything that the Government can do to help you will, of course, be done, for save only the crime of assault upon women there is none so dreadful as that which brought heartbreaking sorrow to your household. I have at once communicated with the Post Office Department asking that all aid we have in our power to give along the line you mention [posting of a description of the victim], or in any others that may prove practicable be given to you.

Theodore Roosevelt [5]

The Marvin case dropped from view in April 1907, with private detectives expressing the belief that the child probably had been murdered and his body buried.

There were legislative reactions to the case. The Indiana legislature increased the term of years provided for conviction of ransom kidnapping. The New Jersey legislature increased its penalty to forty years in order "to guard against a similar offense in New Jersey by making the penalty as severe as possible." [6] The Alabama legislature increased the penalty for ransom kidnapping to death.

The Whitla Case: The First Attempt at a Federal Death Penalty

In March 1909, Willie Whitla, eight-year-old son of a wealthy Sharon, Pennsylvania, attorney, and nephew of Frank H. Buhl, steel millionaire, was released from school to the custody of a man claiming he had been sent from the boy's father. A few hours later, a letter was received by the Whitlas stating that their son had been abducted and would be returned for $10,000 ransom. The letter closed with the phrase: "Dead boys are not desirable." [7]

The initial report of the case, including the text of the ransom note, appeared in a front-page story in the *Times*. The newspaper coverage emphasized that the victim was the nephew of Frank Buhl, and the day following the kidnapping, the press reported that Buhl intended to ask the aid of the state militia of both Pennsylvania and Ohio for the purpose of raiding "Black Hand" camps in the area (settlements of Italian laborers who worked in the steel mills). The press reported a rumor that Buhl had offered a reward of $10,000 for the return of the child, and $20,000 for each of the kidnappers, "dead or alive" (10 Mar. 1909).

Law enforcement efforts were reported not only from the vicinity of the crime but from as far away as Chicago. A state's attorney of that city issued a highly publicized statement labeling the kidnapping of a child as "the worst offense that can be committed,"[8] and calling for a death penalty for ransom kidnapping.

Public reaction to the kidnapping also was intense. The reaction of the citizens of the victim's hometown was described by the *Times* as follows: "Never in the history of Sharon has the town had such a remarkable appearance on a Sunday, which is usually a quiet day here. Today the streets have been alive with people since early morning, groups being seen in all parts of the town eagerly discussing the case and the various rumors. . . . Ministers in all the churches of the city have made the kidnapping the subject for prayers and sermons today. . . . Showmen have already taken advantage of the sensational crime for their own profit. A firm of Pittsburgh moving picture men has its representatives here preparing plans for making moving pictures of the kidnapping, and a local man has purchased the horse and rig in which the boy was taken away, and will exhibit it next week in one of the Pittsburgh theatres" (22 Mar. 1909, p. 1). From Pittsburgh, it was reported that fifty thousand people had joined in the search for Willie who, it was rumored, was hidden somewhere in the city.

In addition to its intensive coverage, the press reacted by offering rewards for the capture of the kidnappers. The Hearst newspapers posted a reward of $10,000. The Scripps-McRae League of Newspapers put up $2,500. The *Pittsburgh Dispatch* and the *Pittsburgh Press* each contributed $1,000. The Pennsylvania legislature adopted a concurrent resolution empowering the governor to offer a reward of $15,000 for information leading to the arrest and conviction of the kidnappers.

The Pennsylvania legislature went beyond the posting of a reward. A bill was introduced to make kidnapping a felony punishable only by hanging, to replace the existing legislation which provided a penalty of life imprisonment or a term of years as the court may direct. The bill further provided that a person convicted of assisting in a kidnapping be imprisoned for life or for such term as the court may direct. The bill was not enacted.

The New York state legislature also reacted. One bill was introduced to raise the maximum penalty from twenty-five year's imprisonment to life; another proposed that the penalty should be life imprisonment or death, at the option of a jury. The chairman of the senate committee which would consider the bills was quoted as follows: "Kidnapping is one of the most serious problems with which we are confronted today. Our present laws, in view of the Whitla and other prominent cases, seem to be insufficient for dealing with that which in all civilized countries is regarded as a most heinous offense." [9] Less than a month later, the New York senate passed a bill increasing the penalty for kidnapping to fifty years.

The Whitla kidnapping also generated the first legislative attempt to make kidnapping for ransom a federal capital offense. Datelined Washington, 23 March 1909, a news report began: "The story of the kidnapping . . . of Willie Whitla had its effect in the House today, when Representative Rodenberg of Illinois introduced a bill making the kidnapping of children and holding them for ransom a capital offense." [10] Since the interstate commerce powers of the federal government had not yet been utilized to any great extent for the purpose of curtailing this type of crime, the Rodenberg bill would apply only to the District of Columbia and the territories. The bill provided that the kidnapping of a child below the age of twelve years and holding it for ransom would be punished either by death or life imprisonment. The kidnapping of a child below this age, without a ransom demand and carrying it out of the district, would be punishable either by life imprisonment or by imprisonment for a term of years.

The *Times* was pessimistic about any action being taken at the present session of Congress, but stated: "The dramatic story of the adventure of the stolen boy at Sharon has created much feeling in Congress, and at the next session, when general legislation is taken up, it is considered likely that a bill similar to this . . . will be passed" (24 Mar. 1909, p. 2). The Rodenberg bill never was reported out of committee. A year later, however, the 1901 abduction legislation applicable to the District of Columbia was amended to include kidnapping for ransom in the district and the territories.

Following four days of complicated negotiations, trips by the victim's father and uncle to several cities, and unsuccessful attempts to deliver the ransom, Willie was returned to his father in a Cleveland hotel, following the payment of $10,000. His return was announced in the *Times* on page 1, with a two-column picture of Willie on page 2. A large crowd was reported in and around the hotel cheering the victim and his father. Congratulatory mail, containing some threats from cranks, began to arrive at the Whitla home and was to total over four thousand pieces within a few weeks.

From Chicago it was reported: "Moving picture exhibitions of kidnappings in five-cent theatres were forbidden by the Police Department today in view of the strong public sentiment growing out of the Whitla kidnapping case. . . . Two films portraying the kidnapping of a child were confiscated today" (*New York Times,* 23 Mar. 1909, p. 2).

The public reaction to the return of Willie and his father to Sharon was tumultuous: "Never was this prosperous little city so stirred as it was this morning while most of its population awaited the homecoming of the kidnapped boy. Never was such a remarkable scene enacted here as that witnessed . . . upon the arrival of the train. . . . The President could not have received a greater demonstration. The celebration of the boy's return was continued tonight. The city was in carnival attire, flags and bunting being placed throughout. The Buhl Independent Rifles, a military organization which was formed by the boy's uncle, paraded the streets headed by a brass band and serenaded the Whitla and Buhl families. Business was practically at a standstill all day and the schools were closed" (ibid., 24 Mar. 1909, p. 2).

Later on the day of Willie's triumphant return to Sharon,

two suspects were arrested in Cleveland, with over $9,000 of the marked ransom money in their possession. One was identified as James Boyle, son of a respected Sharon plumber. He was known in Sharon as being a wild youth, and he had a police record for petty offenses. The woman was Helen Boyle, his wife. Her background was somewhat mysterious and provided ground for considerable speculation in the press. She, too, was known to the police in the Midwest in connection with minor offenses.

After grand jury indictments in Ohio and in Pennsylvania, surreptitious transfers of the defendants from jail to jail to avoid mob action, and a delay caused by James Boyle's suffering a nervous breakdown, the trial of James Boyle began in Sharon, Pennsylvania, almost two months after the kidnapping. No defense was presented, and the trial lasted only a few hours. After being out less than an hour, a jury convicted him of kidnapping, which could carry a maximum sentence of life imprisonment. Immediately upon the conclusion of his trial, the trial of Helen Boyle began in the same court on charges of aiding and abetting the kidnapping. As in her husband's trial, no defense was presented. She was convicted of aiding and abetting which carried a maximum penalty of twenty-five years. Both of the offenders were sentenced to the maximum terms.

The "Black Hand" Ransomings: Victimization of the Working Class

While kidnapping cases involving the children of wealthy and prominent families had been receiving the bulk of the attention from the press, the public, and legislators, children of working-class Italian families in large American cities also were being victimized. Cases were reported from New York City, Philadelphia, and Detroit. The New York cases, however, received much more extensive coverage in the *Times*. As a result, our description of Black Hand cases focuses on the New York City experience.

Periodic reports of ransom kidnappings perpetrated by ethnic criminal societies known as the Black Hand had appeared in the *Times* since 1904. It was the juxtaposition of one such case with the Whitla case in 1909, however, in terms of the disparity between the reactions to the Whitla case and the reactions to the kidnapping of Tony Reddes, that brought the Black Hand ransomings to public attention.

Tony Reddes was the four-year-old son of the owner of a small Italian meat shop on New York City's lower east side, a business which barely produced a living for the family. In February 1909, the boy disappeared while playing on the street in front of the shop. His parents at once reported the matter to the police. Reddes posted a reward of $50. No response was forthcoming to his offer, however, and no demand for ransom had been received a month later. The police expressed the opinion that Tony had been taken not for ransom but by somebody who wanted him for their own child.

An editorial in the *Times* of March 29 noted the disparity between the reactions generated by the Whitla and Reddes cases and offered an explanation. In the opinion of the writer, it was not a matter of the relative wealth of the respective families that made the difference but rather the respective settings of the two crimes. The Whitla family was prominent in a small town, a setting in which the disappearance of children for whatever reason was rare and the cause of great alarm. The Reddes case transpired in a section of a large city whose residents have become inured to tragedies, even those involving children.

By 1909, Black Hand ransomings had generated sufficient reaction to result in legislation being passed in an attempt to curtail them. In April, when the New York state senate in reaction to the Whitla case had passed a bill increasing the penalty for kidnapping to fifty years, the senate also had passed a bill increasing to twenty-five years the maximum penalty "for blackmail, extortion, and Black Hand practices." [11] In the same month, a *Times* editorial comment called attention to Black Hand activities, urging the Italian community not to look upon the extortionists as countrymen but as criminals who could and must be resisted. The writer concluded: "Nothing more than that is needed to put an end to Black Hand outrages, for they would not be committed after they had ceased to pay. Now is the time for the honest Italians in the United States to free themselves from a humiliating slavery" (12 Apr. 1909, p. 8).

Black Hand kidnappings continued unabated throughout 1910 and 1911. Raids by the New York City Police Department's "Italian Squad," a special detail of Italian-speaking detectives who specialized in criminal activities in the Italian community, were common. The usual practice was to raid known Black Hand hangouts, take suspects to the local police station, and bring to the station known or suspected victims of Black Hand ransomings to identify the suspects. Typically, the ransoms involved were under $5,000, the victims were treated roughly, and trials resulted in maximum terms of years. However, intimidation of victims by the Black Hand and the conspiracy of silence characteristic of the community made such trials rare.

Ransom kidnapping constituted only a small but important part of Black Hand activities. Other activities consisted of extorting money by threats to kidnap, by threats of grievous bodily harm to oneself or members of one's family, and by threats to dynamite business establishments and homes. When the threats were not successful, the threatened consequences frequently were carried out. It was in the context of this full range of activities that additional legislation was signed into law by New York Governor Dix in July 1911. One bill increased the minimum penalty for Black Hand kidnapping from five years to ten years, leaving the fifty-year maximum unchanged. A companion bill, directed at extortion through threats to kidnap or to dynamite shops or dwellings, raised the penalty from a fifteen-year maximum with no minimum, to a minimum of five years and a maximum of twenty years.

Black Hand ransomings, extortions, bombings, and murders reached a climax in the summer of 1911. A *New York Times* article of August 30, stated: "[T]he Little Italy of the lower east side is almost in a state of panic. Fathers and mothers, never able to tell where the 'Black Hander's' lightning will strike next, live in dread that at any hour their child may be snatched up and carried off" (p. 4). In quoting the uncle of a recent Black Hand victim in the neighborhood, the article continued: " 'Black Handers when caught are not punished enough here,' he said angrily. 'You put them in prison for ten or fifteen years, but that doesn't do any good. They ought to be put on the shelf for life. Then the others would be frightened and go out of the business. You don't hear anything in the old country about kidnapping children. They hold up and rob men, but they are afraid to kidnap children.' "

Police activity increased significantly after the intervention into the situation of the Italian consulate in New York City. The consul general wrote to the police commissioner asking for information on the bombings, homicides, and kidnappings plaguing Italian residents of the city. Other leaders of the Italian community also were heard from. The publisher of a leading Italian-language newspaper in the city blamed the failure of the police to protect Black Hand victims from retaliation for the lack of cooperation of victims with the police. He also criticized laws against kidnapping that provided inadequate sentences and expressed his preference for life sentences. The police commissioner countered with his remedy for the situation: "The ports of Europe are the places to deal the black-mailers their severest blow. . . . Let the United States Government put capable agents in these ports of departure to demand of every male immigrant his police record. Criminals would then be kept out, and the serious imported crimes by imported criminals would cease." [12]

At this point, the federal government became involved to counter a rumor apparently generated by the police commissioner's statements. A news item datelined Washington, D.C., read: "A report from New York that the Federal Government is contemplating drastic restrictions on Italian immigration beginning Jan. 1 on account of criminal outrages frequent among immigrants from Italy is not credited here. Already immigrants with police records are debarred, and that regulation is enforced as far as possible. Even legislation singling out Italians for particularly severe measures would lead to great diplomatic inconvenience owing to treaties with Italy on the subject. " [13]

On 1 September 1911, the *Times* noted that kidnappers and Black Hand extortionists "are admittedly more active in this city than for many months" (p. 5) but optimistically reminded its readers that on this date the new laws against Black Hand activities, including ransom kidnapping, went into effect. These were the laws signed by Governor Dix in July. Despite the increased legal punishment threats, Black Hand ransomings continued until the summer of 1914, when they subsided, temporarily.

In the last five years of the decade, the ransoming of wealthy victims again became the center of attention. Plots, attempts, or actual ransomings were reported from Idaho, Colorado, Michigan, and Missouri. Only the Missouri case, however, attracted national attention.

The Keet Case: A Ransom Murder

Lloyd Keet, fourteen-months-old, was the son of a wealthy Springfield, Missouri, banker, and grandson of a millionaire. On the evening of 30 May 1917, while in the care of a servant, the baby was stolen. The next day, the parents received a letter demanding $6,000 and threatening to torture the child unless the ransom demand was met quickly. As per instructions, the father delivered the ransom into the Ozark hills on the night of June 1, but the abductors did not appear, probably because a severe rainstorm had made many of the roads in the area impassable. Authorities and volunteers searched the hills for four days without success.

Within the week, Springfield authorities arrested six persons who denied any involvement in the Keet case. They did admit that they had planned to abduct a local jeweler, the child of another Springfield family, and a St. Louis munitions manufacturer. In order to avoid threatened mob violence, a local sheriff set out with the prisoners for the state prison in Jefferson City.

On June 9, the infant's body was found in the well of an abandoned farm. A news item in the *Times* described the reaction in Springfield as follows: "Tonight scores of Springfield men in automobiles were hurrying in pursuit of the County Sheriff's automobile, in which seven [*sic*] persons suspected of the kidnapping and murder were being sped to the State prison in Jefferson City. The pursuers have declared their intention of taking summary vengeance upon the perpetrators of the crime. . . . Springfield tonight was a city in which any eventuality seemed a possibility. The Mayor ordered the saloons closed when it became apparent that the city had not quieted down after the stirring events of the day. All street cars were ordered to remain in the barns, and a company of the Second Missouri Infantry stationed here was held at the arsenal ready to answer any call" (10 June 1917, p. 8).

On June 10, the mob of forty-five Springfield citizens who had been pursuing the sheriff and his prisoners overtook them about forty miles northwest of Springfield. One of the suspects, named Piersol, was given the following treatment, as reported in the *Times*: "[W]ith a rope around his neck, [he] . . . was led to a tree and got an opportunity to confess. Stoutly denying his guilt, he was swung up from the ground and hanged until he was black in the face. His captors lowered him and offered him one more chance for life. Piersol insisted upon not only his own innocence, but that of the four men and one woman who also were prisoners. The mob pulled the rope again, declaring that he would die anyhow, and Piersol remained silent. Sheriff Webb again pleaded with the mob, and the swinging man was released, the mob leaders declaring that they did not intend to punish an innocent man, but did not intend to let Piersol go until they were satisfied of a reasonable doubt of his guilt. Piersol was given back to the Sheriff's custody and the mob dispersed" (11 June 1917, p. 2).

Thousands of Springfield citizens attended the infant's burial. According to news reports, the funeral was but an intermission from "the lust for vengeance" which had been manifested on the previous night, "when 10,000 persons, parading the streets demanded the lives of the six persons suspected in the crime." [14] Missouri, in 1917, legally was no longer prepared to slake the lust of the Springfield mob. Although in 1901 (in reaction to the Cudahy case), it had been one of the few states to provide a death penalty for ransom kidnapping in which the victim was harmed, Missouri, a few months before the Keet case, had abolished capital punishment for all crimes. Two years later, it would be reinstated.

The distance of the case from New York City and the *Times* resulted in sketchy details of the prosecution of the suspects, but the indication was that the case against Piersol and his associates was not strong. Initially, Piersol was indicted for first degree murder of the Keet infant, but apparently he was never brought to trial on the indictment. Eventually, he was convicted of kidnapping and sentenced to thirty-five years' imprisonment.

Summary

Between 1900 and 1919, a number of significant developments occurred with regard to the crime and the societal reaction to it. The number of cases increased and occurred over a much wider geographical area than in the nineteenth century. The victims in the twentieth century represented the extremes of wealth and prominence. The Black Hand ransomings had no precedent in the nineteenth century, and for the first time, a kidnapper in a major case was successful in obtaining a large ransom. On the whole, however, such cases continued to be rare. Finally, a kidnap victim was murdered; although this may have been the fate of Charles Ross, the fact never was determined.

Reactions to the crime also differed in comparison to reactions in the nineteenth century. The assessment of the crime by the social audience as heinous became more widespread. Calls from several reactive sectors for more severe punishment of ransom kidnappers mounted. The belief in the deterrent efficacy of more severe punishments consistently was more in evidence among reactors, although retribution also was cited.

The most striking development in the first two decades of the twentieth century was the creation or modification of legislation in reaction to the crime. In response to the Cudahy case, the legislatures of seven states created their original ransom kidnapping laws. Four other states threatened the death penalty in their original legislation. In reaction to the Marvin case, two states modified existing legislation by increasing the maximum penalty to death. Reactions to the Whitla case resulted in two more states increasing their penalties, and the case produced the first attempt to provide the death penalty on the federal level for ransom kidnapping. In response to the Black Hand cases, New York doubled its term of years for the crime. All in all, nineteen state legislatures and the Congress of the United States participated in creating or modifying kidnapping legislation between 1900 and 1919.

2

Slain Children

and Unharmed Businessmen:

1920-32

Two types of cases predominated in this thirteen-year period: the ransom slayings of children and the ransoming of prominent businessmen who were not harmed. Because of the increased incidence of reported ransomings in the period, only selected cases of each type are described.

The Kidnap Murder of Blakely Coughlin

During the early morning hours of 2 June 1920, Blakely Coughlin, thirteen-month-old son of a wealthy Norristown, Pennsylvania, family, was abducted from his crib. The police were notified immediately and were supplemented by Burns private detectives from Philadelphia, lured into action by rewards offered by the county commissioners and the victim's parents. After the receipt of a series of ransom letters, and the fifteen crank letters received by June 6, U.S. postal authorities entered the case.

The Coughlins commenced traveling around the area looking at "located" children thought to be their son, a precedent established in the Ross and Marvin cases. By June 8, over thirty crank letters had been received, and Coughlin collapsed. On this date, the *Times* took its initial editorial notice of the case. Titled "No Crime Worse Than This" (p. 10), the editorial noted the intense public indignation and sympathy being generated by the case. The editorial attempted to reassure the public that, although heinous, kidnapping for ransom still was quite rare and lent its support to the parents paying a ransom with minimum police interference, as long as concentrated police action followed the return of the victim.

On June 16, it was announced that Coughlin had paid a ransom of $12,000, but that his son had not been returned. He now turned the whole matter over to the police. Little was known about the recipient of the ransom, since only his voice had been heard by Coughlin. The rumor, however, was that the offender was "a man with a foreign dialect, probably Italian." [1]

The combined efforts of local authorities, state police, federal postal authorities, and Secret Service agents, resulted in the arrest of August Pascal in August. The arrest came when Pascal attempted to extort an additional $10,000 from the victim's father. The press reported that the suspect was neither black nor an Italian, as reported earlier, but was "of foreign descent, probably French." [2] A *Times* editorial felt that the capture was quite irrelevant to the main feature of the case—the recovery of the victim. Another editorial addressed the feasibility of the death penalty as a deterrent to ransom kidnapping. The writer adhered to the position that ransom kidnappers lacked sufficient intelligence and humaneness to give much thought to the legal consequences of the act; hence, they were not deterrable by threats of execution.

Shortly after his arrest, Pascal began a practice which infuriated the public and the media. Initially, he admitted involvement in the kidnapping but refused to reveal the whereabouts of the Coughlin infant unless he was granted immunity from prosecution. Four months later, the case continued to receive national press primarily as a result of Pascal's cruel game of alternately claiming the child was dead and then claiming it was alive. Eventually he claimed that the child had smothered during the abduction and that he had thrown the weighted body into the Schuykill River. A search of the river failed to recover the body. Some authorities expressed the opinion that the body had decomposed in the water and that the case was now closed as far as they were concerned.

In October, the decomposed body of a male child about the age of the Coughlin baby was found near the town from which Pascal had written the ransom letter. The police believed it to be the body of Blakely Coughlin, but the parents did not. They continued traveling about the eastern seaboard looking at children put forward as their son.

In November, Pascal was indicted on charges of first degree murder, kidnapping, burglary, and extortion. He pleaded guilty to second degree murder and kidnapping for extortion and was sentenced to life imprisonment on the kidnapping charge, the maximum penalty available under Pennsylvania law. The first degree murder charge was not pressed because it couldn't be proved without the body of the child. The sentencing judge was quoted as follows: "I am sorry that I cannot impose the most extreme penalty known in law, the electric chair, because your crimes richly deserve such a penalty." [3]

Coughlin stated that he was satisfied with the sentence. The *Times*, however, was not satisfied. An editorial titled "An Obvious Failure of Justice" (22 Nov. 1920, p. 14) took the position that never was capital punishment better deserved than in this case, purely on grounds of protecting society from Pascal, who conceivably might be paroled someday.

The Reemergence of the Black Hand: The Verotta Case

In May 1921, the Verotta case occurred in New York City. Other kidnapped children had died in the course of ransomings—the Keet infant in Missouri, and the Coughlin child in Pennsylvania. However, it was never clear whether or not the Keet child had died accidently, and in the Coughlin case, Pascal claimed at least that the killing of the victim was accidental. The Verotta case "was the first case on record in the country where blackmailers had actually carried out their threat to kill when ransom was not paid." [4]

Giuseppi Verotta, five-year-old son of an Italian pushcart merchant, was abducted from in front of his home by members of a Black Hand organization. Two days later, a letter was received by the parents notifying them that their son had been kidnapped, demanding $2,500 ransom, and threatening to drown the victim, kill the rest of the family, and burn down their house. Although a rumor had been circulating in the neighborhood that Verotta had recently collected $50,000 from a lawsuit resulting from serious injury to an older son in an auto accident the previous year, the father could not raise the $2,500 ransom demanded. Verotta did not notify the police, but his neighbors did.

Despite an intensive search by the police, hundreds of neighborhood schoolchildren, and neighbors, there were no developments in the case for over a week. On June 2, a development occurred which captivated the press. Cooperating with the police (itself an unusual circumstance), Verotta single-handedly captured an intermediary who had come to collect the $500 agreed upon as the ransom for his son. In addition to the intermediary, four other arrests were made by the police. The whereabouts of the victim, however, remained a mystery. A *Times* editorial on Verotta's action was titled "A Reminder of Roman Fortitude" (4 June 1921, p. 12), and in it the writer congratulated the father who, at great risk to the life of his son, had acted to protect the children of other parents from ransom kidnappers.

The search for the victim ended a week later, when the strangled body of the child was found washed up on an island in the Hudson River. The reaction of the *Times* was to publish an editorial which indicated a weakening of the newspaper's resistance to capital punishment as a deterrent to ransom kidnapping. Titled simply "Giuseppi Verotta," the editorial concluded: "Few crimes are so atrocious, so agonizing, as that of the kidnapper, and the fiends who practice it are to be deterred only by fear of the ultimate penalty" (14 June 1921, p. 14).

The penalty for ransom kidnapping in New York State at

this time was ten to fifty years' imprisonment. The five defendants pleaded not guilty. At the arraignment, the district attorney announced his intention to pursue indictments for first degree murder which did carry the death penalty. In addition, he called the judge's attention to the fact that this was the first case on record in the United States where blackmailers had actually carried out their death threat when the ransom was not paid.

There was speculation that the boy had been transported between New York and New Jersey. Based upon this speculation, U.S. Representative Siegel of New York announced to the press that he was preparing a bill which would provide the death sentence for persons who kidnap children and transport them from one state to another. Representative Siegel introduced the bill designed to make interstate transportation of child kidnap-victims a federal crime, but it died in the House Judiciary Committee.

Ten weeks after the abduction, a jury took seven hours to find the first of the four defendants guilty of complicity in kidnapping and murder; he was sentenced to death on the murder conviction. The *Times* published two editorials supporting the sentence. Prosecution of the remaining defendants was delayed until the conviction and death sentence of the first defendant could be reviewed by the New York Court of Appeals. When the higher court confirmed the conviction and sentence, the condemned offender confessed his role in the Verotta kidnap murder and implicated forty others. Because of his confession and cooperation with the state, he received a reprieve from the governor. Two of the remaining defendants also received death sentences, and the third was committed to a state hospital for the criminally insane before he could be tried.

Reprieves and rescheduled execution dates kept the case in the press for two more years. Ultimately, all of the condemned offenders had their sentences commuted to life imprisonment in the hope that they would reveal the identity of the other Black Handers involved. New York City law enforcement officials had resisted the commutations on the ground that there had been no Black Hand ransomings in the Italian community since the Verotta offenders had been sentenced to death. The officials had contended that if the sentences were carried out, "such kidnappings, not unusual heretofore, will become rare." [5]

The Kidnap Murder of Bobby Franks: The Death Penalty on Trial

In 1924, only one major case of ransom kidnapping was reported, but it was the most sensational case since the kidnapping of Charles Ross a half century before. That a wealthy victim could be kidnapped and slain by wealthy offenders was incomprehensible. In fact, the killing of any ransom victim was difficult for the public to fathom. The Franks case could not be explained by greed or stereotypically in terms of the criminal customs of "foreigners," as with the Black Hand cases. When the offenders were portrayed in the press as conscienceless experimenters with human life, bewilderment turned to fear.

In Illinois, the death penalty was available either for a ransom kidnapping leading to the death of a victim or for murder. When life sentences were handed down to the offenders the bewilderment turned into cynicism about equal justice for the rich and the poor.

On the afternoon of 21 May 1924, Robert Franks, fourteen-year-old son of a Chicago millionaire, was lured into a car by eighteen-year-old Richard Loeb and nineteen-year-old Nathan Leopold, Jr., the sons of wealthy Chicago families. When the abductors placed the ransom call that evening, threatening death to the victim if the ransom was not paid, Bobby Franks already was dead. Upon receipt of the call, the Frankses secretly notified the police, but also prepared the ransom for delivery. While the parents were waiting for further instructions from the kidnappers, a passerby found the body of Bobby Franks in a culvert.

Rewards totalling $15,000 were forthcoming immediately from the parents of the victim and Chicago newspapers. Franks stated his willingness to spend $1 million to bring the slayers to justice. The *Times* published two editorials on May 24 in reaction to the case. The first, titled "Of All Crimes the Most Abhorrent" (p. 14), reviewed the Verotta and Coughlin cases and reassured the public that ransom kidnappings were rare and those in which the victims were killed were even rarer. It also expressed the opinion that the death of Bobby Franks was probably accidental, but even if it was, the death penalty still would be justified. The second editorial revived the familiar theme of *Times* editorialists concerning the private versus public responsibilities of parents of kidnap victims.

On May 30, Chicago police arrested Nathan Leopold, Jr., and his friend, Richard Loeb. Initial press reports on the suspects immediately featured two themes: that both the suspects were sons of Chicago millionaires and both were "advanced thinkers," having compiled brilliant academic records at the University of Chicago and University of Michigan. The day following their arrest, both offenders confessed. The *Times*, in a front-page article on June 1, reported: "Ransom and the 'adventure' of crime were the motives for the deed, although both received liberal allowances from their parents. Long having had kidnapping in mind, they had discussed making a victim of the grandson of Julius Rosenwald, head of Sears, Roebuck & Company, of which firm young Loeb's father, Albert H. Loeb, is Vice President. . . . The killing was deliberate and decided on in advance of the seizure of the boy, murder as well as ransom being part of the 'adventure.' Failing in other means, they had intended to kill him with ether or acid."

The judicial process quickly went into motion. It was publicized widely that kidnapping was a capital offense under Illinois law, and if Leopold and Loeb were found guilty of the kidnapping and the murder, they could be sentenced to death on two counts. State's Attorney Crowe stated: "I have a hanging case. . . . The State is ready to go to trial immediately." [6] Chief Justice Caverly of the criminal court announced that he would urge an immediate trial and that "Justice shall be served within thirty days." [7]

On the day of the first preliminary hearing, the role which wealth was expected to play in the trial was the topic of speculation by Chicago newsmen: "The beginning of the reported

'$15,000,000 defense' planned by the parents, whose wealth aggregates easily that sum, was indicated when Clarence S. Darrow went to the State's Attorney's office with a demand to be permitted to talk with his clients. The prediction was made that the defense would be insanity, due to overstudy and education. . . . When Leopold and Loeb are placed on trial there will be millions aligned on each side of the counsel table. The two families have combined fortunes conservatively estimated at $15,000,000 and perhaps more. . . . On the other side is Jacob Franks, retired manufacturer and former Loop pawnbroker, whose wealth is set at a minimum figure at $10,000,000." [8]

Although it reprinted the above speculation out of Chicago, the *Times's* position on the matter was one of disapproval, made known in an editorial titled "No Millions Should be Mentioned" (5 June 1924, p. 20). The writer severely criticized the emphasis being placed on the wealth of the parties involved and maintained that in America criminal justice was the same for the rich and the poor. To allege otherwise, demeans the entire American system of justice.

As the defense and prosecution prepared their cases, the press kept the case before the public with a variety of background material. On June 18, the *Times* carried an article, datelined Chicago, headlined: "Loeb's Cousin, a 'Red,' Wants 'Blind Justice'—He Works for a Paper Which Denounces the 'Crimes of Chicago Capitalists.' " The article concerned Moritz J. Loeb, first cousin of the defendant, who worked for the Communist newspaper the *Daily Worker*. The article stated, in part: "His paper's editorial eye is on the Franks murder prosecution. It is warning the Communists of Chicago and the West that 'capitalistic justice is blind, yes, blind to the crimes of the rich' " (p. 11). The *Times* reviewed previous ransomings under the headline: "Charley Ross Stolen Just Fifty Years Ago—Most Famous Case of Kidnapping in Country's History." The five-column article began: "It is just fifty years since a little boy in Philadelphia went for a ride with two strange men, and thereby gave the world the most celebrated of its kidnapping cases. Charley Ross has never come back. Yet whatever happened to him, he still lives, for he has become a legend and his name is known to the very youngsters of today" (29 June 1924, sec. 8, p. 4).

In July, the court proceedings began with Clarence Darrow announcing that the defense would not ask for acquittal but would focus exclusively on an insanity defense in an effort to save the defendants from the death sentence. Pursuant to Darrow's strategy, Leopold and Loeb pleaded guilty to kidnapping for ransom and murder, waived a jury trial, and threw themselves on the mercy of the court. On August 5, Judge Caverly ruled that Leopold and Loeb were sane.

The remaining two weeks of the trial were devoted to Darrow's efforts to save his clients from the death penalty. When the trial ended on August 28, the concluding paragraph of a *Times* editorial summarized the decision facing Judge Caverly: "What Mr. Darrow is really appealing to is not the Judge's mercy but his sense of social responsibility. By what method can the monstrous nature of the Chicago crime be most sharply etched into the public consciousness—by death or life imprisonment? Which stroke will bring most sharply home to parents their responsibilities to society and to their own children—the noose or the prison. That is the real question which the Chicago Judge faces" (28 Aug. 1924, p. 16).

On September 10, Judge Caverly handed down his decision—life terms for murder, and ninety-nine years for the kidnapping for ransom prior to the slaying. The judge made it plain that by life imprisonment he meant the full term of the natural life of the defendants, and he expressed the hope that any attempt in the future to obtain a reduction of the sentence would be futile. Although he could find no mitigating circumstances in the crimes of Leopold and Loeb, he saved them from the death penalty "in accordance with the progress of criminal law all over the world" and "the dictates of enlightened humanity." [9]

After five months of speculation about the influence of wealth on American criminal justice and about the reactions that would be generated by any decision other than the death penalty, life sentences had been handed down.

A Chicago attorney representing a nineteen-year-old client under a sentence of death for killing a Chicago policeman stated: "If after Leopold Jr., and Loeb were given life imprisonment Krauser is hanged, the justice of Illinois will be discredited for a thousand years to come." [10] State's Attorney Crowe, when consulted about the Krauser case, stated: "One judicial error does not pave the way for others. Leopold and Loeb should have been hanged, and their escape, instead of making it easy for others to evade the noose, should point out the need for death penalties more clearly." [11]

U.S. Representative Emanuel Celler, of New York, who in a few years would become a major congressional opponent of federal capital legislation for ransom kidnapping, urged that the Leopold and Loeb sentence be considered as grounds for commuting the death sentence of a nineteen-year-old black girl in Philadelphia. From Philadelphia itself, a prominent defense attorney interpreted Judge Caverly's decision as an act of mercy for two young "special" children and speculated that its effect on "youth of this type in Illinois may be to convince them that they can do the things these boys did without losing their lives." [12] Another Philadelphia criminal attorney admitted that he was surprised by the verdict but respected the decision of the court. He also stated, however: "In behalf of the late Willie Morgan [a former client] I can only regret that he chose Philadelphia instead of Chicago as the scene of his last abnormality." [13]

Reactions from law enforcement authorities were mixed. The New York City police commissioner labeled Judge Caverly's decision as "substantial justice," as "all right thinking people" would probably agree. "Of course," the commissioner admitted, "there will be godless people who will use the judgement in this case to reiterate that there is one law for the poor and another for the rich." [14] Law enforcement sentiment in Philadelphia was summed up in the headline of the news report: "Criticize Penalty—Philadelphia Sentiment was Strong for Hanging Youths." [15] Mayor J. Hampton Moore echoed the sentiments of Philadelphia authorities: "Is it any wonder the plain people of this Country who have not large fortunes to back them up are inclined to be critical of authority? No good citizen will fail to support and defend the Constitution, the law and the courts, but there is always an ever personal equation or personal interest which makes the ordinary voter wonder whether the ideas we believe in are always upheld in practice. But this outrage in Chicago makes me actually wonder whether Justice is blind." [16]

Response of the general public in the form of letters to the editor of the *Times* manifested itself in four letters critical of the decision and one in support of it. A prominent Philadelphia club woman expressed concern that the offenders' wealth would result in their release from prison: "Unfortunately, life imprisonment does not mean life imprisonment these days. Good behavior or money will get them out. Money ruined them, money got them the verdict, and money will get them out. . . . Every mother should be incensed over this miscarriage of justice" (11 Sept. 1924, p. 2).

Reaction of the press was surveyed by the *Times*, which republished editorials from newspapers throughout the eastern half of the nation: New York's *World* approved of Judge Caverly's decision as being in the best interests of public policy. The *New York Herald Tribune* evaluated the sentence as "inadequate justice," an evaluation which the writer believed was shared by most people. The *Chicago Tribune* stated that if the sentence met the approval of the people in Illinois, "the retention of punishment by death in any case in this State is wrong." The *Boston Herald* saw the sentence as "an unfortunate conclusion to one of the most hideous crimes committed in America." The *Baltimore Sun* expressed concern over the effects of the sentence in reinforcing cynicism about the influence of wealth on justice. The *Atlanta Constitution* felt that execution in the case would have been justified. The *Washington Post* felt that the defendants' youth probably justified the life sentence. Louisville's *Courier-Journal* titled their editorial, "A Victory for Murder." The *Indianapolis Star* felt that the public would be more impressed with the sentence if they could be sure that a sentence to life meant life, a sentiment shared by the *Chattanooga Times*. The *Hartford* (Connecticut) *Courant* stated that wealth was all that kept the offenders from being hanged (ibid.).

The editorial reaction in the *Times* itself focused primarily on the implications of Judge Caverly's decision for capital punishment. Three closely spaced editorials reflected cynicism toward American justice, a cynicism which the editorial staff had found repugnant just a few months earlier. The first editorial stated that Judge Caverly did his judicial duty as he saw it, even though the deterrent effect on the criminally disposed may not be as effective as hanging might have been, and the craving of the public for full retributive justice may not have been fully satisfied. The second and third editorials expressed regret that the sentences would be interpreted by millions as evidence of discrimination in the administration of American criminal justice.

In September 1925, one year after the conclusion of the Leopold-Loeb trial, Mary Daly, six-year-old daughter of a wealthy Montclair, New Jersey, businessman, was kidnapped and murdered by Harrison Noel, the twenty-year-old son of an attorney. Noel was described in the press as a brilliant student who had suffered a mental breakdown from overstudy, which resulted in his commitment to an asylum. He admitted having studied the details of the Franks case, and his attorney employed an insanity plea. All of these similarities combined to render the Daly case, at least in the mind of the public, a rerun of the kidnap murder of Bobby Franks.

Reactions to the Daly case were intense, widespread among the sectors, and publicized highly in the national press. A significant difference from the Franks case, however, was that a jury sentenced Noel to death, not for the ransom killing of the Daly girl, but for shooting to death a black taxi-driver whose vehicle was used by Noel in the Daly kidnapping. Noel's conviction was reversed on appeal, and he was committed to an asylum. A *Times* editorial agreed that the place for Noel was in an asylum but also maintained that the case may have been deprived of some of its general deterrent impact by the court's action.

More Child Victims: The Frazier, Parker, and Jamieson Cases

In 1927, the maximum penalty for ransom kidnapping in Tennessee was ten to twenty years, as a result of legislation created in 1901 in reaction to the Cudahy case. In March of the year, a case transpired which prompted an unsuccessful legislative effort to provide the death penalty, an effort which failed only after it had passed the Tennessee senate. The victim was two-year-old Virginia Jo Frazier, daughter of a Chattanooga City Commissioner. Although she wasn't harmed, the case was reacted to with the same intensity as if another kidnap murder had transpired. Following the abduction of the victim from her home, her father received a letter demanding a ransom of $3,333. The father delivered the ransom to a "negro man." Within the hour, the ransomer left the victim on the porch of a minister's home in the city. She was unharmed, but most of her clothes were gone, and she appeared to have been drugged.

Law enforcement activity was intense. The city of Chattanooga offered $5,000 for the capture of the ransomer, "dead or alive," [17] and private citizens supplemented the reward fund as well as participated in the intensive search for the kidnapper. The arrest of early suspects in the case generated such public reaction that the police were forced to remove the suspects from the city as a precaution against mob action. The *Times* called attention to the intense reaction from the public and press of Chattanooga; a spot check of the local press verified it. That the frustration produced by the Leopold-Loeb case remained alive in the minds of many was evidenced by the editorials.

Two weeks after the abduction, a seventeen-year-old black male was arrested for the crime. He stated that he had planned and perpetrated the ransoming because of an urge to travel and to enjoy the good life. Indicted for kidnapping and for burglarizing a store a short time before the abduction, he pleaded guilty and was sentenced to fifteen years for kidnapping and five years for burglary. A defense plea that the offender be sent to a juvenile institution rather than to a penitentiary was rejected.

As was the case in Tennessee, California also was without a death penalty for kidnapping for ransom in 1927. Until December of that year, the state's experience with the crime had been so limited that few felt a death penalty was needed, either as a deterrent, as a means of retribution, or for societal protection. California's only verified case had been the attempt to ransom Gladys Julia Witherall in 1921. Although $50,000 had been demanded, it was not collected. The victim was rescued unharmed, and the offenders received the maximum indeterminate sentence of ten years to life, which for all practical purposes was a life sentence. In 1925, a $200,000 ransom plot concerning Mary Pickford had been frustrated even before it could get underway, and here, too, the offenders had received the maximum sentence. Finally, the Aimee Semple McPherson kidnapping hoax of 1926 had resulted in many Californians coming to view ransom kidnapping more as a publicity gimmick than a realistic threat.

On 14 December 1927, however, the kidnap slaying of children reached a new height of heinousness when twelve-year-old Marian Parker, daughter of a Los Angeles bank official, was ransomed and murdered. When she failed to return home from school, her father immediately notified the police. Over two hundred law enforcement authorities began the search. The next day Parker received the first of four telegrams demanding $1,500 ransom and threatening to kill the victim. The *Times* published the details of the ransom notes on the front page.

Parker's first attempt to deliver the money was frustrated when the abductor saw police in the vicinity. On the second attempt, the abductor appeared in a car with the victim, apparently asleep, seated beside him. He took the ransom and told the father that he would release the victim a short distance down the street, which he did. When Parker lifted the blanket in which the victim was wrapped, he found her dead, having had both legs amputated. An autopsy later revealed that she had been strangled before the amputation. Authorities professed to see in the offender "a self-fancied arch-criminal of the Loeb and Leopold type." [18]

The *Times* carried a front-page story on the case accompanied by pictures of the victim and her parents. A manhunt extending throughout California and nearby states was initiated, and reports began to come in from sections of Los Angeles of the finding of the dismembered parts of the victim's body wrapped in boxes and newspapers. California Lieutenant Governor Burton Fitts wired Governor C. C. Young in Sacramento stating that "without any doubt the murder of Marian Parker is the most vicious and atrocious crime in California history" (19 Dec. 1927, p. 4) and urged that the state offer a substantial reward for the apprehension and conviction of the offender. Rewards to total $100,000 were posted by citizens, film actors, and newspapers, including a contribution from the Angelus Temple of Aimee Semple McPherson. Articles in the *Times* recalled the 1917 Keet case in Springfield, Missouri, the Franks case of 1924, and the Verotta case.

Datelined Los Angeles, December 19, and headlined "Child Slayer Clues Fail in Los Angeles—Terror Grips the City," a *Times* story began: "With . . . the mocking murderer of little Marian Parker, still at large tonight . . . every newspaper, every school room, and every pulpit urged the mothers of the city to keep their children behind locked doors" (20 Dec. 1927, p. 1). Adding to the national alarm was a report from Chicago that a wealthy manufacturer was making arrangements to send his children out of the city after a third letter had been received threatening to kidnap his seven-year-old son unless $5,000 was paid. Another Chicago report stated that the estate of another wealthy family had been "turned into the semblance of a fortress" to guard against the kidnapping of the children.

On December 20, William Edward Hickman was named as the prime suspect. Hickman was nineteen years old and had come to Los Angeles after graduating from high school in Kansas City. He had been employed at Parker's bank, but had been discharged over a check forgery incident. A picture of Hickman appeared in the *Times* of December 21 along with the report that thousands were searching for him in a nationwide manhunt. In addition to local and state law enforcement authorities, the "entire force of the Federal Secret Service Bureau" (22 Dec. 1927, p. 1) was reputed to have been enlisted.

In Los Angeles, young men who resembled Hickman's picture were appealing to the police for protection "as angry mobs quickly gather every time a boy resembling Hickman is stopped and questioned by an officer or citizen who believes he recognizes the fugitive" (ibid.). Exemption cards were being issued to Hickman look-alikes, stating that the bearer had been questioned by the police, identified, and released. One young man reportedly was arrested five times before he was issued his card. One look-alike, rescued from a mob who believed him to be Hickman, was jailed. The next morning he was found hanged in his cell.

Eight days after the abduction, Hickman was arrested by local authorities in Echo, Oregon. The arresting officers became instant celebrities and looked forward to collecting the sizeable rewards that had been pledged. They were to experience considerable frustration when much of the pledged money failed to materialize. They were compensated somewhat, however, by a contract for a week's performance at a Los Angeles vaudeville theater.

Los Angeles District Attorney Keyes stated, upon being informed of Hickman's capture, "We know that we have the arch criminal in California murder history. . . . The entire force of the prosecutor's office in Los Angeles County will be devoted to speeding this case to trial." [19] Parker's reaction was: "I am not only thankful for myself, but for the parents of all other children that such a dangerous man has been apprehended. This thing is too terrible to talk about adequate punishment for the man." [20]

A special session of a Los Angeles grand jury was called. The governor of California promised immediate attention to the extradition papers needed to bring Hickman from Oregon, and California officers were dispatched to bring him back on board a special railroad coach.

Hickman's confession was printed across four columns on page 4 of the December 22 edition of the *New York Times*. A three-column picture accompanied a front-page story in the December 24 edition. Although it originally had been believed that Hickman's only previous involvement with the law had been the check forgery incident, he confessed to a cross-country crime spree on his way from Missouri to California. Later in the judicial proceedings of the Parker case, Hickman confessed to the holdup murder of a Los Angeles druggist and also was implicated in a third murder.

By the time that Los Angeles officers arrived in Oregon to bring Hickman back, it was reported that Hickman had been viewed, filmed, photographed, or questioned by four thousand persons. As the train departed, reactions to the case continued to come in from across the country, many of them having to do with the action of school officials to institute psychiatric screening systems to detect students like Hickman and with the adoption of measures to ensure that teachers would not release pupils to the custody of a stranger.

As the train carrying Hickman proceeded down the coast toward Los Angeles, the *Times* carried special reports datelined from various stops along the route. One report stated that Hickman had told officials that he would "adopt the Leopold and Loeb program" as a defense (28 Dec. 1927, p. 11).

The arrival of Hickman's train in Los Angeles on December 27 was greeted by a crowd of four thousand which accompanied him to the County Building for his arraignment. The presiding judge assured one and all that Hickman's constitutional rights would be safeguarded, while a police official was quoted as stating: "You can say for me that no penalty the law will exact is sufficient for a fiend like Hickman. Hanging is too good for him and anything short of hanging would be a gross miscarriage of justice." [21]

Hickman's attorney announced that he would make an insanity plea in the trial under an untested California law which made the plea an admission of the crime charged. As the trial began, reporters were in attendance from most of the major newspapers throughout the country. One well-known writer did not participate, however, as indicated in a letter to the *Times*, dated February 3: "To the Editor of the New York Times; Beverly Hills Cal., Feb. 13—I want to die claiming only one distinction, the only writer to refuse newspaper offers to cover the Hickman trial. Instead of being ashamed of it, it looks like every town tries to make their murder the biggest one of the year. . . . Yours, Will Rogers" (4 Feb. 1928, p. 17).

After deliberating thirty-six minutes, a jury pronounced Hickman legally sane. The verdict automatically established Hickman's guilt of the kidnapping and murder as a function of the plea. The penalty would be death or life imprisonment on the combined verdicts. On February 13, Hickman was sentenced to hang at San Quentin for first degree murder. Immediately prior to this sentence, he had been sentenced to the term provided by law for the kidnapping, ten years to life.

Since the insanity plea upon which Hickman's defense was based never had been tested in the courts, a lengthy appeals process began. The California Supreme Court unanimously upheld the constitutionality of the plea and Hickman's attorney announced his intention to take the case to the United States Supreme Court. The attempt to have the case heard by the United States Supreme Court was unsuccessful. After California Governor C. C. Young refused to grant a commutation of sentence, Hickman was hanged on 16 October 1928. He was the first person put to death for a crime developing out of a ransom kidnapping. Death sentences for first-degree murder in the course of a kidnapping had been handed down in the Verotta case in 1921 and in the Daly case in 1925, but in both cases the sentences never were executed. The execution of Hickman apparently satisfied the public, press, and legislators of California, even though the criminal justice system had not acted as swiftly as some would have liked. No agitation was forthcoming to increase California's ten-years-to-life penalty for ransom kidnapping.

A little more than a year later, a nineteen-year-old offender was executed in Hawaii for the ransom murder of Gill Jamieson, ten-year-old son of a bank vice-president. Identified in the press as a drug addict, the offender admitted that he had planned the crime after studying the details of the Leopold-Loeb case and of Hickman's kidnap slaying of Marian Parker. Before settling on the Jamieson boy, he had looked over a list of all vice-presidents of Honolulu banks. He needed the money, he stated, to send his parents to Japan. When asked why he had killed the boy, even before receiving the ransom, Fukunaga stated that "he killed the boy because kidnapping never works unless you do." [22]

The Victimization of Midwestern Businessmen

During the late 1920s, while the bulk of public attention was focused on the kidnap murders of children, another form of kidnapping intruded. It began with reports of gangsters ransoming other gangsters. Most of the reports came from Chicago, although others came from New York City, Detroit, and Los Angeles. Many of the cases occurred in the context of power struggles among bootleg gangs.

From case to case, there were several commonalities: children as victims were avoided; large initial ransom demands typically were negotiated downward to comparatively modest sums; threats to victims of diabolical tortures to persuade them to cooperate were common, but seldom carried out; successful prosecutions were rare, largely because of the successful intimidations of the victims and witnesses; and convictions typically were obtained on lesser charges, such as firearm violations. The most consistent factor, however, was the absence of societal reaction to the cases.

When gangster kidnappers began to turn their attention to wealthy members of the respectable community, however, reactions from the press, public, authorities, and, eventually, the lawmakers, were strong. A Detroit report on the 1928 ransoming of a retired hotel proprietor stated that "the police believe [the case] to be a continuation of the activities of a gang of extortionists who have mulcted local persons of thousands of dollars during the last few months." [23] Law enforcement reaction was intense but unsuccessful.

In reaction to the 1928 kidnapping of a wealthy Chicago auto dealer, the *Chicago Tribune* devoted five columns of text to his rescue, accompanied by four columns of pictures of the victim, the police, prosecuting authorities, and the offenders. The offenders were described in the press as "ex-convicts and desperate criminals" (10 Apr. 1928, p. 12) and were thought to be members of a union of kidnapping rings operating in Chicago, Detroit, New York, Boston, and Philadelphia. Authorities claimed and the press publicized that the gang had had "definite plans for abducting a score or more of Chicagoans for ransoms totaling $1,000,000." [24] Even mere rumors of planned kidnappings of wealthy individuals by organized gangs generated much concern and action as illustrated by a rumored plot to ransom the great-grandchildren of John D. Rockefeller in 1929.

By 1930, the pattern of kidnap gangs preying upon wealthy members of the respectable community began to show a clear concentration in the American Midwest. Local businessmen were the prime targets, businessmen already frustrated by the economic rigors of the depression. Cases of this type were reported from Granite City, Illinois; Kansas City, Missouri; Des Moines, Iowa; and Detroit. Many cases became known only in connection with reports of other more sensational cases, and again we must conclude that many more of these cases occurred than those on which we have information.

The $40,000 ransoming of Charles Pershall, wealthy grocer and banker of Granite City, Illinois, in February, was important because of the geographical location of the case. Granite City, Illinois, is just across the Mississippi River from St. Louis, Missouri, which had been experiencing a rash of kidnappings of bookmakers and gamblers at this time. The reaction to these cases, however, had been minimal. This was not the case with the Pershall kidnapping. The local business community reacted strongly. Two hundred and fifty businessmen from Granite City and surrounding communities in the St. Louis vicinity held a meeting at the local Masonic Temple. The chairman of the meeting, the president of a Granite City bank, stated: "We've been held up, bulldozed, and kidnapped long enough." [25] Out of the meeting came a citizen's investigating committee to look into local crime conditions and to organize a movement to support a reform candidate for sheriff.

The victimization of Kansas City businessmen was noteworthy because it produced the first sale of kidnapping insurance in the United States, at a premium of 1 percent for $50,000 maximum coverage. Finally, a Des Moines, Iowa, case illustrated the obstacles for local law enforcement created by the transportation of the victim across the borders of several states.

In April 1931, Fred Blumer, president of a brewery in

Monroe, Wisconsin, was abducted at gunpoint and driven twenty miles south to Freeport, Illinois. A ransom of $150,000 was demanded. An undisclosed amount was paid for his release, and the ransomers escaped. A St. Louis physician was ransomed eleven days later. Authorities believed that the kidnappers were the same gang that had recently ransomed several bankers and businessmen across the river in Illinois. This ransoming was the tenth to occur in the St. Louis area within a year. The victim was released in East St. Louis, Illinois, and authorities cited the interstate transportation of the victim as a major obstacle to their efforts.

In October, St. Paul, Minnesota, authorities reported that city's second kidnapping of a local businessman within two weeks. In November, a wealthy St. Louis fur merchant was abducted from his car by gunmen and a ransom of $100,000 demanded but not collected. The police immediately suspected the Cuckoo Gang of St. Louis and elements of the Capone gang from Chicago.

In November, Chicago police claimed that they were close to apprehending members of a gang "believed to have extorted large sums from 100 or more victims in several States in the last year." [26] Several members of the gang were arrested and tried. One defendant was convicted and sentenced to ninety-nine years, but the other trials all resulted in hung juries. The single conviction was the first for ransom kidnapping in Missouri in ten years, according to St. Louis police. In December, a Chicago physician and his wife were abducted and $25,000 set as the price for their release; $2,000 was collected. One of the defendants broke jail before trial, two were acquitted, and two were given life sentences in return for guilty pleas.

Six days after the abduction of the Chicago physician and his wife, a case to be mentioned prominently before Congress was reported from Kansas City. The victim was Nell Quinlan Donnelly, wealthy head of a clothing company. She and her chauffeur were kidnapped on December 16, and a ransom demand for $75,000 was sent to her husband threatening to blind the victim with acid and to kill the chauffeur. The kidnapping received nationwide press coverage, including a picture of the victim in the *Times.* The husband and a friend of the family, former U.S. Senator James A. Reed, expressed their willingness to negotiate with the kidnappers. Former Senator Reed received wide press coverage for his statement that if Nell Donnelly was harmed, "he would spend the rest of his life, if necessary, to run down the kidnappers and send them to the gallows" (18 Dec. 1931, p. 13).

After being held for thirty-four hours, Nell Donnelly and the chauffeur were released, without the ransom being paid. Police believed that their release came about at the urging of the local underworld to avoid any more publicity being focused on their Kansas City activities. Four persons, all claiming poverty as their motivation, eventually were convicted. Although the press made much of the fact that kidnapping for ransom was a capital offense in Missouri and that the prosecution would ask for the death penalty, two of the offenders received life terms in return for guilty pleas, another received thirty-five years, and the fourth was sentenced to twenty-five years.

The St. Louis and Chicago Chambers of Commerce Go to Washington

By December 1931, much of the American public, the press, and especially Midwest business and law enforcement leaders, were convinced that organized criminal gangs, whose bootlegging profits soon would be curtailed by repeal of Prohibition, were turning to the ransoming of wealthy members of the respectable community. Midwest business leaders had witnessed a significant rise in the number of major kidnappings for ransom, especially in their section of the country. They were especially alarmed by the increase in the number of cases in which prominent businessmen were being victimized. Local and state law enforcement authorities in the Midwest were becoming increasingly frustrated by the legal obstacles created by the interstate movement of victims by their kidnappers. Thus armed, the St. Louis Chamber of Commerce, with the blessings of chambers from other Midwest cities, sought congressional assistance to solve the problem. The remedy they sought was a federal death penalty for ransom kidnapping.

Officers of the St. Louis Chamber of Commerce, the mayor, the chief of police, and others, organized a committee. They selected Cleveland Newton, former U.S. representative from Missouri, as their spokesman and sent him to Washington to lobby Congress. The committee remained behind in St. Louis to draft a bill of the legislation desired and sent one copy to Senator Patterson of Missouri and the other to Missouri Representative Cochran for the purpose of introducing the bills. The bills were introduced and were before the appropriate judiciary subcommittees in early December 1931.

The St. Louis lobbyists perceived the crime of kidnapping for ransom as patently deliberate and rational, as a cost-benefits business transaction perpetrated by organized crime. As such, they believed it to be highly deterrable by the threat of legal execution. The fact that the significant rise in kidnappings to which they were reacting had occurred in Illinois and Missouri—two states that had had the death penalty for the crime since 1901—was dismissed as an artifact of local politics, the susceptibility of local police to corruption by the gangs, and interstate legal complexities. They were firmly committed to the belief that federal legislation, backed up by a federal enforcement and prosecution capability, would remove these obstacles to the deterrent efficacy of the death penalty.

On the second day of 1932, the activities of both kidnappers and law enforcement authorities provided additional support for the lobbyist's cause. Chicago authorities reported that they had arrested six men who comprised "the worst gang of extortioners and kidnappers ever organized." [27] On the nineteenth of January, the $50,000 ransom kidnapping of Benjamin Bower, a wealthy baking company executive, was reported *from Colorado,* one of the few states that still provided only the common-law penalty of seven years for ransom kidnapping. On January 23, while Bower was still being held captive in the mountains of Colorado, a Chicago newspaper correspondent telephoned U.S. Senator Patterson in Washington, informing him that kidnapping investigations in that city had uncovered a plot to kidnap Gen. Charles G. Dawes, recently appointed head of the Federal Reconstruction Finance Corporation. Although Dawes was unperturbed by the plot, the *Times* reported that the story spurred the introduction of a bill in the Senate by Senator Patterson of Missouri "to put interstate kidnapping under Federal jurisdiction and to empower Federal judges to impose sentences, including the death penalty, for the offense" (24 Jan. 1932, p. 1). Testifying to the role of coincidence in the emergence of criminal legislation, the *Times* report continued: "The measure, sponsored by St. Louis and Chicago organizations, is due for hearings soon before a judiciary subcommittee headed by Senator Waterman *of Colorado,* in whose state, as well as in Missouri and Illinois, kidnapping outrages have recently occurred [emphasis added]."

The apparent source of the Chicago reporter's information was revealed on January 24, when Alexander Jamie, chief investigator for the Chicago Chamber of Commerce's "Citizens Committee for the Prevention and Punishment of Crime"—known in the press as the "Secret Six"—announced that the committee had developed evidence against the leaders of a huge kidnapping syndicate. The *Times* reported: "This evidence might be used, other workers of the Secret Six said, in supporting the movement for a Federal law providing the death penalty for kidnappers" (25 Jan. 1932, p. 10). Two days after the revelations by the Secret Six in Chicago, another ransom kidnapping of a prominent businessman occurred, this time in South Bend, Indiana, right in the Secret Six's backyard; on February 2, a prominent Tucson, Arizona, banker was abducted and a ransom of $60,000 demanded.

As the time approached for the Midwest lobbyists to testify before congressional committees, data they had gathered in support of their case began to appear in the press. The results of a survey by St. Louis Police Chief Joseph Gerk of kidnapping activities in 501 American cities were published in the *Times* of January 27. According to Chief Gerk's data, 279 persons were kidnapped in twenty-eight states in 1931, with Illinois leading the list with 49 cases (p. 44). Col. Robert Isham Randolph and Alexander Jamie of the Chicago Secret Six reported to the press that 5 wealthy citizens in that city had been threatened with kidnapping in recent weeks and that detectives of their organization had been assigned to guard several other prominent businessmen. "The field of underworld victims has been exhausted and every reputable businessman is now subject to kidnapping, according to the Secret Six officials" (30 Jan. 1932, p. 36).

In addition to efforts in support of the legislation, alternatives or supplements to it also began to be reported in the press as the date of the congressional hearings approached. Frank J. Loesch, seventy-nine-year-old president of the Chicago Crime Commission, advocated the establishment of an interstate secret organization to combat kidnappers. "The prevalence of the kidnappings for ransom, 'the most detestable of crimes and wholly foreign to American thought,' has created a condition that must be met by businessmen as well as public officials, Mr. Loesch said." [28]

Congressional Hearings on the Kidnapping Legislation

On 26 February 1932, the proposed capital kidnapping legislation came to a hearing before the House Committee on the Judiciary. Titled "A Bill Forbidding the Transportation of Any Person or Persons in Interstate or Foreign Commerce, Kidnapped or Otherwise Unlawfully Detained," the bill contained a clause specifying that, upon conviction, a person shall "be punished by death or imprisonment in the penitentiary for such term of years as the court in its discretion shall determine." [29] Representative Cochran of Missouri opened the hearing with a brief statement in which he reminded his colleagues of his consistent opposition to centralization of power in the federal government and to the creation of overdependency of the states on the federal government. The kidnapping situation had developed to a point, however, that, in his opinion, only the invoking of the government's power to regulate interstate commerce could remedy the situation.

Cochran then introduced Cleveland A. Newton, former congressman from Missouri, who would conduct the hearing and introduce witnesses in support of the proposed legislation. Newton assured the committee that the testimony of the witnesses would convince them of the necessity for a capital law, reviewed a number of recent ransomings in the general vicinity of St. Louis, and stressed the legal obstacles to successful prosecution created by the interstate aspects of the crimes. According to Newton, a federal force, beyond local influence and control, was required. He cited as precedent the existing activities of federal agents directed at such crimes as prohibition violations, mail fraud, white slavery, and the interstate transportation of stolen autos, none of which, according to Newton, began to compare with the crime of ransom kidnapping.

Newton then presented Chief Gerk's statistics. Assuming that seven to ten persons participated in each of the 279 cases reported to Chief Gerk, Newton claimed that nearly two thousand people were involved. He continued: "And this is a crime of such enormous and terrible character that the Federal Government ought to step into that gap and aid the State forces in apprehending and punishing the criminal bands of this character. . . . Because the police officers and the prosecuting officers tell us that, in such cases as I have described, if they had had the cooperation furnished by a Federal law and by the Federal officers, I do not think there is any doubt that there would have been an enormous increase in the number of arrests and convictions. . . . We get reports of conferences that have been held among these criminals, where the leaders will say to the younger fellows, 'Do not fool with "whiskers." ' That is the way they put it—'Do not fool with "whiskers." ' 'Whiskers' means Uncle Sam." [30]

Newton then addressed himself to a report by U.S. Attorney General Mitchell. In the report, the attorney general had agreed that kidnapping was a more serious offense than those for which the federal government already had invoked its interstate commerce powers, but he also stated: "In the present state of the National Treasury, I do not see how I can recommend the passage of a measure of this kind, and it should not be passed unless Congress is ready immediately to provide the additional money necessary to enforce it." [31] Newton commented that it seemed to him "rather a pitiful situation that with a crime that is worse than murder—that the Federal Government, when it has this power over the activities between the States, should hesitate on the ground of economy." [32]

Representative Sumners, committee chairman, interrupted Newton's testimony to address one of the sources of opposition to the bill—the overdependency of the states on the federal government in the control of crime. The *House Journal* recorded the exchange as follows:

THE CHAIRMAN. . . . How long are we to continue our present constitutional system of Government, with its dual relationship, if the people of the States will not gird up their loins and perform their duty of making their State laws effective, instead of leaving everything to the Federal Government?

MR. NEWTON. I think there are a good many acts that provide for Federal action and Federal appropriations that this Congress could very well repeal. . . .

THE CHAIRMAN. Now, the question is, Are we, as a self-governing people, . . . going to tackle the job of making the States as efficient as the Federal Government, or are we going ahead and overload the Federal Government until we make it as inefficient as the States? . . .

MR. NEWTON. Yes, I think that such a movement ought to be discouraged as much as possible. . . . But here, in view of the heinous character of the offense and its far reaching ramifications, I think the Federal Government should do its part.

THE CHAIRMAN. Yes, I think the committee recognizes that basically, there is a good deal in your position. When the States came into the Federal Union they not only surrendered some of the elements of sovereignty, the commerce clause of the Constitution, for instance, but by reason of that surrender, they do not in all cases exercise the same independent police powers that a nation does. They have no frontier to guard as do independent nations.

MR. NEWTON. Yes, sir.

THE CHAIRMAN. And, therefore, there is some obligation on the part of the Federal Government to guard the borders of the

States. But what I am interested in is to see if we can not utilize these crimes that are becoming so frequent, and that are so widespread and so heinous, . . . to stir up the interest of the people in making use of the reserved powers of the States, instead of having our States, whenever they get up against a big proposition, send a delegation of forceful and impressive gentlemen, like those who are here this morning, to the National Capitol to try to secure Federal legislation and Federal absorption of governmental power.

Mr. NEWTON. Yes, Mr. Chairman, but I do not believe that the Federal Government, in its desire and its duty to protect its citizens, ought to hesitate in a case where criminals of the most ruthless kind will take a child into another State, out of the jurisdiction of the State where it was kidnapped, and leave it to that State to follow and punish the criminals. I think the character of this crime is so terrible that the Government ought to make an exception in this case.[33]

Newton's next witness was Walter B. Weisenberger, president of the St. Louis Chamber of Commerce, "who represents the great mass of our business people, who are vitally concerned about this measure." [34] Weisenberger concerned himself not with the text of the bill but with presenting "some of the public sentiment that demands consideration and punishment of the heinous crime of kidnapping." [35] He emphasized that ransom kidnapping was a new crime, that it was national in its extent, that "public enemies No. 1" [36] were using interstate legal technicalities to avoid prosecution, that the crime is highly planned and premeditated, and that it could not be compared in heinousness with other crimes in which the federal government already had taken action. Throughout his testimony, Weisenberger made frequent references to specific cases involving the victimization of prominent business people, including Nell Quinlan Donnelly of Kansas City.

Weisenberger was followed before the committee by St. Louis Police Chief Joseph A. Gerk, who had recently retired as president of the International Police Chiefs Association. Chief Gerk emphasized the ease with which ransom kidnapping could be committed and the ease with which prosecution could be avoided in those cases involving the interstate transportation of the victim. He also focused upon the ease with which local law enforcement officers could be corrupted. Chief Gerk's testimony was interrupted on one occasion by a query from Congressman Dyer concerning how much support the proposed legislation had from other chiefs of police throughout the country. Chief Gerk responded by calling the attention of the committee to communications which had been read into the committee record by Newton. Letters had been received from the police chiefs of twenty American cities unanimously supporting the legislation.

The next witness was Robert Isham Randolph, past chairman of the Chicago Association of Commerce. Randolph informed the committee of the kidnapping situation in Chicago, which had prompted the formation of the association's Secret Six to combat the problem, and emphasized the need for federal legislation and enforcement to combat the interstate crime that kidnapping had become. Rather than getting into a detailed discussion of Chicago's experience, however, Randolph left this task to the final witness, Sgt. Leroy Steffens, a Chicago police officer assigned exclusively to the Secret Six to investigate ransom kidnapping. Sergeant Steffens emphasized the brutality to which prosecution witnesses in kidnapping trials were subjected by friends of kidnappers to prevent them from testifying. His description of such tortures as lowering victims into water, strangling them, soaking them with gasoline, threatening to put them into vats of lime, were vivid.

The hearings before the House Committee were widely publicized in the press, especially such remarks as that by Randolph that he "always drove 'with the doors of my car locked and my gun in a position to shoot,' " [37] and Sergeant Steffen's vivid torture descriptions. Much publicity also resulted from the testimony of many of the same witnesses before the Senate Judiciary Committee in support of a companion bill, introduced by Senator Patterson of Missouri, that would make it a federal offense to demand a ransom through the mails.

At the beginning of March 1932, Congress was not prepared to move rapidly on a federal kidnapping law. In both houses, the bills were still in committee, where concerns had been raised about the death penalty clause, about creating overdependency of the states on the federal government, about encroaching upon States' Rights and centralization of power in the federal government, and about the expense of enforcing such legislation. Most congressmen agreed that ransom kidnapping was heinous, that it had reached problematic proportions in America, and that the federal government had to lend some aid to the states to combat it. Many others, however, particularly in the Senate, did not agree that kidnapping for ransom should be made a federal crime, especially a federal capital crime.

On the state level at the beginning of March 1932, the death penalty was available for ransom kidnapping, at least under some conditions, in seven states. In all seven jurisdictions, it constituted an alternative to life imprisonment or a term of years at the discretion of either the court or a jury. Sixteen other states provided life imprisonment as the maximum sentence, while in the remaining twenty-five states, terms of years were provided ranging from one to seven years in Colorado, to ten to ninety-nine years in New Mexico. Although all forty-eight states had kidnapping laws, laws specifically recognizing kidnapping for ransom existed in only twenty-five jurisdictions.[38]

The Lindbergh Case

On the night of 1 March, 1932, twenty-month-old Charles A. Lindbergh, Jr., was stolen from his second-floor bedroom of the Lindbergh home in Hopewell, New Jersey. In their search of the house and grounds, the parents found a note demanding a ransom of $50,000. When the kidnapping was revealed to the public, the societal reaction was the most intense that had ever been generated by a ransom kidnapping. Charles Lindbergh, Sr., was a heroic figure not only in the U. S. but throughout the world. The victim's grandfather, U. S. Senator Dwight Morrow, may have been the most esteemed public servant in the country. He had died only five months before the ransom slaying of his grandson.

President Herbert Hoover was among the first to receive

an official version of the crime when U. S. Attorney General Mitchell met with him early on the morning of March 2 to discuss "the measures the government would take to help in the solution of the crime and the arrest of the criminals." [39] The measures were announced by Attorney General Mitchell after the meeting. "Although there is no development to suggest that the case is one within Federal jurisdiction," [40] the attorney general reported, on the chance that federal laws may have been violated, federal law enforcement machinery was being mobilized. The mobilization included the full cooperation with New Jersey authorities of the Department of Justice, with young J. Edgar Hoover's Bureau of Investigation as "the backbone of the Federal cooperation," [41] the services of the U. S. Post Office Department, and the full cooperation of the 563 agents of the U. S. Prohibition Bureau, as well as that of the Coast Guard, the Customs and Immigration Services, and the Washington, D. C., police force.

Frank L. Loesch of the Chicago Crime Commission also visited President Hoover on the morning of March 2, expressed his opinion "that the Government crime detection agencies were almost helpless before the machinery of professional kidnapping" [42] and again pushed for the formation of a private antikidnapping organization "along the lines of the Secret Six in Chicago." [43] Other Midwestern proponents of the pending federal kidnapping legislation also were heard from. The *Times* reported extensively on the denouncing of the crime from the floors of both houses of Congress.

As police throughout the eastern states attempted to pick up the trail of the Lindbergh kidnapper and the victim, James DeJute, eleven-year-old son of a wealthy Niles, Ohio, contractor was abducted and a ransom demand for $10,000 received. The words "remember Marian Parker" [44] were printed on the top of the letter.

In addition to reporting the federal law enforcement efforts mobilized by President Hoover and the congressional reactions, the national press launched into a campaign in support of the pending federal legislation. The *Times* published an article titled "Kidnapping Wave Sweeps the Nation" (4 Mar. 1932, p. 9), in which the kidnapping statistics presented before Congressional committees by Chief Gerk again were featured. A *Times* editorial, titled "A New Crime" (3 Mar. 1932, p. 18), called for a few instances of exemplary punishment as a deterrent. In the same issue, the *Times* reprinted editorials from five New York City newspapers, the *Newark News,* the *Washington Post,* and the *Washington Evening Star,* supporting federal capital ransom legislation. In a letter to the editor of the *New York Times,* Will Rogers, who had earlier looked with disdain on the sensation caused by the Marian Parker kidnap murder in Los Angeles, wrote: "Why don't lynching parties widen their scope and take in kidnapping? They are ten times more premeditated and performed by more normal people" (p. 8).

Reactions from opponents of capital legislation covered in the press were few. Among them was Professor Felix Frankfurter of the Harvard Law School, who stated: "The proposed kidnapping law is an example of the tendency to add to the already great burden of the Federal courts" (ibid.).

In Congress, the push for federal capital legislation gained momentum. On March 4, three days after the kidnapping of the Lindbergh child, Congressman Nelson of Missouri received unanimous consent to read into the *Congressional Record* an article he had written twenty years previous titled "Babies and Daddies." [45] Representative Cochran of Missouri read into the *Record* a speech he had delivered the evening before in a nationwide radio address, parts of which appear below.

Ladies and Gentleman [*sic*] of the radio audience. I am indebted to the Columbia Broadcasting System for this opportunity to explain the bill I have introduced . . . .

I can appreciate why some Members of Congress oppose the enactment of this bill because there is no Member who has more vigorously opposed the efforts to centralize power in the Federal Government than I have. However, we are confronted with a situation that the State police are unable to control, especially along the borders of a State. . . .

Early yesterday morning the President, through the Attorney General, placed Department of Justice agents at work on the

Lindbergh case and instructed them to make every effort to apprehend the kidnappers. Everyone will applaud the action of the President, but I can tell you he acted without any authority of law. I seek to give that authority in my bill.

It is not always Colonel Lindbergh's child that is kidnapped. God knows I would never object to the President taking this action. I commend him even though he had no authority. But yesterday another child was kidnapped, this time in Ohio. What I seek to do is to assure every mother that her child will be accorded the same attention from the Government of the United States as the President provided in the Lindbergh case. . . .

Would you, who have seen the shadow of death to bring into this world your dear baby or babies, want brave officers stopped at State lines because of red tape, professional jealousy, or for any cause, or do you want a situation where State lines are no barriers? Do you want ferreted out that lowest of all criminals regardless in what State he or his foul companions seek refuge? Of course you do, and that is just what I am trying to do by my bill. . . .

I say when the time arrives that mothers fear to send their children to school, then the time has arrived when thoughts of State rights and centralization of power must be forgotten; then, I say, we must go back to the thought of preservation of the family, the foundation and unit of all government of all civilization.[46]

In state legislatures, half of which had not been moved in the preceding twenty years to seek more severe penalties for kidnapping for ransom, despite the kidnap murders of child victims in the 1920s and the victimization of businessmen more recently, calls for such action now were heard. Within days of the Lindbergh kidnapping, a death penalty bill was introduced in the New Jersey legislature but was delayed upon the request of Colonel Lindbergh, who feared that the passage of the legislation would endanger the life of his child. Death penalty bills were introduced in the legislatures of New York, Virginia, Mississippi, and Louisiana. In Massachusetts, a bill to raise the maximum sentence to life imprisonment was introduced as was the case in Rhode Island, an abolition state.

Attorney General Mitchell went on national radio under the auspices of the American Bar Association. In the address, the attorney general warned the public not to expect too much from the proposed federal kidnapping legislation. He emphasized that the federal government was under severe constitutional restrictions concerning law enforcement matters. At most, according to Mitchell, the federal government could only supplement, not replace, local law enforcement efforts. He emphasized that if the proposed legislation had been in effect at the time of the Lindbergh case, it would not have enabled federal help because no interstate aspect of the crime apparently was involved.

Despite the pressure being mounted by the proponents of the federal legislation, the bill was still in committee in both houses of Congress. On March 8, it was further delayed when the Senate Judiciary Committee announced that it was postponing action on the bill so as not to hamper Colonel Lindbergh's efforts to communicate with the kidnappers. Senator Norris, chairman of the committee, assured the American people, however, that the committee emphatically favored federal legislation on the interstate transportation of kidnap victims, and would move on the bill after the Lindbergh case was cleared up. However, Senator Norris stated that he, personally, opposed making interstate kidnapping a capital offense because of the risk to the victim that such legislation would create. The House Committee on the Judiciary also delayed action on the bill before it in response to the request from Colonel Lindbergh.

Congressional supporters, meanwhile, continued to take the floor and speak eloquently for the legislation. Although the federal kidnapping legislation remained stalled, congressional action was forthcoming on companion bills. On March 10, the House passed, without discussion and by unanimous consent, Representative Cochran's bill providing for twenty years' imprisonment or a $5,000 fine for using the mails to extort or demand money on threat of harm.

On April 10 Colonel Lindbergh handed over $50,000 ransom to a person believed to be an emissary of the kidnappers on the promise that his child would be returned. When the child did not appear, however, Colonel Lindbergh announced that he had been swindled. Reaction swelled again.

On May 11, the body of the Lindbergh child was discovered in a field not far from the Lindbergh home. Societal reaction now reached even greater heights. The *Times* published a brief editorial titled "The Tragic Ending" (13 May 1932, p. 18), predicting that the world would open its heart in deepest sympathy. In the same issue, other ransomings were reviewed in which the victims had been slain, including the Ross (1874), Franks (1924), Daly (1925), and Parker (1927) cases. Messages arrived from all over the world in response to finding the body of the victim. An article in *Osservatore Romana*, the Vatican City newspaper, expressed the outraged sentiments of the pope and the holy see: "Such a 'monstrous offense' against all the finer feelings of modern civilization, says *Osservatore*, calls for immediate exemplary punishment." [47] From Washington came the report: "Disregarding the fact that the Federal Government, under existing law, has no jurisdiction in the kidnapping and murder of the Lindbergh baby, President Hoover today ordered all Secret Service agencies of the United States 'to make the kidnapping and murder of the Lindbergh baby a live and never-to-be-forgotten case until the criminals are implacably brought to justice.' " [48]

The *Times* of May 14 reported that congressional action on the federal kidnapping legislation now appeared imminent. Senator Patterson, expressing hope for swift action on his bill in the Judiciary Committee, stated: "Death is the only kind of punishment these racketeers can understand" (15 May 1932, p. 2). In the House, a $100,000 reward to be provided by the government was urged, and on May 19, the Judiciary Subcommittee of the House voted to report out favorably the kidnapping bill to the full committee. There was no longer any reason to delay action in order to protect the Lindbergh baby. Although the report on the House Subcommittee action also stated that some members had reserved the right to challenge the death penalty provision of the bill in the full debate, Representative Cochran stated: "The bill is something that is being demanded by every mother in the nation, and if enacted will cause future kidnappers to think deeply before committing such another crime as the Lindbergh tragedy." [49]

On June 2, the House passed the threatening letter bill, already approved by the Senate, and sent it to President Hoover for his signature. On the same date, the House Committee on the Judiciary approved the Cochran bill to make interstate kidnapping a federal crime, punishable by death. The death penalty provision was softened somewhat, however, by an amendment which provided that the death penalty should not apply when a jury recommends mercy. The next day, the Senate Judiciary Committee recommended to the full Senate the passage of an amended version of the federal kidnapping bill *with no death penalty provision.* The amended bill substituted "imprisonment in the penitentiary for such term of years as the court, in its discretion, shall determine." [50] On June 9, the Senate passed the amended bill and the scene was set for the debate before the full House of Representatives, in which support for the death penalty consistently had been stronger than in the Senate.

The House's version of the federal kidnapping bill, which included a death penalty provision, was called to the floor for debate on June 17. Two aspects of the bill received primary attention—the death penalty provision and the implications of the legislation for the creation of a federal police force. It was immediately called to the attention of the House that the Senate had passed a version of the bill which provided a term of imprisonment instead of the death penalty, and an amendment was made to substitute the Senate version for the House bill.

Support for deleting the death penalty provision came from Representative Celler of New York; and opposition, from Representative Dyer of Missouri. The *Congressional Record* reported the exchange.

MR. CELLER. Mr. Speaker, as a member of the Judiciary Committee, I am in favor of this bill, on the condition, however, that the provision for the death penalty be stricken out. If the object of punishment is vengeance or personal hatred or personal venom . . . I would say leave in the death penalty. . . . but that is not the modern conception of punishment. It is the barbarous, savage idea of punishment. We want to deter and prevent other people from committing like crimes and at the same time reform the criminal. . . . We are in the twentieth century, and we must show some enlightenment. . . . The important thing is certainty, not severity, of punishment. Swift justice will do the trick—nothing else. . . .

If you insist upon the death penalty, I wager that you will inflict a penalty on the victim who is kidnapped. . . . The person kidnapped is the witness who, even when rescued, can always point the accusing finger at the guilty. Doing away with the victim would save the life of the guilty. We must be careful, gentlemen. We must be realists, and not let our feelings get the better of us. . . .

Mr. Dyer. . . . I disagree with the gentleman from New York . . . when he states that we should not provide the death penalty. The object or purpose of this legislation is purely to deter kidnapping. The States have been pretty well able in all other respects to take care of this crime, and this is for the purpose of providing a death penalty because a number of States do not provide such a penalty in kidnapping cases, and I would ask the gentleman whether or not he would be in favor of the death penalty for the kidnappers of the Lindbergh baby. . . .

It is foolish to enact legislation to deter kidnapping and not make it punishable by death. What would happen in the case of the kidnappers of the Lindbergh baby, if they could be shown to be the ones that did it? We would have no law probably in the State where the prosecution occurred, and none in Federal law, if this bill should leave out the death penalty they richly deserve.

What would be the result? Nothing more nor less than the uprising of the people, and you would have probably a repetition of what we have had in the country many times—lynching.

Let us provide laws that will give the punishment that is deserved by those guilty of this horrible offense, where they had kidnapped and death results.

. . . I am in favor of this bill, if you will pass it with teeth in it and provide the death penalty.[51]

After further discussion of the death penalty provision of the House bill, including amendments that would provide a death penalty only if recommended by a jury, the debate turned to the second main point of contention—the potential of the bill for creating a federal police force. Basically the question was whether, under section 2 of the bill, a newly created body of federal agents would enforce the legislation, or whether existing state and local police would be given federal authority to enforce the kidnapping legislation. Amendments favoring each alternative were offered. Abstracted portions of an exchange between Representatives Oliver of New York and Cochran of Missouri illustrate the concern.

MR. OLIVER OF NEW YORK. . . . [W]e should check the establishment of a Federal police force under the control of political officials who will use this force not for the enforcement of laws but for political purposes, as is the case in Europe. . . .

You have got to give the Federal Government a police force to carry out the responsibility. . . . If you should give the Federal Government the responsibility without giving it a police force, then you are perpetrating a fraud on the Government and you are only passing a fake statute. . . . [Y]ou will find the people of the States, now in turmoil over a Federal police force enforcing prohibition, rising up to strike down this kind of a police force if it is to be paid for out of the Federal Treasury and controlled as a political police force by the United States Government.

MR. COCHRAN OF MISSOURI. Does not the gentleman feel the crime warrants such action?

MR. OLIVER OF NEW YORK. I do not feel it warrants the overturning of the entire police control to the Nation. However, I believe that laws should be enforced, and I say give us Federal authority and give us State police clothed to exercise that Federal authority.[52]

After several unsuccessful attempts to amend the various provisions of the House bill recommended by the Committee on the Judiciary, with lengthy debate on each amendment, the House voted to substitute the Senate bill, *which did not provide a death penalty.* A flurry of amendments was offered to amend the Senate bill so as to incorporate a death penalty provision, even if only as an option available to a jury. It was quickly recognized by the proponents of the bill, however, that if such an amended bill were sent back to the Senate for conference, all might be lost. To the accompaniment of predictions that without the death penalty the federal ransom laws would prove ineffective, the Senate's noncapital version of the bill passed the House without a dissenting vote. Five days later, on 22 June 1932, President Hoover signed the bill into law.

Eight days later, Haskell Bohn, twenty-year-old son of a wealthy St. Paul, Minnesota, manufacturer, was kidnapped. The ransom note demanded $35,000 and cautioned the father to "Remember what happened in the Lindbergh case." [53] Through further negotiations with the abductors, the ransom was reduced to $12,000 and, after it was paid, the victim was released. No arrests were made.

In the next six months, ransomings claimed the eight-year-old son of a wealthy partner in the New York Stock Exchange, a wealthy Chicago couple, and an alleged New York City bootlegger. None of these cases, however, involved the interstate transportation of the victim and, therefore, provided no opportunity for invoking the new federal legislation.

Summary

In the latter years covered in this chapter, the victimization of adults generated the drive for federal legislation, something the kidnapping and, in some cases even the murder, of children in the 1920s had not been able to accomplish. It was not the kidnapping of just any adults which produced the legislation, however. When gangsters ransomed gangsters, little reaction was generated. It was only when gangsters turned their attention to prominent midwestern businessmen that societal reaction became intense.

Under severe economic pressure, reading accounts in the press about persons like themselves falling prey to ransom kidnappers, witnessing the inability of local and state police to deal with interstate kidnapping, and being convinced that organized crime was turning from bootlegging to ransom kidnapping, the chambers of commerce of St. Louis and Chicago went to Congress. There they encountered a generally sympathetic ear to the idea that the government should do something, but encountered stiff resistance to their specific proposal that ransom kidnapping should be made a federal capital crime.

When the Lindbergh tragedy occurred, the proposed federal legislation was languishing in subcommittees of both houses of Congress. The case created societal reaction of an intensity sufficient to overcome the congressional resistance to making the interstate transportation of a kidnap victim a federal crime; however, it was not sufficient to overcome resistance to making it a federal capital crime.

Supporters of a federal death penalty had argued, unsuccessfully, that the death penalty was the vital element in deterring kidnappers. They prominently cited the Lindbergh case as a "cost" of congressional delay in passing the legislation which had been before them for at least three months prior to the Lindbergh case. The ransom cases that occurred in 1932, following the passage of the federal legislation, now were tallied as additional "costs" of not including a death penalty.

3

The Federal War on

Ransom Kidnapping:

1933-39

The belief that the noncapital federal legislation would not deter ransom kidnappers received much support during 1933. Twenty-seven major cases would be reported, more than twice the number in any previous year, and the use of the phrase "kidnapping epidemic" would become widespread. In response to a combination of continued frustration over the lack of progress in the Lindbergh case and the apparent inability of the noncapital federal legislation to deter kidnapping, state legislators continued to increase the penalties. Each legislative action was widely publicized, as evidenced by a front-page *Times* article of February 5, which began: "Society, aroused in feverish anxiety . . . is slowly but surely increasing penalties against the [kidnapping] evil so drastically revealed" (sec. 2, p. 1). Legislation to strengthen existing laws had been recently passed, was being considered, or was in prospect in twenty-three states. In some states, such as Minnesota, it had been found that ransom kidnapping was not a crime under existing legislation. Most legislatures amended existing laws by increasing the term of years for kidnapping. A minority, such as Wyoming, Ohio, Virginia, and South Carolina, were proposing a death penalty.

Federal Forces Try Out the 1932 Legislation

On February 12, Charles Boettcher II, millionaire broker from Denver, Colorado, was ransomed for $60,000. The Boettcher case established several firsts: federal forces actively became involved under the 1932 legislation, federal charges were filed against the defendants under the legislation, and it was the first ransoming in which the involvement of the Midwest bandit gangs of the depression became known. In a relatively short time, the names of Machine Gun Kelly, Alvin Karpis, Ma Barker, Gordon Alcorn, and Verne Sankey were to become daily topics for front-page coverage.

Boettcher and his wife were accosted by two gunmen as they drove into the driveway of their home, robbed, and Charles Boettcher kidnapped. A ransom note left with Mrs. Boettcher demanded $60,000 and stated: "Remember the Lindbergh baby would still be alive if ransom had been paid." [1] J. Edgar Hoover, in charge of a meagerly staffed and underfinanced squad of agents in the Department of Justice, ordered his men into the case three days after the abduction, on the invitation of Denver authorities. Hoover's agents took an active role in the case from the beginning, despite the fact that the seven-day waiting period provided in the 1932 legislation had not elapsed, and interstate transportation had yet to be established.

Local reactions to the kidnapping were intense. A $5,000 reward was offered by the Denver City Council for the arrest and conviction of the perpetrators, the governor of Colorado and the mayor of Denver issued a proclamation asking all citizens to be on the lookout, and four thousand Denver citizens combed the city. State legislators hastened to take action on a pending bill making ransom kidnapping a capital offense if the victim was killed. The legislation was held in abeyance, however, at the request of Mrs. Boettcher. The press covered the ransom negotiations daily, and on February 20, the victim was released unharmed following the payment of $60,000 ransom. The seven-day waiting period having passed, and it having been learned from the victim that he had been transported into South Dakota, federal forces took full jurisdiction.

An informer told authorities that the abductors had been the Verne Sankey-Gordon Alcorn gang, well-known desperadoes wanted for bank robbery in the United States and Canada. Local authorities arrested four members of the gang on March 6 in Denver and South Dakota, but Alcorn and Sankey escaped. As federal agents began a nationwide manhunt for them, federal kidnapping charges were filed against the defendants in custody.

Legislative reaction in western states was swift. On March 9, the governor of Montana signed into law the state's first ransom kidnapping legislation with life imprisonment as the maximum penalty. Nine days later, the governor of Utah signed into law ransom kidnapping legislation which provided either death or life imprisonment as the maximum penalty.

Two months passed before further developments in the Boettcher case were reported. During the interim, $50,000 ransom was demanded for the return of the nineteen-year-old son of a Chicago underworld figure; $250,000 was demanded for the ten-year-old daughter of a prominent Massachusetts family, and $60,000 was collected; and an Iowa-Illinois ransom gang were apprehended by federal authorities for ransoming two Illinois men.

In May 1933, two of the Boettcher ransomers pleaded guilty to Lindbergh Law charges in a Denver federal court. One received sixteen years for conspiracy to kidnap, sixteen years for the actual kidnapping, and a $1,000 fine for using the mails to extort. Another defendant was sentenced to a federal penitentiary for twenty-six years under the conspiracy clause of the 1932 legislation. One of the two women defendants was not prosecuted. Conspiracy charges against the other were dismissed, although charges of extortion by mails were continued against her, to be revived when her husband and leader of the gang, Verne Sankey, was apprehended.

Other kidnappings in which the victim had been killed had resulted in death sentences, but the sentences had resulted from the murder and not from the kidnapping itself. In the McElroy case in Kansas City, Missouri, in May 1933, the victim was not killed, but a death verdict was pronounced.

The four abductors were inspired, according to their testimony, by reports of two earlier ransomings. They demanded

$60,000 for the return of Mary McElroy, twenty-five-year-old daughter of the city manager of Kansas City. They accepted $30,000, and released the victim, unharmed, from the Kansas farm on which she had been held for twenty-nine hours.

The agents of J. Edgar Hoover's squad entered the case immediately upon its being revealed that the victim had been transported across state lines, and they participated in the arrests of the offenders in Texas, Kansas, and Virginia within a matter of days. Assistant U. S. Attorney General Joseph D. Keenan was dispatched from Washington to assist state officials in prosecuting the case. The county prosecutor proclaimed that the state would demand the death penalty under Missouri law and Keenan agreed to hold federal charges in abeyance and to assist in the state prosecution.

The Height of the Kidnapping Epidemic: The Summer of 1933

Within a five-week period during the summer of 1933, six ransom kidnappings were reported, along with other less publicized extortions and attempts. The impression was growing that state and federal legislative actions were not having the deterrent effect intended by their sponsors. The 1932 federal laws had enabled the Department of Justice enforcement and prosecuting forces to make significant contributions in a number of cases after they had occured, but new cases kept occurring. The nationally publicized capital prosecution in Missouri, as a result of the McElroy kidnapping, likewise was perceived as exercising little deterrent effect.

In June, St. Paul, Minnesota, contributed the Hamm case which, together with a subsequent Oklahoma City ransoming, was to catapult the rise to prominence of J. Edgar Hoover and the FBI. Five days before the Hamm kidnapping, Hoover's force had received a titular boost from an executive order by President Roosevelt creating the Division of Investigation within the Justice Department. It was Joseph Keenan, however, and not Hoover, who was named to direct it.

On June 15, William Hamm, Jr., wealthy brewer in St. Paul,

was abducted. Although it was not to become known for some weeks, Hamm's abductors were the notorious Alvin Karpis-Ma Barker gang. The next day, the U.S. mails were used to deliver a $100,000 ransom demand. Following the payment of the sum, the victim was released unharmed three days later. When it was suspected that the victim had been carried across state lines, in addition to the fact that the mails had been used, Melvin Purvis, chief Department of Justice enforcement agent in the Midwest, entered the case.

While federal investigators concentrated on apprehending the known offenders in the Boettcher case and the as yet unidentified kidnappers of Hamm, a Chicago underworld figure, whose son had been ransomed three months earlier, alleged that he had been ransomed for $70,000. Federal authorities added the case to their agenda. Five days later, John King Ottley, wealthy Atlanta banker, and a former appointee of President Hoover to a national advisory commission, was the victim of an unsuccessful $40,000 ransoming. Federal agents took up the investigation, but withdrew after assisting in the arrest of the defendants, when it was determined that no interstate transportation had occurred.

One day after the Ottley case was reported from Atlanta, the O'Connell case was reported from Albany, New York. It was to appear regularly in the *Times* for six years. The victim was John J. O'Connell, Jr., twenty-four-year-old son and nephew of the political bosses of the Albany County Democratic machine. The price demanded for his release was $250,000. New York Governor Lehman mobilized all state resources, and U.S. Senator Copeland of New York, at this time heading up a Senate Crime Investigating Committee, requested the attorney general to send in Department of Justice agents. They made their appearance the next day.

When the O'Connell case was reported in the national press, it had to share coverage with the attempted $100,000 ransoming of Alton, Illinois, businessman and banker, August Luer. Hoover's squad now had another case. The *Times* reported that Luer was highly respected in Alton for his efforts to keep workers employed in his businesses throughout the depression, even to the extent of substituting his own money for depositors' assets frozen in his bank. After having been held captive for five days, Luer was released without any ransom having been paid. Federal agents arrested two suspects and charged them under federal extortion laws. Four other arrests quickly followed and Department of Justice prosecutors announced that they would hold the federal charges in abeyance to allow Illinois authorities to prosecute under the state capital kidnapping law, with federal prosecutors assisting them.

The final event of this five-week period in the summer of 1933 was the kidnapping of millionaire oil man Charles F. Urschel of Oklahoma City on July 22. Eventually to become interwined with federal action in the Hamm case, the Urschel kidnapping was to ensure the rise to prominence of the FBI. The Urschel case added to the registry of depression-era banditry the names of Harvey Bailey and George "Machine Gun" Kelly. In addition, it provided the first opportunity for demonstrating the effectiveness of a complete federal effort under the 1932 legislation.

On the night of July 22, Urschel, his wife, and neighbors were playing bridge on the porch of the Urschel home. The screen door opened and two armed men entered and demanded that Urschel come with them. Mrs. Urschel notified authorities immediately. Reporters were next to arrive, and the kidnapping gained nationwide headlines. Hoover's agents took complete charge of the investigation on the next day. A $200,000 ransom was delivered to Kansas City and Urschel returned home unharmed.

Federal agents pulled out all stops in their attempt to locate the spot where Urschel had been held. Urschel was a prominent person. Not only was he a millionaire, but he was a personal friend of newly-elected President Franklin Delano Roosevelt.

Press coverage of the Urschel case was diverted by the trial of Walter McGee in Kansas City for the McElroy kidnapping. The state was seeking the death penalty under Missouri law, the first such attempt for a kidnapping in which the victim was neither killed nor harmed. Assistant U.S. Attorney General Joseph B. Keenan had been sent to Kansas City to assist in the state prosecution. The prosecution took two days to present its case and in his closing argument to the jury on July 26, the prosecutor stated: "The nation is watching this courtroom today. . . . As soon as a message is sent out from this room that a jury has said a man shall hang by the neck until he is dead for this kidnapping, you will have taken a big step to stop this wave of kidnapping." [2]

The testimony of the victim, Mary McElroy, was largely responsible for the jury's death verdict. The *Times* described the reaction of both the state and federal prosecutors to the verdict as follows: "The influence as a deterrent to criminals and as an aid to public protection of one hanging verdict in a kidnapping case is greater than the influence of penitentiary sentences to twenty kidnappers. . . . The infliction of the penalty of death in this case will serve notice to gangsters and kidnappers throughout the nation that the Federal authorities are presently engaged in close cooperation with the police and the prosecuting forces of the various States" (27 July 1933, p. 4).

The death sentence handed down in the McElroy case was not carried out. The victim suffered great anguish over the role that her testimony had played in the sentence. Eventually she appeared before the governor of Missouri and pleaded with him to commute the sentence, which he did.

Throughout July and August 1933, developments in other outstanding cases were reported. John J. O'Connell, Jr., was released after the payment of $42,500 ransom, having been held captive for twenty-three days in New Jersey. Federal authorities joined local law enforcement forces in a massive manhunt. Hoover's agents located the spot where Charles F. Urschel had been held during his ransoming—a ranch near Paradise, Texas, belonging to R. G. Shannon, stepfather of Mrs. George "Machine Gun" Kelly, one of the FBI's "Ten Most Wanted" men. At the scene, Harvey Bailey, another notorious outlaw of the period, Shannon, his wife and son, were arrested, and the testimony of the Shannons implicated Kelly and another well-known outlaw, Albert Bates. A nationwide manhunt for Kelly and Bates was launched with daily reports appearing in the press. The cases of the summer of '33 came to an end with the abortive attempt to collect $10,000 ransom for William Wood Foristal, retired capitalist and cousin of former President Taft, in San Francisco.

An indication of the widely shared perception that the nation was in the grip of a kidnapping epidemic was the appearance in July of the *Times* kidnapping "box score." The box score appeared July 11, under the title "Recent Kidnappings in America," and listed seventeen cases under the column headings of "Name," "Date Stolen," and "Returned." The box scores were updated on a regular basis throughout July, August, September, and October, along with summaries of sentences handed down to convicted kidnappers. In the July 25 edition of the *Times*, coverage devoted to kidnapping was as follows: A front-page box score titled "The Drive on Crime"; a front-page article on the arrest of a Chicago gang suspected of the Hamm kidnapping; five of the eight columns of page 4 devoted to the hunt for the Urschel kidnappers, a progress report on the O'Connell case, the denial of a request for a new trial in the McMath case in Massachusetts, the trial in Kansas City for the McElroy kidnapping, a report of a foiled kidnapping attempt in Upstate New York, an article on federal activities to combat kidnapping, and an article listing sixteen major ransomings that had occurred between 1931 and 1933.

Reports also appeared in the *Times* on steps being taken by and in behalf of wealthy and prominent people to protect themselves and their families from kidnappers. On July 10, Governor Horner of Illinois ordered the formation of a special squad of state highway patrolmen to aid in breaking up kidnapping rings. The governor's action was in response to information he had received that gangsters planned "wholesale kidnapping of wealthy citizens in several sections of the State" (11 July 1933, p. 3). On July 15, the *Times* reported that "in the latest step in the Federal Government's war against the reign of terror invoked by kidnappers, forty wealthy Chicago men were put under guard" (p. 2). City and state police were reported to be patroling various estates of wealthy men in that city. On July 20, the two grandchildren of Henry W. Taft, law partner of federal crime commission head George W. Wickersham, were secretly placed aboard a steamship bound for Europe "because the family was in constant dread of a kidnapping" (21 July 1933, p. 6). An August 15 report, datelined Chicago, related that Lloyds of London was writing kidnapping insurance for wealthy adults and their children. A policy rider was available to provide compensation for injuries incurred while the victim was in the hands of kidnappers. Business was reported as brisk.

An indication of the perceptions of the situation by law enforcement officials from twenty-four states was provided by a *Times* survey of August 21. The officials' assessments showed that although ransom kidnapping was the most spectacular crime, it was only part of the total crime situation in America at the time. The comments of the officials surveyed indicated their explanations of the perceived crime wave and their proposed remedies. Cited causes were lack of jobs, the parole and pardoning of hardened criminals, and juries failing to return convictions. Proposed remedies focused on law enforcement: taking politics out of law enforcement; providing peace officers with more sophisticated weaponry; establishing secret police, state police, and federal police; and regulation of firearms and ammunition.

While several factors were believed to be responsible for the crime situation in general, the perceived causes of ransom kidnapping were more focused. One of them was the willingness of families of victims to pay ransom. Local, state, and federal police officials, legal scholars, and members of the general public (via letters to the editor) proposed legislation that would make payment of ransom a crime. The *Times* predicted a "kidnapping epidemic" unless the encouragement of the crime by the payment of ransom was stopped (28 July 1933, p. 2).

The perceived need to prohibit the payment of ransom took concrete form in the recommendations to the legislature by New York Governor Lehman in August. He recommended as part of a legislative package needed to combat kidnapping that it be made "a felony to agree to or to pay a ransom, or to negotiate for the payment thereof, or to participate in such negotiations." [3] The governor stated that he was aware of the probable difficulty of getting convictions under such a law, but that it was necessary to destroy the "wrong psychology which has been allowed to develop"[4] concerning the payment of ransom. Both Republican and Democratic legislators made it known to the governor, however, that since the law would apply to members of the family of a kidnapped person, "conviction would be impossible and the legislation would be useless."[5] The bill died in committee.

Another factor perceived as being implicated in the ransoming epidemic was the ineffectiveness of the federal noncapital laws of 1932. The belief of the opponents of a federal death penalty that the mere specter of "Whiskers" ready to apprehend and prosecute kidnappers was all that was needed to deter kidnapping had lost credibility as a result of recent events. Federal powers created by the 1932 legislation had led to the successful apprehension and prosecution of kidnappers after the fact but was perceived as possessing little deterrent efficacy. In addition, federal law enforcers were chafing under the seven-day waiting period dictated by the 1932 legislation. Finally, federal prosecutors, too, found the 1932 legislation annoying. Even when federal jurisdiction clearly had been established, it rarely had been used other than as a holding action until local prosecutors could assess their chances of going for the death penalty under state law.

During the summer of 1933, the belief that a death penalty would stem the epidemic was more in evidence on the state level than on the federal level. The California legislature, which had stood by its indeterminate sentencing policy even in the face of the mutilation kidnapping of Marian Parker in 1927, now provided a death penalty or life imprisonment for kidnappers who killed or mutilated their victims. New York created a death penalty to be applied if a ransom victim was not returned before the trial began. A special session of the Ohio legislature created a death penalty for the kidnapper whose victim died as the result of ransom kidnapping; and the Texas legislature, which already had provided a death penalty if the victim was harmed, passed a bill making the death penalty possible even if the victim was not harmed.

The Strengthening of Federal Efforts against Kidnapping

In the late summer and fall of 1933, the federal government mobilized to strengthen its efforts against kidnapping. The mobilization initially took place on two fronts: an antikidnapping and racketeering legislative package and the creation of a federal police force. Eventually both fronts were to merge as the foundation for the government's "War on Kidnapping."

The need to strengthen the 1932 kidnapping legislation had been recognized in the Senate as early as the spring of 1933. At that time the Senate appointed a select crime investigating committee, headed by Senator Copeland of New York, to look into racketeering and kidnapping. Throughout the summer, the Copeland committee held hearings in various cities. As the events of the summer unfolded, the Copeland committee came more and more into the public eye, highlighted by presidential action summed up in front-page headlines of the *Times* of July 11: "Roosevelt to Aid War on Racketeer/Copeland Gets Promise of Every Government Facility to Help Investigation/Warns of Kidnappings/He Says 'Easy Money' Men Will Turn to Such Crimes." The next day, a report from Washington, D.C., stated that Senator Ashurst, chairman of the Senate Judiciary Committee, "said that the Federal Anti-Kidnapping Laws might have to be drastically altered at the next session of Congress to cope with the growing evil." [6] One day later, the same objective on the part of the Department of Justice was announced: "In an effort to speed apprehension of kidnappers and the return of their victims, Attorney General Cummings offered several suggestions to the public today, and made known that new legislation to deal with kidnapping and racketeering was being drafted." [7]

Also in July 1933, there was a revival of interest in the creation of a national police force—an "American Scotland Yard" as its proponents were fond of calling it—a suggestion that had met severe opposition in Congress in 1932. When the idea was revived in 1933, however, it came not only from lobbyists representing Midwestern business and law enforcement interests but as the result of a widely perceived need for such action, action backed by the Roosevelt administration. A front-page headline of the July 27 edition of the *Times* read: "Roosevelt Orders War on Kidnapping by Federal Forces: Cummings Is Instructed to Increase Agents and Push Fight on Racketeers: 'Super-Police' in Wind." The article stated, in part:

> President Roosevelt, in a conference today with Attorney General Cummings, instructed the Department of Justice to make an intensive study of recent kidnappings throughout the country and to report on the advisability of creating a super-police force to check the growth of organized crime.
>
> "The racketeering must stop," the Attorney General said after his conference with the President. "The Department of Justice will build up its force and increase its activities, in cooperation with the States, to crush the bands of kidnappers and racketeers. These crimes apparently are increasing and the Federal and State Governments must cooperate to the utmost in necessary investigations and prosecutions. . . .
>
> "We intend to spend as much money as needed and when needed to fight kidnapping and punish criminals," the Attorney General said. He explained that the Bureau of Investigation of the Department of Justice would be expanded; that some of the investigators of the Prohibition Bureau would be taken over, and that the enlarged force will devote itself chiefly to interstate crime such as kidnapping.
>
> President Roosevelt is expected to recommend legislation in the next session of Congress which will ask the States to surrender their authority in cases of kidnapping. State lines must be ignored, it is held, if the fight on kidnapping is to succeed.

Support for a federal police force came from several sectors. Governors, attending their national conference, requested that President Roosevelt speed the organization of a national police force. The World Association of Detectives, convened in Chicago, wholeheartedly endorsed the administration's plans. Senator Copeland, in an address before a New York City advertising club, urged a "Scotland Yard" in the United States to fight kidnapping, but admitted that "it is impossible under our form of government." [8] A committee of the Federal Bar Association recommended to the parent body that it go on record in favor of a constitutional amendment which would allow the creation of an "American Scotland Yard." [9] Resistance to the creation of a national police force was lacking in comparison. The American Bar Association, however, did voice opposition to what they perceived as a move by the Roosevelt administration to federalize prerogatives belonging to the states.

Four days after President Roosevelt announced his "plans" for a federal police force, it was a reality. It was announced that Attorney General Cummings, backed by the president, had set up a nucleus, "the purpose of which is to drive the racketeer, gangster, kidnapper, extortionist, bomber and hoodlum into subjection and prison." [10] A *Times* report on the action, datelined Washington, D. C., July 29, stated: "J. Edgar Hoover, Chief of the Justice Department's Bureau of Investigation, was appointed by Attorney General Cummings today as director of the Division of Investigation created by the President's executive order of June 10. The new division will include the present bureaus of investigation, identification and prohibition, effective Aug. 10. . . . The new division of the Justice Department will conduct the nation-wide warfare against racketeers, kidnappers and other criminals" (30 July 1933, p. 2).

Other steps in support of the federal war quickly followed. Raymond F. Moley, assistant secretary of state and "known as the chief member of the President's 'brain trust,' " was temporarily relieved of his State Department duties by Roosevelt and transferred to the Department of Justice. Moley, described as "one of the country's leading students of crimes," [11] was charged with conducting a special survey of crime-prevention measures for the Department of Justice, including an intensive study of all laws, state and federal. Attorney General Cummings delivered a national radio address in support of the federal government's plans to combat the "real warfare which an armed underworld is waging upon organized society" [12] and mentioned prominently that additional legislation soon would be recommended to Congress by the Department of Justice. The attorney general made it clear that, in the interim, state capital legislation would continue to be utilized against kidnappers in the effort of the Department "to seek the most severe penalties for all kidnappers." [13]

Using the powers provided by the 1932 legislation to the utmost, federal investigative and prosecution forces went into action. In August, a Chicago gang was indicted by a federal grand jury in Milwaukee for conspiracy to kidnap for ransom and transport in interstate commerce William Hamm, Jr. In his instructions to the grand jury, the judge termed kidnapping a "vicious" crime and told the jurors it was "extremely dangerous to the welfare of society." [14] A *Times* article lauded the work on the case by Melvin Purvis's Division of Investigation office in Chicago, which "has become a new cause for fear among gangsters, the kidnappers and the gunmen of Chicago and the Mid-West," and which kidnappers have come to recognize as "the Federal Government's personal weapon against them" (21 Aug. 1933, p. 30).

Two days later, Hoover's agents, in cooperation with local authorities, accomplished the "first major triumph in the recently undertaken war against kidnapping and racketeering" [15] with the arrest of Harvey Bailey and a dozen other suspects in the Urschel kidnapping. Attorney General Cummings immediately wired congratulations to Hoover's men for their success in breaking up a gang "which has been terrorizing Kansas, Missouri, Oklahoma, and Texas with shootings and kidnappings." [16] All the defendants were charged under the 1932 Lindbergh Law.

Hoover's forces having made the arrests in the Urschel case, federal prosecutors of the Department of Justice then took over. An Oklahoma City federal grand jury indicted the defendants, whose ranks by now had swelled to fourteen. The press publicized the claims of the prosecutors that they had enough evidence against the defendants to put them away for life, and that federal authorities had named Albert Bates and George "Machine Gun" Kelly, still at large, as the actual kidnappers of Urschel. Joseph B. Keenan, special U. S. attorney general, who would prosecute in the Oklahoma City federal court, stated that life terms would be sought for all of the defendants whether they had been principals or accomplices.

During federal preparations for the trial in the Urschel case, Keenan traveled from Oklahoma City to Alton, Illinois, to assist in the state prosecution of the defendants accused of kidnapping August Luer. The *Times* reported: "Mr. Keenan's visit was in fulfillment of his plan actively and personally to interest himself in kidnapping prosecutions over the country" (16 Sept. 1933, p. 8). All six defendants were convicted by a jury, but the death penalty asked for by the state was not recommended. Two offenders were sentenced to life, one to twenty years, and two others to five years.

The federal trial of the Urschel defendants began on September 18 in a heavily guarded Oklahoma City courtroom, with Keenan heading the prosecution. Shortly after the trial began, more machine-gun toting guards were added to the security force when Kelly, still at large, began sending threatening letters to the principals in the trial. Early in the proceedings, Federal Judge Edgar S. Vaught ruled that under the 1932 Lindbergh Law a kidnapping conspiracy continued until all the ransom paid had been located, thus linking seven Minnesota money-changers with the conspiracy and establishing a legal precedent for subsequent federal prosecutions. In turning down a defense motion for dismissal on the ground that the prosecution testimony had been insufficient to convict, Judge Vaught, according to the *Times*, stated: "This is a revolutionary proceeding today. . . . Kidnapping is as bad as murder, if not worse. . . . There is no greater menace to the country today. In interpreting the act under which this case is heard I bear in mind that its purpose is to prevent all kidnapping" (24 Sept. 1933, p. 3).

The federal district attorney concluded his closing argument to the jury with the plea: "I beg of you, in the name of my government, to return a verdict of guilty against these defendants. This is one of the most important cases ever tried. Precedents are being set that will guide the courts and the bar in all future trials growing out of this determined effort of your government to stamp out this damnable of crimes—kidnapping" (30 Sept. 1933, p. 1).

After deliberating two and a half hours, the jury returned verdicts of guilty against all the defendants except three of the money changers. The verdicts were announced on the front page of the *Times*.

The first Federal Court jury to act under the "Lindbergh Federal Kidnapping Law" convicted not only the actual gunmen who abducted Mr. Urschel, but also persons who participated in guarding him during his nine day's imprisonment, and two of those who took part in attempts to change the $200,000 of ransom money paid for his return. . . .

The result of this first major test of the "Lindbergh" law, passed by Congress in June, 1932, was hailed jubilantly by Herbert K. Hyde, District Attorney, and Joseph B. Keenan, assistant to the Attorney General, who were in charge of the prosecution.

"The verdict means the government is on top of this fight against kidnapping and we are ready to shoot the works," said Mr. Hyde. . . .

"This is just a skirmish," declared Mr. Keenan. "The government is not through. We are going right on down the line until we get every criminal and gangster in the United States. The new law has proved a powerful weapon and we are prepared and eager to use it to the finish."

With this trial out of the way, Mr. Hyde plunged immediately into other phases of the Urschel kidnapping.

George Kelley and his wife will be brought there soon from Memphis to stand trial [the Kellys had been apprehended by federal and local authorities on September 27]. (1 Oct. 1933)

The successful prosecutions in the Urschel and Luer cases, occurring almost simultaneously, were celebrated as a single achievement. The Justice Department regarded the convictions "as the most important victories for law enforcement in a decade" (ibid., p. 34). Attorney General Cummings extended congratulations to Hoover's investigative forces and to Keenan's prosecutors. As a reward for his efforts, Keenan was appointed assistant attorney general in charge of the criminal division of the Department of Justice. Hoover himself expressed the belief that the successful conclusion of the two cases would have "a wholesome influence on the general crime drive and will be important in convincing criminals that kidnapping is not a 'safe racket' " (ibid.). Keenan reiterated the position of his department that prosecutions would generally be pursued in the state courts, even if federal jurisdiction was available, where the state law provided a death penalty. In early October, sentences were pronounced in the Urschel case by Judge Vaught. Four defendants received the maximum penalty of life imprisonment; the sentences of the remaining defendants ranged from five years to a suspended ten-year sentence.

At the Kellys' trial, lasting three days, a federal court jury deliberated one hour and pronounced them guilty under the Lindbergh Law. The next day Kelly and his wife each were sentenced to life imprisonment, with U. S. Attorney Hyde asking the court to give him an unqualified recommendation that no clemency be shown at any time to any of those convicted in the Urschel case. On the same page of the *Times* announcing the conclusion of the Kellys' trial, there appeared an aerial view of the newest federal acquisition in the crime war—Alcatraz Penitentiary. The picture was captioned: "Where Government Will Exile Kidnapping Prisoners" (12 Oct. 1933, p. 52).

The Department of Justice forces did not rest on the laurels garnered in the Urschel and Luer cases. In October, the Lindbergh case, now in its seventeenth month, was taken from the Special Intelligence Section of the Internal Revenue Service and given to Hoover's Department of Justice division. Hoover immediately convened a closed-door conference of all federal personnel working on the investigation and expressed confidence that the case eventually would be solved.

Venting of National Frustrations: The Brooke Hart Case

Brooke Hart, of San Jose, California, was the twenty-two-year-old son of a wealthy department-store owner. On the night of 9 November, 1933, he was kidnapped, and a ransom of $40,000 was demanded for his safe return. Local authorities were notified immediately and they, in turn, notified the Division of Investigation. Hoover's men entered the case immediately. Four days of ransom negotiations were conducted by telephone. By tracing the calls, federal agents and local authorities arrested the two suspects on November 16—Thomas M. Thurmond and J. M. Holmes. They admitted that they had kidnapped Hart, killed him immediately, and had thrown his weighted body into San Francisco Bay. According to a federal agent's statement to reporters, Thurmond and Holmes told him: "We thought it would be easier with Hart out of the way. We didn't want to bother lugging him around the countryside and we didn't want to take the chance of his escaping and giving us away. So we just bumped him off." [17] The suspects were confined in the San Jose jail to await judicial proceedings.

Holmes and Thurmond were indicted by a San Francisco federal grand jury on November 22 for using the mails in an attempt to extort. Consistent with their policy, federal authorities agreed to hold their charges in abeyance so that the state could prosecute under California's new "Little Lindbergh Law" which provided death for kidnapping where either a demand was made for ransom or violence was done to the victim. The available penalty provided in the federal extortion law was a maximum of twenty years and a fine of $5,000. There was to be no prosecution in this case; on November 26, the day that the victim's body washed ashore, Holmes and Thurmond were lynched. A mob overpowered the jailers and dragged the defendants across the street to a city park where they were stripped, beaten, and hanged. An article in the *Times* of November 28 described the event in vivid detail.

The societal reaction to the event was triggered by the comments of California Governor James Rolph: "This is the best lesson that California has ever given the country. We show the country that the State is not going to tolerate kidnapping" (27 Nov. 1933, p. 3). A front-page *Times* report on the governor's comment related that Governor Rolph had said he would like to place all kidnappers serving time in California prisons into the custody of "those fine, patriotic San Jose citizens who know how to handle such a situation," and that he had refused to send in the National Guard when San Jose authorities had called for assistance before the lynchings. The report quoted the governor liberally: "If anyone is arrested for the good job I'll pardon them all. . . . No kidnapper will ever be turned loose or pardoned while I am Governor. . . . Kidnappers will learn they're not safe even in our penitentiaries. . . . It is about time the people should have comfort in their homes. This kidnapping business has become so bad that mothers and fathers are afraid to let their children out of their homes. . . . The Sheriff and the law enforcement officers of that community did all they could to preserve order and uphold due respect for the law. They did their duty as far as it was possible, but the might of the people was determined to serve notice to the world that kidnapping and murder will not be tolerated in California" (28 Nov. 1933).

The governor's initial statement and subsequent ones produced a wave of reaction throughout the nation, much of it initially favorable. The governor's office in Sacramento claimed it had received in a single day more than eighty telegrams from thirty states supporting Rolph's stand. Under a Cambridge, Massachusetts, dateline, the *Times* reported: "Editors of the *Harvard Crimson* in today's issue of the undergraduate daily, praised Governor Rolph of California for his stand on the lynchings of the Brooke Hart slayers at San Jose. 'Thurmond and Holmes were too guilty to be accorded the delightful interlude called American criminal justice,' said the editorial. 'The mob was sick of a system that convicts 299 out of 300 law abiding citizens for violating traffic regulations and then refuses to convict seventy-nine out of eighty accused murderers' " (29 Nov. 1933, p. 3).

Negative reaction to Governor Rolph's position was expressed in a *Times* editorial titled "A Fine Lesson," which concluded by calling the governor "Governor Lynch" (28 Nov. 1933, p. 20). The foreign press was represented by a critical editorial in the *London Daily Express;* the *London Mirror* wrote that America "has not yet escaped from the psychology of the pioneers whose idea of law was necessarily primitive" (ibid., p. 3). Organizations of a variety of ideological persuasions were quick to express their criticism, including the National Committee for the Defense of Political Prisoners, the International Labor Defense, the NAACP, the Commission on Interracial

Cooperation, the American Civil Liberties Union, and the American Federation of Labor.

By November 29, the governor's office claimed that the mail was running 267 in favor to 57 against Rolph's stand. However, letters to the editor of the *Times*, critical of the governor, were in the majority. A group of faculty members of the University of California issued a call for Rolph's resignation. The San Francisco Chamber of Commerce prepared a statement deploring the lynching and the governor's sanctioning of it; among the signatories was former President Herbert Hoover. Religious leaders from across the country issued organized criticism. Members of the criminal justice system came forward to criticize Rolph's stand, including the California Bar Association. The governor of Pennsylvania expressed his abhorrence, and Norman Thomas of the American Socialist Party sent a telegram to President Roosevelt calling for federal antilynching legislation. The president expressed his abhorrence in a December 6 radio broadcast of an address before the Federal Council of Churches of Christ in America.

The Federal Crime War Legislation of 1934

As 1933 came to a close, federal efforts in prosecuting kidnappers to the limit of the law received a setback in a St. Paul federal court when a jury acquitted members of a Chicago gang of the ransoming of William Hamm, Jr. As announced in the *Times*: "The Federal Government encountered in this case its first defeat in a kidnapping prosecution since the passage of the Lindbergh Kidnapping Law" (29 Nov. 1933, p. 1). Frustrated in the Hamm case, federal forces continued to run down every last person involved in the Urschel kidnapping and to recover all of the ransom.

From Washington, progress was reported on the proposed antikidnapping and racketeering legislation. Senator Copeland had met with President Roosevelt to discuss plans for a complete revision of the federal criminal law. Senator Copeland reported: "We are determined to perfect the Federal Statutes, and there is an enormous public opinion demanding it." [18] In his annual report to Congress on 5 January 1934, Attorney General Cummings stated that the Department of Justice also would be initiating legislation.

The first of the antikidnapping and racketeering bills were submitted to the Senate on January 11. In introducing the thirteen proposed measures, Senator Copeland listed among the supporters of the legislation: President Roosevelt, the Copeland Senate Crime Committee, the Department of Justice, the International Association of Chiefs of Police, federal and state prosecutors, and the American Bar Association. As to the support of the president, Senator Copeland stated: "I would not wish to close this preliminary statement without referring to the fact that the President of the United States is tremendously interested in what we are attempting to do. No later than this morning he has told me of his desire to have adopted a program which will make safer the citizens of America. There is not a mother in this country who is not alarmed over the possibility of kidnapping in her family; and, in that connection, I may say that there is not a family in America safe against the menace of kidnapping." [19]

S. 2252, the bill amending the 1932 Lindbergh Law, was remanded to the Senate Judiciary Committee. In addition to an amendment that would shorten the waiting period for FBI intervention in a kidnapping from seven to three days, the bill contained another amendment. To the wording of the 1932 legislation, "held for ransom," would be added the phrase "or reward or otherwise." Another bill directed at kidnappers would extend federal jurisdiction from the use of the mails to communicate ransom demands to the use of the telephone, telegraph, radio, oral message, or otherwise.

It was another piece of proposed legislation, however, which generated the most discussion in the Senate, a bill requested by the Department of Justice to aid its efforts at creating a national police force. Specifically, the bill would empower the president, by executive order, to consolidate the investigative arms of various federal departments into a single force. Senator Copeland did not speak strongly on behalf of the measure and stated that he expected some resistance to it. Senator McKellar's comments illustrated the nature of the resistance.

MR. MCKELLAR. Before the Senator leaves that, are we to build up a Russian checa in this country? We are getting to have a tremendous secret-service organization, or perhaps should I say organizations. I think they are frequently used as a means of doing great wrong, and I have my doubts about secret-service systems in a republican form of government like ours. . . .

MR. COPELAND. Mr. President, the Senator has asked a question, and I must answer it in all frankness. . . .

I know what evils have crept into the system in the past, and I want to avoid them so far as possible, but the Senator would be amazed, perhaps, to hear the responses to a questionnaire which I sent out to the 48 Governors of the States of this Union. . . . I asked, "Do you believe that it would be advantageous to have the Federal Government cooperate more closely with the States in the administration of criminal justice so far as those matters are concerned which might possibly have an interstate significance?" I asked a similar question looking to what I called an American Scotland Yard, using the term in . . . legendary sense, because, as a matter of fact, I say in all truth that I believe that the Division of Investigation of the Department of Justice in the Federal Government of the United States is unsurpassed in this world as an investigative body and an institution for running down criminal activities. . . .

MR. MCKELLAR. It was alleged in the newspapers at one time that this secret service body of the Department of Justice investigated and rifled certain Senators' offices here in the Capitol. The Senator does not approve of that, I know.

MR. COPELAND. I certainly do not approve of it, and I have some very profound convictions about certain personnel which I will discuss in private with the Senator. But honestly administered and capably administered, this Division of Investigation can be made a more powerful agency for good in its field than any other arrangement that could be suggested. That is my opinion. . . .

The response has been amazing. I expected to have protests from many States where there was a firm conviction of States' rights. . . . Out of 48 Governors, 36 have responded, and 34 of them are in favor of the plan.[20]

Nowhere among the bills introduced on January 11 was there a measure amending the 1932 Lindbergh Law so as to provide for a federal death penalty for ransom kidnapping. The matter came up only obliquely when Senator Walsh of Massachusetts wanted to know the conclusions reached by the Copeland committee regarding the adequacy of punishment for crimes arising out of acts of violence. Senator Copeland's reply revealed why such a recommendation would not be forthcoming from his committee: "Personally—and I speak only for myself and not for the committee in this—I do not believe that punishment of crime is a deterrent." [21]

On the morning of January 17, Edward Bremer, president of a St. Paul, Minnesota, bank, became the city's fifth kidnapping victim in two years. A $200,000 ransom note was sent to his father, the majority stockholder in the Jacob Schmidt Brewing Company, "prominent Democrat," and "personal friend of President Roosevelt." [22] The victim was driven to Freeport, Illinois, and held in the same house that had been used in the Hamm kidnapping; this was no coincidence since the abductors of Hamm also were the abductors of Bremer—the Alvin Karpis-Ma Barker gang.

The case immediately became front-page news. "Kidnapping experts of the Department of Justice" [23] were ordered into the case by President Roosevelt. On January 19, the finding of the victim's car with blood stains on the seat prompted Joseph B. Keenan, assistant attorney general in charge of the Division of Criminal Prosecution, to express fear that Bremer had been killed. Keenan said that he was afraid that "in the Bremer case we may have the misfortune of experiencing another Lindbergh situation." [24] Such reports facilitated immediate reactions, among which was the introduction of a bill by a U. S. representative calling for "death at the hands of an army firing squad as the mandatory sentence for a kidnapper convicted and sentenced before the return of his victim." [25] The bill died in committee, but it had its impact.

While pessimism reigned as to the possible fate of Bremer, federal authorities generated some optimism by their continued efforts in the Boettcher case. Datelined Chicago, January 31, a news release reported that federal agents had arrested Verne Sankey, "America's public enemy No. 1." [26] Sankey confessed to taking part in the ransoming of Charles Boettcher of Denver in 1933 and to having transported the victim into South Dakota. Sankey also confessed to having been involved in the ransoming of Haskell Bohn of St. Paul in 1932. Federal prosecutors immediately arraigned Sankey under Lindbergh Law charges and sped him on his way to South Dakota for trial. Three days later, federal agents in Chicago arrested Gordon Alcorn, the only other fugitive suspect in the Boettcher kidnapping. Alcorn also confessed.

Federal plans to prosecute Sankey to the fullest extent under the Lindbergh Law were frustrated when he hanged himself in his cell on the eve of his appearance in court. This left only Gordon Alcorn to be dealt with for the Boettcher kidnapping, and on February 9 he pleaded guilty and was sentenced to life in Leavenworth. The entire proceeding took less than fifteen minutes. When Alcorn arrived at Leavenworth to begin his life term, the *Times* pointed out that he was the fifth kidnapper to be confined in that federal facility under the government's drive against the "snatch racket" (11 Feb. 1934, p. 34). He joined such select Lindbergh Law company as Harvey Bailey, George "Machine Gun" Kelly, and Albert Bates, all of whom had been convicted for the Urschel ransoming.

As federal prosecutors wrapped up the Boettcher case, Hoover's investigators took full charge of the Bremer ransoming. Hoover announced that strict censorship would be imposed on any developments in the case and any word of progress would come from the attorney general. After seventeen days of silence, the Bremer kidnappers at last established contact with the victim's family, the $200,000 ransom was paid, and Bremer was released on February 7. His release, as reported in the *Times,* "was followed immediately by the starting of one of the most intensive manhunts in the history of the Northwest" (9 Feb. 1934, p. 1). Governor Floyd B. Olson of Minnesota announced that all law enforcement officials of the state would attend a conference in his office to make plans "to crush the menace of kidnapping" (ibid.). The range of the publicity was indicated by a report that the *London Daily Mail* had contacted the Bremer home by transoceanic telephone to ask for an interview with the victim.

To add impetus to the federal antikidnapping and racketeering bills submitted by Senator Copeland, on February 20 the Department of Justice submitted twelve proposed measures of its own. On March 22, the Senate Judiciary Committee, without amendment, favorably reported out a number of the anticrime bills including the bill which would amend the Lindbergh Law by allowing the FBI to enter a case after three days instead of seven and by expanding the definition of kidnapping from "for ransom" to "ransom, reward, or otherwise." Eight of the anticrime bills were considered on the floor of the Senate one week later. There was little discussion of any of the measures and no discussion at all of S. 2252. Accounts of major ransom kidnappings, especially of the Urschel case, were cited liberally in support of the bills. The bills were passed by the full Senate and referred to the House Judiciary Committee. A federal death penalty for ransom kidnapping still was not included in the legislative package.

As the proposed kidnapping legislation became the business of the House, Hoover's investigators and Keenan's prosecutors continued to garner headlines. The *Times* published another box score, this time titled "One Day in Kidnapping War," in which the accomplishments of the federal forces were summarized (14 Mar. 1934, p. 1). Federal authorities released for the first time the names of the two chief suspects in the Bremer kidnapping: Arthur "Doc" Barker and Alvin Karpis. Fred Barker, another member of the notorious Karpis-Barker gang, also was being sought in connection with the case.

On April 25, a particularly cruel kidnapping of a child in Tucson, Arizona, created more work for federal forces. June Robles was the six-year-old daughter of a prominent Mexican-American family. She was kidnapped while walking home from school, and a ransom note demanding $15,000 was received a few hours later. Local reaction was intense. A thousand Arizona ranchers joined in a search for the girl amid threats of lynching. The governor mobilized the state police and requested Washington to send in federal forces. The Department of Justice responded with twelve Division of Investigation agents. On April 27, all of the news on page 5 of the *Times* dealt with kidnapping: the Bremer case, the Lindbergh case, and the Robles case. In the Bremer case, it was reported that several men had been charged on federal warrants in Chicago for possession of some of the ransom money. The next day a front-page story reported more arrests in Chicago by Hoover's agents of persons found with over $50,000 of the ransom. On April 29, the Bremer and Robles cases were linked when a rumor was published that the Dillinger gang had been involved in both kidnappings. This week of intense federal activity concluded with the following announcement from Washington: "Fast armored cars, airplanes, machine guns and special rifles are to be turned loose in a great drive against the underworld if plans of the Department of Justice are approved. Attorney General Cummings made this announcement today, together with the fact that he is seeking funds with which to add 270 men to his forces. . . . The War Department had already agreed to furnish the airplanes." [27]

A Federal Death Penalty from the House

During the intense publicity being given to kidnapping developments in the last week of April 1934, a news item had appeared in the *Times* concerning the work of the House Judiciary Committee on the anticrime legislation then before it. The item contained the first public mention that a federal death penalty for ransom kidnapping was going to be part of the government's anticrime legislative package. The source of the proposal was the same as in 1932—the House Judiciary Committee.

On May 3, the House Judiciary Committee submitted a report to accompany S. 2252 recommending eight amendments to the Senate bill. One of the amendments would maintain the seven-day waiting period for federal intervention in a kidnapping rather than the three-day period suggested by the Senate. The other amendment called for the insertion of the following wording in the penalty provision of the bill: "or . . . by death if the verdict of the jury shall so recommend, provided that the sentence of death shall not be imposed by the court if, prior to its imposition, the kidnapped person shall have been liberated unharmed." [28]

On May 5, the House passed five of the anticrime bills, including S. 2252 containing the death penalty amendment. There was no discussion. On May 7, the progress of the anticrime legislation hit a snag when the Senate moved to disagree to all the House amendments, sending all the bills to a House-Senate conference committee.

As the House and Senate conferees debated the legislation, particularly the House's death penalty amendment to S. 2252, a ransom kidnapping case was reported from Arcadia, California. On May 9, two masked gunmen kidnapped William F. Gettle, retired oil millionaire. A front-page story in the *Times* labeled the case "one of the boldest kidnappings thus far written on the country's records" (11 May 1934, p. 1). Accompanied by pictures of Gettle and simultaneous coverage of the Robles case, the receipt of an $80,000 ransom demand was reported. The story concluded with the statement: "a grimly determined force of Department of Justice agents, acting on instructions from Washington, and State and county police officers today had taken up the search for Mr. Gettle" (ibid.).

Two days after the report of the Gettle ransoming, the House and Senate conference committee released their report. It recommended that the Senate recede from its disagreement to the House amendments to the bill, including the death penalty amendment and the retention of the seven-day waiting period. The Senate and House agreed to the recommendations, and while final arrangements for enacting the bills into law were being completed, the national press reported that the victims in the Robles and in the Gettle cases both were rescued on May 14.

The Robles child was rescued from a pit dug into the floor of the desert outside of Tucson. She had been chained to the wall of the pit for nineteen days, subsisting on various food items left with her by the kidnappers. When rescued she was suffering from starvation and exposure, but recovered. No ransom had been paid. Her rescue received international press coverage. The *London Times* reported that the story of her "cruel imprisonment was 'sweeping the world,' " and the *London Daily Mail* telephoned for an interview with the victim.[29] A local district attorney expressed his wish that Arizona had capital punishment for kidnapping, and U. S. Attorney General Cummings pledged the cooperation of his forces in an effort to bring the abductors to justice, a goal which was never accomplished.[30]

Gettle's rescue from a small town north of Los Angeles came when authorities traced a ransom call. The *Times* carried a three-column picture of the victim and his family, as well as a report of the arrest by local authorities of six suspects. The Los Angeles district attorney immediately announced that he would seek at least life sentences for the abductors under California's "Little Lindbergh Law." The death penalty was possible if the victim had been injured, and Gettle had injured his side during the kidnapping. Twenty-four hours after the rescue and arrests, three of the suspects pleaded guilty and were sentenced to life terms in San Quentin. According to the *Times*, the three men were told bluntly by authorities that their choice was to plead guilty to kidnapping or stand trial on a capital charge. As put by the district attorney, the threat of "the shadow of the noose looming about their ears" was the deciding factor in the defendants' decision (16 May 1934, p. 1). Crowds of souvenir hunters were reported massing around the house in which Gettle had been held for five days, "making away with whatever could be torn loose," and a sign appeared on the house reading: "See the room where Gettle was held. Admission two cents" (17 May 1934, p. 19).

On 17 May 1934, the anticrime bills were sent to President Roosevelt for his signature. As the long congressional process neared a conclusion, the new legislation was highly publicized in a front-page article in the *Times*. The president's signing of the bills on May 18 also was heralded on the front page. The article featured the death penalty amendment and reported that of the original twelve measures six had been dropped, including the bill to give the president the power to combine federal forces into a national police force, "partly owing to objections raised in committee by advocates of State's rights who hesitate to grant increased power to the Federal Government" (19 May 1934).[31]

Department of Justice officials were quick to avail themselves of their new powers. A *Times* headline of May 20 read: "New Weapons for the War on Kidnappers"; the article contained three pictures each representing one of the three fronts of the war—local, state, and federal law enforcement authorities. A cartoon accompanying the article showed a sinister figure stretching out his arm over a town; written on the arm was "kidnapper" (sec. 8, p. 1).

In June, a Virginia case looked like it would provide an opportunity for the application of the new federal anticrime powers, but the prosecution was handled by the state. In August, a New York City kidnapping did result in a federal prosecution, but the case would not support a capital trial. In September, a Nashville, Tennessee, abduction murder looked like it would provide the opportunity for the first capital prosecution under the new legislation, but it, too, frustrated federal efforts when it could not be determined if ransoming had been involved. Before the first opportunity could present itself, Bruno Richard Hauptmann was arrested for the Lindbergh kidnapping.

Hauptmann was arrested in September 1934, thirty months after the Lindbergh child was abducted. In the *Times* of September 21, three columns of the front page and the entire second, third, and fourth pages were devoted to his arrest. The articles stressed the fact that federal agents never had abandoned their intensive investigation. Editorials praised the work of local, state, and federal authorities.

Federal authorities rejoiced. The lack of progress in the Lindbergh case had been an embarrassment for over two years. They quickly availed themselves of the opportunity to remedy the situation. The *Times* published the text of a national radio broadcast delivered on the night of September 22 by U. S. Attorney General Cummings detailing local, state, and federal law enforcement efforts in the case. The attorney general emphasized the tenacious, systematic investigation that had led to the arrest of Hauptmann and cited cooperation among law enforcement forces at all levels as the key. He asked for the support of the American public in the federal war against interstate crime and concluded: "The time is ripe for action. The American people, unless I misread the public temper, demand action" (23 Sept. 1934, p. 26).

Although the Lindbergh case had provided an opportunity for federal forces to display their considerable investigative skills, it did not provide a like opportunity for Keenan's prosecutors. The case was clearly within the jurisdiction of the state of New Jersey. As New Jersey prosecutors prepared their case against Hauptmann, a case was reported from Louisville, Kentucky, which would involve both the investigative and prosecuting arms of the federal effort against kidnapping.

On 10 October 1934, the kidnapper entered the Stoll home expecting to find Mrs. Stoll's father-in-law, wealthy president of an oil refining company; instead he found Alice Speed Stoll and her maid. The maid was bound and gagged, and the victim struck with an iron bar and abducted. A ransom note demanding $50,000, prepared in anticipation of kidnapping the father-in-law, was left at the scene. The ransom note was published on the front page of the *Times* of October 17. In it, the writer demonstrated his knowledge of the capital ransom laws of Kentucky and the federal death threat, and claimed that he was a member of a Socialist band of "once-respected workingmen . . . harrassed . . . by capitalists such as Stoll, Mellon, Morgan, Insull, etc."

Alice Stoll, twenty-eight-year-old wife of the vice-president of the Stoll refining company, was a person of considerable prominence. Her late grandfather's estate was estimated at $15,000,000. Her family was a pillar of Louisville society and had been a pioneer family of Kentucky. Her ancestors had been personal friends of Abraham Lincoln. U.S. ambassador to England Robert W. Bingham, himself from Louisville, was a family friend, and former ambassador to Germany Frederic M. Sackett was the victim's uncle.

Federal agents of the Division of Investigation took charge of the case immediately; the seven-day waiting period retained in the recent legislation posed only a technical difficulty. Hoover sent an assistant to Louisville to take charge of the investigation and promised to come to the city himself if necessary. Kentucky Governor Laffoon maintained constant telephone contact with city officials, and the head of the Kentucky National Guard arrived in Louisville to offer the services of his troops.

Three days after the kidnapping it was reported that the $50,000 ransom had been mailed to Nashville, Tennessee. It subsequently was learned that the money had been sent to Thomas Robinson, Sr., the abductor's father, an unwilling accomplice in the kidnapping. On October 16, the victim, bruised and weak, returned home. She had been released in Indianapolis, Indiana. Accompanied by Mrs. Thomas H. Robinson, Jr., her abductor's wife, she had telephoned her home and embarked by automobile for Louisville. Mrs. Robinson claimed that when her husband had wanted to abandon the victim in a locked closet in the Indianapolis apartment, she had refused and stayed with Mrs. Stoll to protect her. Her husband had fled with the ransom money.

Thomas H. Robinson, Jr., twenty-seven-years-of-age, son of a Nashville contractor, had graduated from college and had been a student in the Law School of Vanderbilt University when he began experiencing emotional problems. After dropping out of Law School, he had worked at one of the filling stations owned by the victim's family. Five years before the Stoll kidnapping he had been tried for impersonating a police officer and robbery, but the charges were annulled when he pleaded insanity. He was placed in a state hospital from which he had been released in 1930. No organized ring of Socialists had been involved, only Robinson. Federal authorities began a nationwide manhunt for the suspect.

A representative of the Department of Justice stated that all persons arrested in connection with the kidnapping would be prosecuted under the amended federal ransom law. On October 20, a federal grand jury indicted Robinson, Jr., his father, and his wife on counts of plotting to kidnap Alice Stoll for ransom; to transport her in interstate commerce; of taking overt acts to carry out the unlawful agreement; of beating, injuring, bruising, and harming her; and of not liberating her unharmed. The complexity of the indictment reflected some of the contingencies that had to be met before the federal death penalty could be imposed: the prosecution had to prove transporation in interstate commerce for federal jurisdiction to arise, and the prosecution had to prove that the victim was not released unharmed. The other contingencies were: the defendant had to request a jury trial rather than either asking for a bench trial or entering a plea of guilty; the jury, in addition to convicting the defendant, had to recommend the death penalty; and the judge had to support the jury's recommendation of a death sentence. Despite a concerted effort by federal prosecutors, not only did the jury not recommend a death penalty for the father and wife of Robinson, Jr., the jury acquitted them of all charges.

The First Federal Kidnapping Execution: Arthur Gooch

As 1934 drew to a close, all indications pointed to the probability that Thomas H. Robinson, Jr., once he was apprehended, would be the first kidnapper executed under the amended federal legislation. The Stoll case had all the earmarks of a classic deterrent example: it involved a major ransom kidnapping; there was no question that the offender had known of the existence of the death penalty and that he was liabling himself to it before he committed the kidnapping; the crime had been deliberated by the offender for weeks prior to its commission; and the execution would receive maximum publicity. Before Robinson, Jr., could be apprehended, however, circumstances thrust southwestern outlaw Arthur Gooch into the role expected to be played by Robinson.

On November 26, Gooch and a confederate were stopped at a gas station for routine questioning by two Paradise, Texas, police officers. Following a fight, during which one of the officers was seriously injured, Gooch and his associate forced the two officers to drive them over the state line into Oklahoma. Federal agents who happened to be in the vicinity of Okemah, Oklahoma, investigating another case, immediately were called in, and Gooch and his confederate were cornered. During the ensuing gun battle the confederate was killed.

This was the case that would provide the federal death penalty for ransom kidnapping with its first opportunity to deter potential offenders by an execution example; but the case was all wrong for the intended purpose. It was not a classic kidnapping of the type which the amended Lindbergh Law was designed to prevent. No ransom was involved. No victim was killed. The locale of the crime was not conducive to extensive press coverage, and the victims were not prominent. Even when the execution eventually took place it would receive little publicity.

The year 1934 ended on a note of continued confidence in the abilities of federal forces to rid the country of kidnappers. On December 11, a *Times* article was headlined: "Federal Crime Drive Nets 74 Kidnappers, Ends Lives of Over a Score of Gangsters" (p. 2). The article applauded the record of the Department of Justice and expressed confidence that Hoover's agents soon would apprehend Thomas H. Robinson, Jr., wanted for the Stoll kidnapping, as well as Alvin Karpis—now "public enemy No. 1"—and Arthur and Fred Barker, under indictment for the Bremer ransoming.

In January 1935, Bruno Hauptmann was brought to trial in Flemington, New Jersey. Amid a circus atmosphere every development in the trial received detailed coverage in the national media. Labeled by the prosecution as "public enemy number 1 in this world,"[32] Hauptmann was sentenced to death in February. *Times* editorials hailed the verdict and sentence as examples of honest and efficient criminal justice, although the writers did acknowledge that Hauptmann's exact role in the crime remained unclear and that the outcome would not satisfy everyone.

Continuing efforts in investigating and prosecuting offenders in federal cases centered on the Bremer case; the developments were sensational. On 8 January 1935, it was reported from Chicago that one of the suspected kidnappers of Bremer "was shot and fatally wounded tonight in a pitched battle with government agents." [33] Eight days later, a report from Florida stated that Ma Barker and her son, Fred, "long sought as members of the gang that kidnapped Edward G. Bremer," [34] had been killed in a machine-gun battle with federal agents. It was rumored that Alvin Karpis and Arthur "Doc" Barker had been in the vicinity but had left shortly before federal agents arrived. Two days later, federal authorities reported that Arthur "Doc" Barker had been arrested more than a week before in Chicago. The sensational series of developments almost included the capture of the only remaining fugitives in the Bremer case, Alvin Karpis—"public enemy No. 1"—and Harry Campbell, when they were cornered in Atlantic City on January 20. In a machine-gun battle with police, however, they eluded capture.

Federal prosecutors moved with dispatch against the suspects in the Bremer case, both those in hand and those still at large. Secret federal grand jury indictments were returned against twenty-two suspects. The trial of the defendants in custody began in St. Paul on April 15 and ended on May 17, with five convictions and two acquittals. Two of the principals immediately were sentenced to life imprisonment, the maximum penalty in effect at the time of the Bremer kidnapping.

The verdict and sentences were widely acclaimed in this, according to the *Times*, "the first case in which the Federal Government has attempted to convict not only the principals but everyone who has any connection with the crime" (18 May 1935, p. 34). J. Edgar Hoover now had less reason for the reticence he had shown in an interview published less than two weeks before: "While there have been no sensational kidnapping cases this year, Mr. Hoover refused to say this crime had been halted. 'It would be silly of me to make such a statement,' he said. 'We probably would get two or three reports the next day. But the large kidnapping gangs are broken'" (5 May 1935, p. 29). Hoover was correct. It would have been silly.

Another Challenge to Federal Forces: The Weyerhaeuser Case

When the victim's grandfather, a timber tycoon, had died on 16 May 1935, his death received national publicity. The fortune he had accumulated was mentioned prominently as were the names of his heirs. Among the readers of the publicity were Harmon Waley, his wife, Margaret, and William Mahan. As they later admitted, it had been the publicity given to the death of the grandfather that had attracted the offenders to nine-year-old George Weyerhaeuser of Tacoma.

Eight days following the death of his grandfather, the victim failed to return home from school and the police were notified. Within hours of the disappearance, his parents received a special delivery letter demanding a ransom of $200,000 and threatening to kill the boy if the ransom was not paid in five days. Agents of the FBI were sent to Tacoma immediately, and local authorities placed their entire force under the direction of Hoover's agents. The case, as reported in the *Times,* was called "the biggest kidnapping case the Northwest has seen" (26 May 1935, p. 2) and prompted the resumption of publication of that newspaper's kidnapping box scores along with the complete text of the ransom note. Pictures of the victim, his family, and his home abounded in the press, and the label "kidnapped heir to millions" appeared on front pages across the country.

Law enforcement forces withdrew to facilitate ransom negotiations amid rumors that remnants of the Karpis-Barker gang were responsible. Even after the seven-day waiting period expired, federal forces continued to remain in the background so as not to endanger the opportunity for successful ransom negotiations and the safe return of the victim.

Elsewhere, federal forces made progress on other outstanding cases. On May 31, they arrested members of a gang in Kansas, accused of the 1933 kidnapping of Alton, Illinois, businessman August Luer. Federal authorities hailed the culmination of their two-year hunt as a "smashing clean-up" of bank robberies and kidnapping in the Middle West (1 June 1935, p. 32). J. Edgar Hoover was quoted liberally in a *Times* article titled "Kidnapping Racket on Downgrade." Hoover credited the certainty and severity of punishment under the amended federal law for the decline in kidnappings, a certainty well known by prospective kidnappers. He concluded: "I know a lot of criminals who are capable of kidnapping and quite a few who have been in the racket. I have spent hours talking with them, and I know what they are afraid of. The thing they are most afraid of is the electric chair. We need more death sentences" (2 June 1935, sec. 4, p. 10). George Weyerhaeuser was released on June 1, unharmed, after the payment of the $200,000 ransom. A news release from Washington, D.C., published in the *Times,* announced that "All the crime fighting forces of the Department of Justice were unleashed today for the capture of the kidnappers" (ibid., p. 3). Ransom bills, the serial numbers of which had been recorded, began appearing throughout the Northwest and one such lead resulted in the capture of Harmon Waley and his wife in Salt Lake City on June 9. Hoover announced the arrests from Washington and added that the Waleys had named William Mahan as their accomplice. "Under orders to kill at the slightest show of resistance" (11 June 1935, p. 3), federal agents began their hunt for Mahan. Hoover's announcement was accompanied in the *Times* by a two-column picture of himself next to a picture of the victim.

Reports of prosecution plans for the Waleys stressed the severity of the penalties they faced. George Weyerhaeuser had not been harmed, so the maximum penalty under the federal Lindbergh Law was life imprisonment. Under Washington State law, however, a death penalty was possible even though the victim had not been harmed. Federal warrants charging conspiracy to use the mails to extort were issued in order to facilitate the removal of the Waleys from Utah back to Tacoma, but it was admitted openly that once back in the jurisdiction of the state of Washington federal charges would be held in abeyance and the Waleys prosecuted under state law. A few days later, however, federal officials alleged that the Waleys and Mahan had transported their victim from Washington into Idaho, and Lindbergh Law charges were filed.

The Waleys pleaded guilty, and a federal judge sentenced Harmon Waley, not to life, as had been the general expectation, but to forty-five years, apparently in return for his guilty plea. Margaret Waley was sentenced to twenty years. It was publicized widely that the Waleys' decision to plead guilty to federal charges was to avoid a possible death sentence under a state prosecution.

While the federal prosecution of the Waleys ran its course, government forces had made progress in the capital prosecution of Arthur Gooch under the amended Lindbergh Law. Their efforts had not been without difficulty. In their first attempt to prosecute Gooch, the indictment had been worded in such a way that a death verdict would not have been possible and trial plans had to be abandoned. An amended indictment resulted in a trial in federal court in Muskogee, Oklahoma. Gooch was convicted and the jury recommended the death penalty. The continued lack of publicity given to the case was indicated by the page 3 placement in the *Times* of the announcement of the death verdict, the first under the amended Lindbergh Law. Gooch's attorney began a process of appeal during which several execution dates were stayed. Eventually his case would be the first before the U. S. Supreme Court involving the death penalty provision of the amended Lindbergh Law.

Final Victory Glimpsed by Federal Forces

Until the final week of December, it looked like 1936 would be the first year in some time in which no major ransom kidnapping would be reported. The freedom of American society from kidnapping was the occasion for much congratulatory stocktaking by, and in behalf of, federal forces. In January, when legislation was passed amending the Lindbergh Law to facilitate the prosecution of handlers of ransom money, it was generally believed that the need for such legislation had passed. In February, the *Times* published an interview with J. Edgar Hoover which reinforced the public perception: "J. Edgar Hoover, Chief of the 'G-men,' said today that 'kidnapping is well in hand in America. I won't say anything about the future,' he added, 'that's always a bad policy. But there's every reason to believe, now, that the kidnapping racket is on the decline. We haven't had a major kidnapping since the Weyerhaeuser case last Spring' " (16 Feb. 1936, sec. 2, p. 2).

In the spring and summer of 1936, some of the earlier cases came to dramatic conclusions. Bruno Hauptmann was executed on April 3, after many months of highly publicized appeals. As had been the case on the occasion of his conviction and sentencing, public reaction was mixed. With the conclusion of the judicial proceedings in the Lindbergh case, there was further reason for public complacency. In response to congressional inquiries about the massive federal force created to deal with kidnapping and racketeering, J. Edgar Hoover warned, however, against too much complacency.

Hoover appeared before a Senate appropriations committee in April. According to the *Times*, he was asked why his bureau claimed credit for solving most of the kidnappings when local authorities and others broke many of them; Hoover replied that due credit had been given. Questions were raised about reports in the press that Hoover had issued shoot-to-kill orders in certain cases, which Hoover denied. The necessity of his agents being armed with machine guns was questioned, to which Hoover replied that the character of the men his agents faced made it necessary. One senator criticized Hoover's bureau for "running wild" in spending money, but a senatorial supporter asked:

> "What would be the effect if word should go out that Congress was withdrawing appropriations for supressing kidnapping?"
> "You would have a wave of kidnapping," Mr. Hoover said.
> "It would start up immediately?"
> \ "Exactly. There would not be the slightest doubt about that. It would cripple law enforcement and place a premium on lawlessness." (17 April 1936, p. 6)

The *Times* reported Hoover's appearance before the committee under the headline "J. E. Hoover Warns of a Kidnap Wave" (ibid.). Not long after this episode, questions about the continued need for Hoover's bureau were put to rest when President Roosevelt "gave the F. B. I. a mandate to seek out Communists, Fascists, and subversives deemed to be threatening to national security."35

Even before the assignment by the president to new duties, the FBI rallied public support for its continued existence when, within the space of two weeks in May, the fugitive suspects in the Hamm, Bremer, Weyerhaeuser, and Stoll kidnappings were apprehended by its agents. On May 1, Alvin Karpis, "the most-wanted man in America," was captured in New Orleans with Hoover himself present at the arrest. Front pages all over America announced the event. Six days after the arrest of Karpis, federal agents in San Francisco arrested William Mahan wanted in the Weyerhaeuser kidnapping. Agents in Toledo arrested Harry Campbell, Karpis's alleged accomplice in the Bremer case, and thereby "wiped the list of unapprehended public enemies almost clean" (8 May 1936, p. 1). Five days after these triumphs, the slate was wiped even cleaner when Hoover announced the capture in California of Thomas H. Robinson, Jr., long sought as the kidnapper of Alice Speed Stoll. Another round of "box scores," now devoted not to new cases but to the fate of kidnappers, was published in the *Times*. Editorial comments titled "The G-Men Score" (13 May 1936, p. 22) and "Swift and Sure" (15 May 1936, p. 24) appeared.

Karpis pleaded guilty to a federal charge of conspiracy in the Hamm kidnapping, indicated that he would be willing to enter a similar plea for his role in the Bremer kidnapping, and was given the maximum sentence possible under the federal legislation in effect at the time of the Hamm ransoming—life. Harry Campbell pleaded guilty to federal charges for his role in the Bremer kidnapping and was sentenced to life. William Mahan pleaded guilty in a Tacoma federal court to the Weyerhaeuser kidnapping and received two concurrent sentences of sixty years on Lindbergh Law charges.

Federal prosecutors had been embarassed by their lack of success against Robinson's wife and father for the Stoll kidnapping and now announced that they would seek the death penalty under the amended Lindbergh Law for Robinson, Jr. Their quest was frustrated again, however, when Robinson, Jr., pleaded guilty, thereby precluding a possible death sentence recommendation by a jury, and was sentenced to life. The entire proceedings were accomplished within forty-eight hours of his arrival in Louisville from California. This should have been the end of the Stoll case, but through his own efforts, Robinson, Jr., was going to give federal prosecutors another opportunity to go for the death penalty a few years later.

While federal prosecutors in June 1936 could not have known what would eventually transpire in the Stoll case, they did know that Arthur Gooch would be the first man executed under the amended Lindbergh Law. Gooch's death sentence had been appealed all the way up to the United States Supreme Court. In February 1936, in its first opportunity to rule on the constitutionality of the amended Lindbergh Law, the Court held unanimously that the kidnapping of a police officer came within the congressional meaning of the phrase "for ransom, reward, or otherwise." [36] Only a grant of executive clemency from President Roosevelt could have saved Gooch from hanging but, in June, the president refused. Gooch's hanging on June 19, the first person executed under the federal ransom law, was relegated to page 7 of the *Times*.

A Flare-Up of the Epidemic

With three days remaining in 1936, Charles Mattson, ten-year-old son of a prominent Tacoma, Washington, surgeon, was kidnapped from his home located in the same general neighborhood as the Weyerhaeuser estate. A ransom note left at the scene demanded $28,000 and included instructions very similar to those used by the kidnappers of George Weyerhaeuser. Local and federal authorities were notified, and Hoover responded. It had been less than a month since Hoover had labeled the Weyerhaeuser kidnapping the last major kidnapping in the nation, and he pledged the full cooperation of the bureau to wipe the slate clean once and for all. Forty-five FBI agents were reported to be in Tacoma by December 31, and Hoover had a private telephone line installed in the Mattson home.

On 11 January 1937, the beaten and frozen body of Charles

Mattson was found near Everett, Washington, about fifty miles from the victim's home. The case never would be solved. When the tragic news was broadcast, a nationwide reaction emerged to this apparent flare-up in the kidnapping situation. From the White House President Roosevelt issued a statement: "The murder of the little Mattson boy has shocked the nation. Every means at our command must be enlisted to capture and punish the perpetrator of this ghastly crime. . . . A crime of this kind is renewed evidence of the need of sustained effort in dealing with the criminal menace." [37]

Legislators in Washington State already had provided the most stringent capital kidnapping legislation in the country, and now they offered a $5,000 reward to supplement the $10,000 put up by the Department of Justice. Nonpayment of ransom legislation was introduced in the Washington State and Massachusetts legislatures and in Congress. Death penalty laws were proposed in the Pennsylvania and Rhode Island legislatures and passed in Georgia and Connecticut. The New Jersey legislature, which had provided a death penalty in 1933, now passed a measure which would provide hanging as the method of execution, and in Congress a New Jersey representative introduced a bill to specify public hanging as the method of execution under the Lindbergh Law. On January 17, the *Times* quoted the father of Charles Mattson: "Is it possible . . . that little Charles was sacrificed to further stimulate a previously enraged public to the enactment of even more drastic laws, both in the prevention and the punishment of this awful crime? If this is true, we feel that Charles shall not have died in vain" (17 Jan. 1937, p. 20).

The year of 1937 was a bad one for federal forces. Their reputation tarnished by lack of progress in solving the Mattson case, the FBI was to encounter another case never to be solved. In addition, they were to be accused of interference with local authorities and of petty rivalry with other federal agencies.

In June, Mrs. William H. Parsons of Long Island, New York, disappeared. Local authorities found a $25,000 ransom note in her abandoned car and called the FBI. Within a week, the *Times* began reporting friction between local authorities and federal agents. Local authorities were pursuing the theory that this was a murder case and wanted to launch an immediate search of the area. Federal agents were convinced that Mrs. Parsons had been kidnapped and wanted all law enforcement authorities to withdraw so as to facilitate ransom negotiations. Relations became so strained that local and state authorities moved out of a headquarters they had been sharing with federal agents. No progress having been made by the end of June, the FBI closed its local headquarters as did their local counterparts down the street. The case never was solved, but did not besmirch the batting average of the Department of Justice who expunged it from their records, since interstate transportation never had been established.

The bureau's next difficulty came when the *Times* published the results of a Brookings Institute study of crime control under the headline: "Federal Agencies on Crime Chided: Brookings Report Charges Jealousies, 'Feverish Outbursts of Self-Advertising' " (29 Sept. 1937, p. 14). The report discussed the rivalry between the FBI and federal postal agents over who actually had been responsible for the capture of Alvin Karpis. The report asserted that not only is there " 'unwillingness on the part of one agency to give credit to another,' but that there are a 'lack of cordial personal contacts among officials' and 'indirect attacks' by one agency upon another" (ibid.).

Adding to federal difficulties, another rash of kidnappings broke out in the fall of 1937. One was strictly a local affair in New York City, but the other, in Chicago, was to result in the first execution under the Lindbergh Law for a classic ransom kidnapping. Ironically, the name of the victim was Charles Ross. Ross was a wealthy, retired manufacturer. On a September evening, in a tactic reminiscent of the gangster kidnappings of the 1920s, his car was pulled over by another vehicle and he was kidnapped. For three weeks the victim's wife pleaded with the abductors to commence ransom negotiations, as Hoover's agents stood by. Eventually a $50,000 ransom was demanded and paid, but the victim was not returned. Again, friction was reported between Hoover's agents and local authorities. A Chicago state's attorney claimed that his "office had been excluded from the Ross case by the government men" (20 Oct. 1937, p. 3). J. Edgar Hoover announced that he was taking personal charge.

Two weeks later, Dr. James Seder of Huntington, West Virginia, was kidnapped for ransom, and federal agents had to divert some of their manpower from the Ross case. The seventy-nine-year-old Seder was held for twelve days in an abandoned coal mine. Before the $50,000 ransom could be paid, however, he was rescued, suffering from shock and exposure. Federal agents participated in the arrest of the three abductors—Arnett Booth, John Travis, and Orville Adkins. No interstate transportation of the victim had occurred. However, the mails had been used to send the ransom note, resulting in federal charges of using the mails for extortion. During preliminary proceedings, Seder died from pneumonia contracted during his captivity in the mine and the federal charges were held in abeyance to facilitate a state capital prosecution for kidnapping and murder. The trial resulted in a guilty verdict which made a death penalty mandatory.

The year ended with a White Plains, New York, ransom slaying which resulted in two more state death sentences, bringing the total to seven that would result from cases during the year.

After the difficulties they had experienced in 1937, federal forces were understandably anxious to avail themselves of opportunities to renew public confidence in their efficiency. Such opportunities were abundant in 1938. In January, Hoover's forces captured Henry Seadlund, suspected kidnapper of Chicago's Charles Ross. Seadlund was apprehended in California, and Hoover, as he had done in the capture of Alvin Karpis, went to California to take personal charge of the case. Seadlund confessed that he and an accomplice had kidnapped Ross and held him captive in a Wisconsin cave. While they were holding Ross, however, the abductors had become involved in a fight over the ransom, Ross had intervened, and he and the accomplice were critically injured. Seadlund maintained that he killed both of them to spare them further suffering.

After deliberating an hour and a half, a federal jury in Chicago decreed that Seadlund should be put to death. Seadlund's attorneys announced that they were going to challenge the constitutionality of the Lindbergh Law, and an automatic stay of execution resulted. While Seadlund was just beginning his appeals process, the condemned ransomers of Dr. James Seder had exhausted theirs. Booth, Travis, and Adkins were hanged on March 21 in West Virginia's first executions growing out of a ransom kidnapping.

In February 1938, the attention of Hoover's agents had been directed to New Rochelle, New York, by the first kidnap murder of a child since the Mattson case in 1936. Twelve-year-old David Levine was abducted while walking home from school. A $30,000 ransom demand was made. Federal agents quickly went into action but were unsuccessful. Three months later, the wirebound, headless torso of the victim washed ashore in Long Island Sound. The case never was solved, although in 1963, on the twenty-fifth anniversary of the abduction, an FBI spokesman would report that the bureau was still working on the case. Only it and the Mattson case, he claimed, prevented the bureau from having solved every major kidnapping for ransom since 1932.

The flare-up of ransom kidnappings after the interlude of 1937 had created a good deal of unanticipated work for federal forces. The work load began to strain the bureau's budget. In May 1938, President Roosevelt asked Congress for an additional appropriation for the FBI to offset unforeseen expenses in connection with the recent cases. Seven days later the financial burden of the Department of Justice was increased when James Bailey Cash, five-year-old son of a Princeton, Florida, grocery store and filling station operator, was stolen from his bed. A ransom of $10,000 was demanded in a note slipped under the door of the Cash home. The father notified the FBI in Miami and J. Edgar Hoover flew in a squad of agents from Washington. Four days later, Cash delivered the ransom as instructed, but his son was not returned.

The Cash family was neither wealthy nor prominent, but the societal reaction was intense nevertheless. The *Times* carried four-column aerial pictures of the 2,000 citizens, American Legionnaires, WPA workers, Boy Scouts, and authorities participating in the "greatest manhunt ever seen in Florida" (2 June 1938, p. 3). The Red Cross set up field kitchens to feed the searchers. J. Edgar Hoover flew down from Washington to take personal charge of the investigation and brought in additional bureau manpower. After almost a month had passed since the kidnapping, hope for finding the child alive was abandoned, and despite the lack of any evidence that a federal law had been violated, Hoover and his men stayed at the scene. By June 7, the bureau was in need of further appropriations. President Roosevelt went back to Congress and received a $50,000 supplement to the $186,000 the bureau had received earlier in the year. The next day, J. Edgar Hoover announced that the body of the Cash boy had been found in dense underbrush about a half mile from his home and that a suspect was in hand.

The abductor was Franklin Pierce McCall, the twenty-one-year-old son of a local minister, who had lived in an apartment in the Cash home a few years before while he and his wife worked as harvesters. Hoover announced that McCall had made a full confession to the kidnapping and murder. According to Hoover, as reported in the *Times*, McCall had been motivated by his desire "for the better things of life for his wife and himself and had been unable to get steady employment" (11 June 1938). The child had been smothered, accidentally, by a handkerchief which McCall had placed over the child's face during the kidnapping. Hoover also announced that as far as federal involvement was concerned the case was closed, leaving the capital prosecution of McCall to the state of Florida. McCall was sentenced to death.

As the appeals process began for McCall, it ran out for John Henry Seadlund, condemned for the kidnap slaying of Charles Ross; Seadlund was electrocuted in Chicago on July 14. After an appeals process that included an unsuccessful attempt to have the verdict and sentence reviewed by the U.S. Supreme Court, McCall was executed on 24 February 1939.

Although it could not have been recognized at the time, the Cash case in May 1938 marked the end of the flare-up of ransom kidnapping. By the last year of the decade, the epidemic which had spawned the federal war truly was over. Two cases were reported in 1939, one in Brooklyn and the other in Port Arthur, Texas, but both were local affairs and generated little societal reaction.

Summary

The years 1933 through 1939 included many of the most dramatic developments in the annals of American ransom kidnapping. The incidence of the crime reached its historic peak in 1933, and the concentration of sensational cases in a seven-week period during the summer of the year gave rise to the general impression that the nation was in the throes of a kidnapping epidemic. The situation provided much support to the claims of the 1932 congressional supporters of a federal death penalty that a noncapital ransom law would prove ineffective as a general deterrent.

In response to the perceived epidemic, the federal government broadened its crime control powers against interstate kidnappers. Initially, action proceeded on two fronts—seeking a comprehensive anti-kidnapping and racketeering legislative package and creating a national police force. In 1934, the two fronts merged in the federal war against ransom kidnapping. Unlike the situation out of which the 1932 federal legislation was created, the crime war legislation had the full backing of the Roosevelt administration, a consensual base that supported drastic federal action, and few detractors.

Two significant developments were spawned by the federal effort. The first was a capital amendment to the 1932 Lindbergh Law, which now would make a death penalty possible if the victim was transported interstate and was harmed. The second development was the creation, by executive order, of a special division within the Department of Justice to enforce the legislation. Charged by the president and the attorney general with the specific duty of waging war against interstate kidnapping, the division was placed under the directorship of J. Edgar Hoover.

Hoover's forces were highly efficient in the use of their expanded crime control powers, especially against the desperado gangs of the Midwest who had turned to ransoming to supplement dwindling bank robbery proceeds. In less than three years, the gangs were decimated through the combined efforts of Hoover's enforcers and Department of Justice prosecutors. Although none of the gang members came within the jurisdiction of the capital amendment, most of them were prosecuted celeritously and incarcerated in the federal facility obtained for the confinement of ransom kidnappers—Alcatraz. After experiencing a good deal of frustration because of the legal complexities of the capital law, the first federal execution for ransom kidnapping took place in 1936, and others followed. State capital prosecutions added to the number.

By 1936, it was widely believed that ransom kidnapping had been vanquished in America, primarily as a result of the efforts of federal forces. A flare-up of ransomings in 1937 shook the confidence of the public in the belief, and state legislators indulged in a flurry of capital law creation. A ransom slaying of a child in Florida in 1938, however, truly marked the end of ransom kidnapping on an epidemic scale. The crime was about to enter a period of dormancy that would last for more than three decades.

4

Decline, Dormancy, and Resurgence: 1940-74

The prevailing opinion during the early 1940s was that ransom kidnapping on an epidemic scale had been vanquished by the federal crime control effort. Even though infrequent, when ransom kidnappings did occur, the federal government was quick to exploit still-fresh memories of earlier periods to gain additional crime control powers. The De Tristan kidnapping in September 1940 is a case in point.

Marc De Tristan was the three-year-old son of a wealthy Hillsborough, California, family. A ransom of $100,000 was demanded for his safe return. Before any ransom was paid, however, the offender and the victim were apprehended in the foothills of the Sierra Nevada. Since no federal statutes had been violated, Hoover's agents withdrew and the defendant was prosecuted by the state of California. He pleaded guilty and was sentenced to life imprisonment.

The De Tristan case received national publicity but generated little concrete societal reaction on the local or state levels. On the federal level, however, the case was cited as additional evidence of the need for federal wiretapping powers, powers already being sought in the Roosevelt administration's efforts against subversives and saboteurs. As subsequent kidnappings occurred, they, too, were cited as supporting evidence.

Robinson Gives Federal Prosecutors Another Chance at the Death Penalty

At the end of 1942, Thomas H. Robinson, Jr., was in the sixth year of his federal life sentence for the kidnapping of Alice Stoll in 1934. In August 1943, the U.S. Supreme Court granted Robinson a new trial to be held in Louisville, the site of his original guilty plea. This time, however, the case would be heard by a federal jury which could recommend a death penalty, a possibility which Robinson's guilty plea in 1936 had precluded, much to the frustration of federal prosecutors.

At his trial in December 1943, Robinson testified that he and Alice Stoll had been intimate on occasions prior to the kidnapping, a claim which she and the state denied vehemently. The effect of Robinson's testimony was devastating in light of the social prominence of the victim and her family. The jury not only convicted Robinson but also recommended that he be put to death. That Robinson's testimony had played no small part in the outcome of the trial was noted by the presiding judge; in sentencing Robinson to death, he set the execution date to allow time for appeal and even for consideration of executive clemency by the president. Federal prosecutors also lacked the zeal which had characterized their earlier antikidnapping efforts.

Appeals of Robinson's death sentence continued for over a year. The process terminated when the U.S. Supreme Court upheld the death sentence. Presidential clemency now was his final hope. In May 1945, President Truman denied clemency, and Robinson was brought back to Louisville for resentencing to the electric chair. Less than a month later, however, the president reversed his earlier decision and commuted Robinson's sentence to life imprisonment. Press reports indicated that the president's decision had come after the recommendation of Attorney General Biddle that the sentence was unduly severe, a recommendation supported by U.S. Senator Chandler of Kentucky. This action on the part of federal officials stood in sharp contrast to the denial by President Roosevelt of executive clemency to Alvin Gooch in 1936.

Six months after Robinson was saved from execution, the federal judiciary also evidenced a departure from its strict interpretation of the Lindbergh Law. The Supreme Court refused to extend the law to three members of the Mormon faith charged with interstate transportation of a fourteen-year-old girl for the purpose of making her a plural wife of one of the defendants. In the Gooch case, the Court had ruled that forcing a law enforcement official to drive Gooch over a state line to avoid arrest came within the meaning of the phrase "for ransom, reward, or otherwise." Now, however, the Court labeled as "absurd"an application of the law to the case before it.[1]

In January 1946, Chicago was the scene of the Suzanne Degnan child murder in which ransom kidnapping was only peripheral. However, the case gained national publicity and served as the occasion for a media revival of the 1924 Franks case in Chicago and the mutilation of kidnap victim Marian Parker in Los Angeles in 1927. There were a number of similarities: the offender was a student at the University of Chicago, the victim was a child taken from a second-floor bedroom, she was slain, and her corpse was cut up and disposed of in the sewers of Chicago.

The FBI was notified but adhered strictly to the seven-day waiting period and remained in the background, a marked change in strategy from earlier years. This policy was to become common in subsequent cases, and the apparent rationale would be revealed two years later. Six months after the Degnan slaying, William Heirens was arrested on suspicion of burglary. The FBI matched his fingerprints with those found on the Degnan note, and he was charged with kidnapping and murder under Illinois statutes. He eventually confessed to the Degnan kidnapping and murder as well as to more than twenty burglaries and the murder of two of his burglary victims. He was sentenced to three consecutive life terms with no chance of parole for at least sixty-one years.

During the three remaining years of the decade, the three ransom cases reported spanned the continent from Lodi, California, to Kearney, New Jersey. None of the cases attracted national attention. The widely separated and sporadic cases did little to challenge the prevailing impression that ransom kidnapping was a crime of the past.

The Decade of the 1950s: The Greenlease and Weinberger Cases

During the 1950s, a total of ten ransom cases was reported from Missouri, New York, New Mexico, California, Arizona, and Washington. The ransoms demanded in two of the cases were newsworthy in that they were the largest ever, but contributing most to the publicity was the execution of three of the kidnappers. All of the executions resulted from the two kidnap murder cases—the 1953 Greenlease case in Kansas City and the 1956 Weinberger case in Westbury, New York.

When the Greenlease case became known in September 1953, it generated the most intense societal reaction since the 1930s. The offenders were Carl Austin Hall and Bonnie B. Heady. Hall reportedly had gone through a $200,000 legacy and then turned to crime. He admitted to having planned the crime while serving a robbery sentence. His accomplice, Heady, was portrayed in the press as a hanger-on to various midwestern criminal gangs.

On 28 September 1953, Bonnie Heady obtained possession of the victim, the six-year-old son of a wealthy Kansas City businessman, by representing herself to school officials as an agent of the boy's parents. The victim was killed by Heady and Hall on the day of the kidnapping and his body buried in a lime-sprayed grave. The next day a letter was received at the Greenlease home demanding $600,000 ransom, the highest in American kidnapping history. The FBI again adhered strictly to the seven-day waiting period dictated by the 1932 Lindbergh Law, and local authorities delayed active intervention for five days at the request of the victim's parents. The $600,000 ransom was paid on October 4. Two days later, local police and federal agents arrested Hall and Heady on a tip from an informer and located the victim's body.

By 1953, the press had adopted the practice of not reporting a case until the fate of the victim had been decided. As a result, the first report in the *Times* did not appear until twelve days after the kidnapping. Accompanying it was an editorial reflecting public sentiment concerning the appropriateness of the death penalty for Hall and Heady, as retribution. It was the first editorial response by the *Times* to a ransom kidnapping in almost twenty years. Other editorials followed which reviewed the ransoming experiences of the 1930s, the federal kidnapping war, and the legendary exploits of the FBI. U.S. Attorney General Herbert Brownell, Jr., reinforced the reputation of the bureau when he told dinner guests at a New York City social function that in the last twenty years the FBI had virtually wiped out the crime. In Congress, Senator Estes Kefauver of Tennessee reacted by announcing that he would introduce legislation to make the bureau even more effective by empowering Hoover's agents to take immediate jurisdiction in kidnapping cases. Kefauver said that the present seven-day waiting period made it "almost impossible" to conduct a thorough, efficient investigation, and two other senators agreed, maintaining that immediate jurisdiction "would be a 'deterrent' to future crimes" (10 Oct. 1953, p. 34).

Soon after their arrest, federal charges of using the mails to send a kidnapping demand were levied against Hall and Heady. These charges, however, were merely a holding action until it could be determined if capital Lindbergh Law charges could be brought. If not, Missouri authorities would prosecute under capital kidnapping or murder statutes. Hall and Heady admitted that they had taken their victim over the Missouri-Kansas line to kill him, thereby justifying federal jurisdiction. They pleaded guilty to the federal kidnapping charges, and their trial in November solely was for the purpose of determining the punishment. The jury's recommendation of death was greeted by applause in the courtroom. The executions were scheduled for December 18.

Ordinarily, the initial execution date would be a mere formality and would be stayed several times by appeals, but not in this instance. On order of the judge and with the concurrence of the defense attorneys, it was agreed that no appeals would be instituted. Hall and Heady, the latter the only woman ever executed for kidnapping, went to the gas chamber on schedule. They were the third and fourth kidnappers put to death under the 1934 amendment to the Lindbergh Law. The *Times* pointed out that the executions took place only eighty-one days after the abduction, constituting "the swiftest punishment ever meted out under the Lindbergh Law" (18 Dec. 1953, p. 30).

The decade's other sensational case occurred in 1956. On July 4, the one-month-old Weinberger infant, son of a wealthy drug firm executive, was taken from his carriage when his mother left him alone momentarily on the patio of their Long Island home. When she returned, Mrs. Weinberger found the carriage empty and a ransom note demanding $2,000. The note threatened to kill the infant if authorities were notified and also contained an apology from the abductor: he wrote that he regretted his action but was in great need of money and was only asking for the amount needed. On July 5, the ransom was left at the designated site near the Weinberger home but was not picked up. It was revealed later that the abductor had driven to the ransom site with the victim in the car but had been frightened off by crowds in the vicinity, crowds which had gathered despite a voluntary media blackout on the case.

When the blackout ended on July 6, media reactions to the kidnapping and public interest were particularly intense, since the Weinberger case occurred in the same locale from which a three-year-old child had disappeared less than a year before. The same intensity characterized New York area law enforcement reactions. Reminiscent of actions taken by his predecessors three decades earlier, the police commissioner of New York City published a list of instructions to parents of kidnap victims and announced that all 2,500 of New York City's detectives would attend a kidnapping investigation procedures course. A *Times* correspondent, sent to cover the course, reported in detail on what the detectives were being taught about motives and types of kidnappers (12 July 1956, p. 51).

The FBI once again adhered strictly to the seven-day waiting period, but entered the case upon its expiration on July 11. Before this time, they had been on the scene but only as observers. J. Edgar Hoover announced that the full resources of the bureau now would be made available but emphasized that the investigation had been made difficult by the wealth of phony tips, extortion attempts, and hoaxes that had plagued the case in the seven days during which his forces were legislatively blocked from taking jurisdiction.

On July 12, the *New York Daily News* published an editorial, later to be read into the *Congressional Record*, calling for the abolition of the statutory waiting period. It concluded: "Why the Lindbergh law was originally written as it is, we don't know. But neither do we know why this statute should any longer be permitted to bar the FBI from any kidnapping case until the trail is cold and amateurs or semipros have handled, or more likely mishandled, what clues there are. In any kidnapping case, time is of the essence" (12 July 1956).

From Washington, it was announced that the House Judiciary Committee would begin hearings on Representative Keating's bill to allow the FBI to enter a kidnapping case twenty-four hours after the abduction. The New York representative's bill, a companion to Senator Kefauver's proposal, had been in committee since its introduction eighteen months earlier, in response to the Greenlease case: " 'The entire nation,' Representative . . . Keating . . . said today, 'has been shocked over the tragic kidnapping of the Weinberger baby. . . . Almost as shocking, is the revelation to the American public that the F.B.I. could not enter the case until one week after the baby disappeared.' " [2]

Action in the House, historically the stronghold of resistance to reducing the seven-day period, was swift. On July 13, a subcommittee on the judiciary approved unanimously the twenty-four-hour period. Five days later, the full Judiciary Committee issued their report in favor of the bill. That the deterrence of potential kidnappers was an intended effect of the legislation is evident in the committee's report which read, in part:

Since the enactment of the act of May 18, 1934, the record of the Federal Bureau of Investigation in the apprehension and conviction of . . . [kidnappers] has been outstanding. . . .

However, during the past few years kidnappings have occurred which have unfortunately resulted in the deaths of innocent victims. Without criticizing any law enforcement agency, it is the opinion of the committee that the efficient work of the Federal Bureau of Investigation, had it been able to initiate its official investigations prior to the statutory period of 7 days after the date of the occurrence, might well have prevented the tragic deaths of the victims. The mere apprehension and conviction of these criminals is one aspect of the problem. The other is to preserve the life of the victim. Another factor to be considered which, in the opinion of the committee, strengthens the need for the proposed bill is the recognition of the worldwide reputation of the Federal Bureau of Investigation for the apprehension and conviction of kidnappers. The fact that a potential kidnapper would be cognizant . . . that the Federal Bureau of Investigation would take up his trail within 24 hours after the commission of the crime should prove to be a deterrent in the minds of those criminals.[3]

The full House passed the Keating bill on July 23, with several representatives speaking in its behalf. The Greenlease and Weinberger cases were cited prominently in support of the legislation. Action in the Senate, too, was swift. With little comment, the measure was passed on July 28 and signed into law on August 6 by President Eisenhower.

While Congress was acting to increase the effectiveness and deterrent impact of the FBI's prowess in kidnapping cases, local and federal investigative efforts in the Weinberger kidnapping had proved ineffective. Throughout July and August the parents of the victim continued to issue appeals over the media but without results. On August 23, the painstaking comparison of the handwriting on the ransom note with signatures on thousands of public records led the FBI to Angelo John Lamarca. Lamarca confessed that the day after the kidnapping he had returned to the vicinity of the Weinberger home to pick up the ransom and to return the victim unharmed. Seeing large crowds in the vicinity, however, he fled and abandoned the baby, alive, in a rural thicket. The day following his arrest, he led authorities to the thicket where the baby was found dead of exposure.

Judicial processing of Lamarca was left to New York authorities and the federal forces withdrew. In December, a jury convicted Lamarca of kidnapping and felony murder. Since the jury did not recommend mercy, a death sentence was mandatory. After six stays of execution, Lamarca died in the electric chair on 7 August 1958, the third kidnapper to die under the kidnapping laws of New York State.

After the Weinberger case, only one other ransom kidnapping was reported during the remainder of the decade. Again the victim was a child, this time eight-year-old Lee Crary of Edmonds, Washington. The $10,000 ransom case attracted little attention outside of the immediate area. It did, however, provide the FBI with an opportunity to begin an investigation after only twenty-four hours rather than seven days, and the case was solved speedily. In addition to their swift initiation of the investigation, federal authorities were aided significantly by the victim. Not only was he able to describe the wooded area in which he had been held for three days but also provided authorities with the license number of his abductor's car.

During the holiday season of 1959, J. Edgar Hoover cautioned parents against leaving their children in the care of persons not well known to the family because of "the baby sitter kidnap menace" (21 Dec. 1959, p. 17). The *Times* relegated the warning to a brief item on page 17; it is doubtful that the general public took the warning even that seriously.

A Reduction in Threatened Punishments: The 1960s

In December 1963, there began a pattern of one major ransoming a year, a pattern that was to persist until 1967. Some of the victims had names of sufficient prominence to catch the attention of the national press and the public, and, together with the regularity of the cases, occasioned references in the press to a possible resurgence of kidnapping in America.

The case which initiated the annual pattern was the kidnapping of Frank Sinatra, Jr., from Stateline, California, on 8 December 1963. The Sinatra name, the size of the ransom, and the well-publicized prosecution under the Lindbergh Law combined to call up America's kidnapping past. The victim was abducted at gunpoint from a Stateline motel. He was driven to a Los Angeles suburb and held for fifty-three hours until a $240,000 ransom demand was met. The FBI entered the case immediately, supervised the ransom delivery and safe return of the victim, and led the hunt for the offenders.

Media publicity was intense and widespread. According to the *Times*, the case even was mentioned in a Moscow radio broadcast as an example of "how business is done in America" (13 Dec. 1963, p. 6). A *Times* editorial treated the kidnapping in the context of the aftermath of the Kennedy assassination in Dallas and civil rights violence in the South. Feature articles reviewed the history of the Lindbergh Law, major cases since its passage in 1932, and praised the efficiency of the FBI against ransom kidnappers.

Five days after the kidnapping, press releases from Washington testified to the efficiency of Hoover's men by announcing the arrest of three suspects. The appropriateness of the accolades was challenged, however, by William H. Parker, Los Angeles chief of police, who charged that his forces and the California Highway Patrol had been unjustifiably excluded from the case by the federal takeover. He recommended a top-level reexamination of relations among federal, state, and local law enforcement agencies.

Prosecution of Sinatra's kidnappers was under the federal Lindbergh Law, since the defendants had taken their victim from California to Nevada. The death penalty, however, never was at issue. Throughout the trial the defendants claimed that the victim had cooperated in the crime as a publicity stunt, and the press played up this aspect; a federal jury thought otherwise and convicted all three defendants on some counts. Two of the offenders were sentenced to life and additional terms totaling seventy-five years, while the other received a sentence of sixteen years, eight months. That the government's case had been less than cut-and-dried, however, was revealed when the life sentences were reduced to terms of years, making two of the offenders eligible for immediate parole. In addition, a subsequent appeal to a higher court resulted in the reversal of the convictions of two of the offenders.

Annual cases for 1964 and 1965 were reported from Hollywood, California, and Tacoma, Washington, respectively. The string of West Coast ransomings was broken by an unsuccessful attempt to ransom the son of a wealthy Surfside, Florida, contractor, but the annual case for 1967 reestablished California as the center of ransomings in the 1960s. The concentration of cases in the Los Angeles area began to generate a good deal of alarm.

The Kenneth Young case of 1967 had the potential for generating a good deal of societal reaction. The victim was a child—the eleven-year-old son of a wealthy Beverly Hills financier. The manner of the abduction recalled earlier sensational cases—the victim was stolen from his second-floor bedroom as he slept. The ransom was large—$250,000. The FBI invested major resources in the case, and the kidnapper escaped with the ransom in what appeared to be the first successful ransom kidnapping in many years. When the offender was apprehended two years later, his identity caused a considerable stir. He had been an Internal Revenue Service agent at the time of the ransoming and after the crime had continued to work for the government. Among his duties was serving as a bodyguard for President Nixon and former Vice-President Humphrey. The case generated only a fraction of the reaction it would have generated if the arrest had come when details of the case were still fresh in the public's mind. Even so, the case made the front page of the *Times* and called forth reviews of earlier ransomings, as well as a recital of the FBI's record against kidnappers.

Concurrent with the beginning of the annual pattern of ransom kidnapping, a concerted effort to abolish capital punishment in America for all crimes had begun, spearheaded by the Legal Defense Fund of the NAACP. Capital kidnapping statutes began to be examined as part of the general abolitionist effort. The execution under California's "Little Lindbergh Law" of Caryl Chessman in 1960, after years of highly publicized appeals, already had brought capital kidnapping laws under scrutiny. Chessman had fallen under the capital punishment provisions of the act not for a classic ransom kidnapping, but for forcing a victim of his sexual attack to move from the car of her boyfriend to Chessman's car—a distance of about thirty feet. To many observers, California's "Little Lindbergh Law" had been exploited solely as a technical means of subjecting Chessman to a capital prosecution.

Efforts to reduce legal punishments for ransom kidnapping, as part of the growing general abolitionist movement, encountered considerable resistance. New York State provided an example of resistance in the legislative sector. In 1963, the legislature eliminated an automatic death penalty for persons found guilty of premeditated murder or kidnapping in which the victim was harmed. Additional changes two years later virtually abolished capital punishment in the state for all crimes. In 1966, however, a legislative effort was mounted to keep kidnapping penalties, short of execution, as severe as possible. The New York senate approved by a vote of fifty-two to six a bill empowering a sentencing judge to provide that a person convicted of kidnapping, murder, or treason shall never be released on parole. The measure passed the assembly by a vote of eighty-six to thirty-eight and appeared well on its way to becoming law, until it was vetoed by Governor Rockefeller.

Resistance in the judicial sector to removing ransom kidnapping from capital status was most evident in California. In 1967, a superior court judge ruled that the death penalty provision of the state's "Little Lindbergh Law," which only required bodily harm and not the death of the victim, did not constitute cruel and unusual punishment as prohibited by the Eighth Amendment to the United States Constitution. The ruling came in response to a constitutional challenge mounted by the American Civil Liberties Union. Two years later, however, the California Supreme Court restricted the scope of the state's kidnapping legislation by ruling that kidnappings "in which movement of victims was merely incidental during the crime," [4] as many had maintained in the Chessman case, was not within the legislative intent of the statute.

As of 1967, the capital status of the crime had changed little despite the growing abolitionist movement. Kidnapping for ransom under certain conditions was still punishable by death in thirty-two states. In the preceding decade only three state legislatures had removed it from capital status and then merely as part of general abolitions. The availability of the death penalty for ransom kidnapping was rendered moot, however, by the de facto situation. American sentiment against carrying out death sentences had been building for several years. Although by 1967 it had yet to make a major impact on removing capital statutes from the books or in having the death penalty struck down by judicial fiat, the movement had had a major impact on the number of condemned offenders actually executed. The execution of a convicted murderer by the state of Colorado on 2 June 1967 marked the beginning of a ten-year hiatus in execution in America.

The death penalty provision of the federal ransom law proved less resistant to abolition pressure than state kidnapping penalties. In January 1967, a federal district court judge in Connecticut handed down a decision which would lead to the federal death penalty for kidnapping being declared unconstitutional. The ruling followed the indictment of three men for hijacking a truck in Connecticut, abducting the driver to New Jersey, and leaving him tied to a tree. The driver suffered rope burns on his wrists. Technically, therefore, he had not been released unharmed rendering the defendants liable to a possible death sentence.

The constitutional challenge was mounted at the point in the judicial process when the three defendants faced the choice between trial by jury or a bench trial. The choice was crucial. If they pleaded guilty or waived their right to a jury trial and had their case heard only by a judge, they ran no risk whatever of being sentenced to death. Hence, in order to exercise their constitutional right to trial by jury, they had to risk a possible death sentence. "Thus," said the federal judge, "the law violates the Sixth Amendment to the Constitution of the United States and is invalid." [5]

In May 1967, the U.S. Supreme Court agreed to review the district court ruling, and in April 1968, the High Court declared the death penalty provision of the Lindbergh Law to be unconstitutional. All other provisions of the law were left in force. Thus, after thirty-four years, during which time six persons had been executed under the law, ransom kidnapping no longer was a federal capital crime. The Supreme Court's decision was publicized widely. The *New York Times* of April 9 announced the ruling on the front page.

The Beginning of the Resurgence in Ransom Kidnapping

During 1967–68, societal reaction to the crime continued to be minimal, sporadic, and unfocused. Several factors were responsible. The cases that now began to number four or five a year, rather than one, occurred in widely separated parts of the country—Texas, California, Illinois, Georgia, and Nevada. None of the victims were prominent on a national scale. None of them were killed. No sensational manhunts or trials resulted which could have demanded major media attention for extended periods of time. In fact, it would not be until the kidnapping of Patty Hearst in 1974 that kidnapping for ransom would once again emerge as a cause for national alarm on a scale that rivaled the situation during the 1930s.

Early in 1968, the media began to carry sporadic reports of ransomings by and against members of organized crime. The *Times* described the phenomenon as something new: "Members of the Mafia are beset by a new problem: They are being kidnapped" (8 Mar. 1968, p. 41). Of course, it was not new. Later in the year, reports of the ransoming of children came in from San Antonio, Texas; Beverly Hills, California; and Oakbrook, Illinois. In none of the cases were the victims killed and in none of them were the ransoms collected. State prosecutions resulted in long prison sentences in all three cases.

It was not until the December 1968 ransoming of Barbara Mackle that the crime came to national attention. The Mackle case had the reaction-generating qualities that the other cases had lacked. Her family was prominent throughout the state of Florida; they were residents of Key Biscayne and neighbors of President Nixon. The method of sequestering the twenty-year-old daughter of one of Miami's richest men was the most sensational yet devised—a buried coffin equipped with a life support system. The ransom was $500,000 and, in sharp contrast to most other cases during the 1960s, the abductors successfully collected it. In addition, J. Edgar Hoover took a personal interest in the case, a nationwide manhunt resulted, and the two suspects were placed on the FBI's "Ten Most Wanted" list. Such are the qualities that attract attention and spawn reactions.

The victim, a student at Emory University, was taking semester examinations, and her mother had been staying in an Atlanta motel from which they were to leave for Florida for Christmas vacation. Early on the morning of December 17, two persons forced their way into the room, bound and gagged the mother and kidnapped her daughter. The mother notified authorities. J. Edgar Hoover sent an agent to Miami to take charge. The victim was taken to a wooded area of Georgia and entombed in a capsule containing elaborate instructions on the operation of the capsule's life support system. The kidnappers then telephoned the victim's father in Florida and demanded a ransom of $500,000. Fifteen hours after supervising the delivery, the FBI received directions to the victim's location. Barbara Mackle was rescued after spending eighty hours entombed.

Five days after the kidnapping, federal and local authorities arrested Gary Steven Krist and began a nationwide hunt for Ruth Eisemann-Schier, his accomplice. Despite being placed on the FBI's "Ten Most Wanted" list, she eluded capture for three months. Initially federal Lindbergh Law charges were brought against the defendants but were dropped when interstate transportation of the victim could not be shown. The willingness of federal authorities to withdraw from such a sensational case may have been prompted, in part, by the fact that the Lindbergh Law had been stripped of its death penalty provision eight months earlier. Georgia kidnapping statutes, however, retained the penalty. A jury convicted Krist of kidnapping, but their recommendation for mercy saved him from the death penalty sought by the prosecution. Eisemann-Schier pleaded guilty. Krist was sentenced to life imprisonment and his accomplice to seven years.

During the last years of the decade, three major ransomings

were reported, two from California and one from Nevada. In none of them was ransom collected, and they attracted little attention outside of their immediate locales.

The American Kidnapping Experience in the Early 1970s

In the first year of the decade, reports of ransomings came from Arkansas, New York, and California. Only the Zeigler case from Los Angeles attracted much national attention and then primarily because the offenders were black, a rarity in ransom kidnappings. Neither did two of the three cases reported from South Carolina, Georgia, and New York, in 1972, prompt much concern. The South Carolina Lindsey case was to attract some attention, retroactively, in the context of kidnappings by political terrorists.[6] Three to four cases a year constituted a real increase in comparison to the annual rate during the preceding forty years, but only if one was counting. Despite the inability of the cases themselves to generate much concern, public attention was directed to the crime by two other matters. Ransom kidnapping occasionally was being mentioned in media coverage of the mounting pressure to abolish the death penalty in America, usually as an example of the type of criminal offense which many believed the death penalty did deter. Ransom kidnapping was brought to the attention of the public more dramatically by alarm over its increasing popularity as a weapon of political terrorists abroad.

During 1970, it was clear to state legislators and executives that it was just a matter of time before the U.S. Supreme Court would consider the constitutionality of the death penalty for all crimes. The Maxwell case, involving a death sentence given in 1961 to a convicted Arkansas rapist, was before the Court early in the year. Many observers believed that the Court would use the Maxwell case to make known its views on capital punishment. In anticipation of the decision, officials in several states called for reviews and, in some cases, revisions of their capital statutes. In June, however, the justices returned the Maxwell case to the trial court, leaving intact the moratorium on executions.

While a majority of political figures quoted in the *Times* favored abolition of the death penalty, as did the *Times* itself, other officials and a large segment of the general public favored its retention. In Illinois, for example, a referendum in December 1970 on a proposed section of the new state constitution that would abolish the death penalty resulted in the rejection of the proposal by voters in all sections of the state. Officials in California, in which state the bulk of the recent ransom cases had occurred, expressed the same sentiment, specifically concerning ransom kidnapping.

In January 1971, the abolition movement was given added momentum when the National Commission on Reform of the Federal Criminal Laws, after a three-and-a-half-year study, called for life imprisonment as the maximum federal penalty.[7] Two of the commission members, Senators Ervin and McClellan, disagreed with the recommendation and contended that the death penalty should at least be retained for intentional murder or treason.[8] The *Times,* on the other hand, characterized the recommendation as "a new message of hope" for the condemned but did note in its article, titled "The Nation against Death," that the recommendation was the only one that was not presented to the president without dissent (10 Jan. 1971, sec. 4, p. 4). The commission's recommendation prompted another flurry of statements from state officials both in support and in opposition.

In May 1971, the Supreme Court handed down another decision which many expected would contain a ruling on whether or not the death penalty itself was cruel and unusual punishment and, hence, a violation of the Eighth Amendment. Once again, however, the ultimate issue was not addressed and, as noted in a front-page *Times* article of May 4, there was no indication in the decision of whether the Justices would now agree to face the ultimate question, even though the question was presented in many of the 120 death cases then pending before the Court.

The *Times* report also noted that there was no indication that the Court's decision which, in effect, upheld the constitutionality of two procedural matters relating to the death penalty, would have any immediate impact on the thirty-eight states which still had death statutes. Officials in most states indicated that they would maintain their wait-and-see posture until the Court did rule on the issue. Another *Times* article of May 4 reviewed the general trend among Western nations to abolish capital punishment but pointed out that the penalty was particularly sensitive to public reaction to dramatic crimes and cited the Lindbergh kidnapping as the most famous American example of this quality.

Although only peripherally involved in the abolition movement in the early years of the decade, ransom kidnapping was a more central part of the national concern over the activities of political terrorists during this period. Eventually the two concerns would merge. In California, for example, much of the support for retaining the death penalty was prompted by a concern with violence associated with political activists. During 1970, the bombing of a San Francisco police station killed an officer, and later in the year, a legislative measure spawned by the incident went into effect. Under the measure, the death penalty or life imprisonment at the discretion of the jury was provided for conviction of willfully and maliciously exploding a destructive device, causing great harm or injury to a person. The same type of concern over terrorist activities was reflected in the actions of federal legislators in October, when both houses of Congress passed a bill, as part of the Omnibus Crime Control and Safe Streets Act, providing the death penalty for persons convicted of fatal terrorist bombings.

Concern over terrorist bombings soon expanded to take in the growing popularity of ransom kidnapping as a terrorist strategy. Initially the alarm was vicarious, since terrorist kidnappings and airplane hijackings usually occurred abroad rather than in the United States. Editorials at various times throughout the year evidenced the concern of the *Times* with the phenomenon. In April, terrorist kidnappings of diplomats in Guatemala and Brazil elicited editorial responses, as did the kidnap murder of a U.S. official in Uruguay in August, and the kidnapping of a British trade representative by Quebec separatists in October. In November, the possible emergence of the problem in the United States was forecast with the announcement by the FBI that a plot had been foiled to kidnap the governor of Minnesota, hijack an airplane, and use the hostages to free black activists under indictment for murder in California.

By December 1970, the federal government was addressing itself to terrorist kidnappings, and Deputy Attorney General Kleindienst recommended that any victims other than the president, vice-president, or their families be sacrificed rather than ransomed. Three months later, it was announced that the administration formally had adopted an across-the-board policy of not paying ransom in cases of political kidnapping, at home or abroad, in an effort to discourage terrorist groups. When the bizarre and abortive South Carolina kidnappings were reported in March 1971 and interpreted by some officials as another attempt by black power groups to secure hostages to trade for imprisoned black activists (see n. 6), concern over a domestic outbreak of terrorist kidnappings increased. Among retentionists who believed in the ability of capital punishment to deter terrorist kidnappings, now there were additional grounds for concern as the time for another Supreme Court ruling drew near.

In January 1972, the cases which would produce the landmark *Furman* decision already were before the Supreme Court. Attorneys for two convicted murderers and two convicted rapists were asking the Court to strike down their death sentences as cruel and unusual punishment. In opposition, attorneys from California, Georgia, and Texas were arguing that death penalty laws reflected the will of the people of their respective states and that the penalty did not violate constitutional prohibitions against cruel and unusual punishment.

During the months of the Supreme Court's deliberations, activity in state legislatures was intense. New Jersey, forever linked with the history of ransom kidnapping in America, and California, the site of many recent cases, are illustrative.

In January 1972, the New Jersey Supreme Court declared the state's capital punishment statute unconstitutional. Ironically, the grounds were the same as in the 1968 *Brady* decision in which the death penalty provision of the federal Lindbergh Law had been struck down—by stipulating that only a jury could decree a death sentence, defendants were coerced from exercising their constitutional right to a jury trial. New Jersey legislators responded by introducing bills that would make a jury trial mandatory in capital first-degree murder cases. Although not proposing that the death penalty be reinstated for ransom kidnapping, proposed legislation would increase the penalty by requiring anyone sentenced to life for the crime be required to serve at least thirty years, rather than being eligible for parole after fourteen years and ten months.

In California, too, the matter was brought to a head by the state supreme court. In February, the court faced the ultimate issue directly, ruled that the death penalty constituted cruel and unusual punishment, and ordered all death sentences commuted to life imprisonment. Reactions in California to the ruling were a microcosm of the reactions that would follow the ruling of the U.S. Supreme Court four months later in *Furman*. As reported in the *Times*, Governor Reagan labeled the decision as "a case of the courts setting themselves up above the people and the legislature" (19 Feb. 1972, p. 1). The governor maintained: "Capital punishment is a deterrent. Society has a right to use it" (1 Mar. 1972, p. 46). California Attorney General Younger reacted in much the same vein. He accused the California court of usurping a function that should be left to the U.S. Supreme Court and of making " 'an inappropriate and unsubstantiated legislative finding' that the death penalty did not deter dangerous criminals" (4 Mar. 1972, p. 56). Attorney General Younger was adamant in his view that the capital punishment issue should be left up to the citizens of California who, he claimed, wanted the death penalty. Mail from voters in response to the decision ran two to one in support of Younger's appraisal. Led by Governor Reagan, the matter eventually was put to the voters in a November referendum; by more than two to one they approved a constitutional amendment that would reinstate the death penalty.

Cases of ransom kidnapping during the first half of 1972 did little to expand the death penalty debate to embrace the crime. Only one major case was reported during the period and then not until June. The victim was the nephew of a reputed

New York City Mafia chieftain. The suspects also were members of the New York City underworld. Consistent with the historical pattern of reactions to such cases, no one got very excited when both victim and offender were reputed to be gangsters.

The Furman Decision and Its Aftermath

On 29 June 1972, the U.S. Supreme Court handed down what was expected to be the definitive ruling on the constitutionality of the death penalty. The nine separate opinions of the justices contained a wealth of social scientific, philosophic, and pragmatic arguments addressed to the ultimate question of whether the death penalty itself was cruel and unusual punishment. This was not the question presented to the Court, however, by the one murder and two rape cases reviewed by the justices. Instead, the question focused on the manner in which the death penalty had been administered; specifically: "Does the imposition and carrying out of the death penalty [in these cases] constitute cruel and unusual punishment in violation of the Eighth and Fourteenth Amendments?" [9]

A five-to-four majority of the Court answered in the affirmative, the majority being persuaded by the wealth of social scientific evidence cited showing that significant bias against minority offenders had occurred in the administration and imposition of the death penalty. Since murder and rape constituted the vast majority of cases for which offenders had been executed, the Court focused almost exclusively on these capital crimes. Ransom kidnapping was mentioned only in the concurring opinion of Justice Marshall and then only in the context of noting that "murder is the crime most often punished by death, followed by kidnapping and treason." [10] Justice Marshall was correct, if he was referring to the fact that kidnapping was a capital crime in more jurisdictions than rape, but of the 3,859 persons executed in the United States since the Justice Department began keeping records in 1930, 3,334 had been for murder, 455 for rape, and only 20 for ransom kidnapping.

Although having played no significant role in the *Furman*

decision, kidnapping was mentioned prominently in initial reactions to the decision, again as an example of the type of crime which many believed to be deterrable by the threat of legal execution even if murder and rape were not. In a nationally televised press conference on the night of the *Furman* decision, President Nixon said he believed the death penalty was needed at the federal level as a deterrent to such capital crimes as kidnapping and air piracy. The president went on to say that he hoped the Court's decision "does not go so far as to rule out capital punishment for kidnapping and hijacking." [11]

The Court, in *Furman*, again had failed to address the ultimate issue of whether or not capital punishment was, in itself, cruel and unusual punishment. The decision, therefore, did not constitute an absolute prohibition on the use of the death penalty. Instead, it merely vacated existing death sentences and placed the burden on the various state and federal jurisdictions to rethink the matter, particularly as to whether the death penalty was a deterrent. The failure of the Court to absolutely prohibit capital punishment was a major factor in generating the societal reaction that followed. A constitutional ban would have satisfied at least the abolitionists, and reactions would have been forthcoming primarily from the retentionists. As it stood, intense media coverage of the decision made both sides aware that the ultimate issue still had not been decided.

The strategy adopted by those legislators committed to reinstating the death penalty had been laid out for them in the opinions of some of the dissenting justices, particularly Chief Justice Burger; namely, design legislation that would lessen the opportunity for discriminatory imposition of capital punishment. Death sentences for clearly specified crimes, under clearly specified conditions, became favored legislative criteria. With these criteria, particularly that relating to specified crimes, the opportunity was presented to legislators to expand their focus beyond murder to include such crimes as ransom kidnapping. The primary focus of legislators remained on murder, however, and specification, for the most part, consisted of distinguishing among different types of murder and situations in which murders occurred. Ransom kidnapping was mentioned occasionally during the remainder of the year by President Nixon and in media reports. In the latter instances, attention was called to the particular ability of the crime to generate both retentionist sentiments, as in the Lindbergh case, and abolitionist sentiments, as in the Chessman case.

In state legislatures, ransom kidnapping received little consideration during the remainder of 1972. In some states, such as Colorado, kidnapping was indirectly involved in legislative proposals to require mandatory death sentences for felony murders. In other states, such as Pennsylvania, kidnapping was specified as one of the crimes for which the death penalty should be reinstated if the victim was killed. Even in California, the site of several of the recent cases, kidnapping was not specified as one of the proposed crimes for which the death penalty was needed.

Considering the actual American experience with ransom kidnappings during the years preceding the *Furman* decision, the lack of legislative attention to the crime was not surprising. The Mackle case in 1968, in which President Nixon had taken a personal interest, had been the last case sensational enough to attract national attention. Few persons were aware of the increase in ransom kidnappings that had been underway since 1968. In the six months immediately prior to the *Furman* decision, only two ransomings had been reported, and the five cases reported for the remainder of 1972 generated little national concern. They were widely separated—Georgia, New York, Texas, Minnesota, and Louisiana. The Piper case from Minneapolis attracted national attention briefly because the kidnappers escaped with a reported $1 million ransom, but no calls for legislative action were precipitated.

The increase in ransom kidnappings during 1973 was significant. The *Times* reported twelve major cases, more than twice the number in any year since 1937. Seven of the cases occurred in the first six months and close enough together to generate speculation in the media about a kidnapping wave.

On February 20, a lone kidnapper ransomed the twelve-year-old son of a Dallas bank president for $200,000, but was apprehended by the FBI only a few hours later. On the evening of the same day, in what "was believed to be the only major kidnapping in recent Washington area history," [12] the sixteen-year-old son of a Bethesda, Maryland, businessman was ransomed for the same amount. Four days later, abductors demanded $40,000 for the return of the wife of a Bath, Pennsylvania, bank president, but released her before picking up the ransom. In March, the wife of a Roanoke, Virginia, businessman was ransomed for $25,000. Despite the fact that the kidnapper was placed on the FBI's "Ten Most Wanted" list, he eluded capture for almost a year. In April, two kidnappers were unsuccessful in their attempt to collect a $20,000 ransom for a Macomb, Illinois, coed. Later in the month, a New Rochelle, New York, gambler was rescued from a Harlem apartment where he was being held for $250,000 ransom by three black offenders.

The wave of ransomings temporarily ended in June, with an unsuccessful attempt to collect a ransom of $1.5 million for the return of Melvin Zahn, president of a Chicago pharmaceutical company. The Zahn case attracted considerable national publicity, initially because of the size of the ransom, and later because of the sentences pronounced. A federal judge sentenced the offenders to twelve and fifteen years, respectively, under a provision of the federal code which made them eligible for parole consideration within three months. Zahn bitterly criticized the sentences, claiming that such leniency could only encourage more kidnappers.

That segment of the public and officialdom favoring reinstatement of the death penalty because of what they considered increasing leniency on the part of courts were sympathetic. Nationally, retentionist sentiment had increased. According to a Harris poll in June 1973, 59 percent of the sample supported capital punishment as a more effective deterrent than a life sentence without parole.

The nation was free of major ransom kidnappings during the next three months, but detailed media coverage of the July 1973 Getty kidnapping in Italy kept the crime before the public.

Of the remaining five cases reported for the year from California to Michigan to New York, only the year's final case generated much reaction. The reaction was intense but confined, for the most part, to the black community of Detroit.

On the afternoon of 1 December 1973, six-year-old Keith Arnold, familiar to many Detroit television viewers from his appearances in a popular television commercial, and eight-year-old Gerald Kraft, were abducted while playing in the neighborhood. Initially, $53,000 was demanded as the price for their safe return, but the demand later was reduced to $15,000. An attempt by authorities to capture the abductors at the ransom site failed, and they escaped with the money. Three days later, the bodies of the two victims were found shot to death.

Community organizations and residents joined with police in the investigation that eventually led to the kidnapping and murder prosecutions of three twenty-one-year-old male residents of the community. The *Detroit News* called the crime "a slaughter of innocents," [13] the Detroit police commissioner labeled the crime "tragedy almost without parallel in our community," [14] and Mayor-Elect Coleman Young called for a new commitment to "reduce the outrageous levels of violence and carnage among our citizenry." [15]

There was little evidence that the publicity received by the cases of 1973 had any major impact on legislators striving to reinstate the death penalty. Over half of the states now were so engaged. As observed by the *New York Times*: "The passage of such legislation may be difficult but the bills introduced, often backed by a governor, indicate that a sizeable proportion of elected officials still consider the death penalty a strong crime deterrent" (11 Mar. 1973, p. 1).

Ransom kidnapping continued to be involved in proposed legislation in most states merely as one of the unspecified felonies which would invoke the death penalty if the victim was killed. The specification of ransom kidnapping as one such felony did appear to be spreading, but whether the ransom cases occurring were responsible could not be determined. Only in a few states, such as Georgia, did the legislature propose the reinstatement of the death penalty for ransom kidnapping if the victim was not killed but suffered lasting mental or physical damage as a result of the crime. Georgia, however, was among the thirteen states which had reenacted capital legislation in May 1973.

Ransom kidnapping occupied a more prominent position in federal capital punishment deliberations and actions during 1973. In January, it was evident that President Nixon's normative evaluation of the *Furman* decision, six months earlier, was going to be acted upon. Attorney General Kleindienst announced that he would ask Congress to enact legislation reinstating the death penalty for certain crimes, as yet unspecified, even if it meant seeking an amendment to the Constitution. L. Patrick Gray, successor to J. Edgar Hoover as director of the FBI, offered encouragement to state legislatures to do likewise.

On March 10, President Nixon, in a national radio address, called on Congress to restore the death penalty for the federal crimes of assassination, treason, air hijacking, murder of law enforcement agents and prison guards, and kidnapping. Four days later, he detailed the proposal in his State of the Union Address to Congress and the American people. The list of suggested capital crimes had been modified somewhat, but kidnapping was still among them. To many of the assembled congressmen and the viewing public, kidnapping may have seemed out of place in the list of acts which focused primarily on the protection of the government and law enforcement authorities. Kidnapping again figured prominently in a report later in March when the president asked Congress to abolish insanity as a defense against charges of murder and related federal crimes. When the administration forwarded the draft legislation to the House and Senate, the status of kidnapping as a proposed capital crime had been modified. Now, only homicide resulting from a kidnapping would invoke the death penalty.

There was a good deal of reaction generated by the Nixon administration's proposed legislation, most of it focusing on the death penalty in general rather than on its application to any specific offense. A feature article in the *New York Times* of

April 1, however, observed that Nixon's proposal made more sense for some crimes than for others, and potential kidnappers were singled out as probably deterrable by fear of capital punishment.

A Centennial Outbreak of Ransom Kidnapping

The peak reported incidence of ransom kidnapping in America occurred during 1933. The twenty-seven cases reported for that year were sufficient to prompt the label "kidnapping epidemic," to launch a federal war on the crime, and to overcome congressional resistance to making kidnapping for ransom a federal capital crime. Twenty-six major cases were reported for 1974, twenty-three of them coming after the February 4 kidnapping of Patricia Hearst. The Hearst case provided a nexus for a range of concerns about the crime of ransom kidnapping, concerns which, until the Hearst case, had lacked a common focus.

In the aftermath of the Hearst case, official and public concerns came together and generated the most intense societal reaction since the 1930s. Among the reactions were proposals for preventing the crime or at least minimizing its import. Statutory regulation of the conditions under which ransom could be paid, a ceiling on the amount paid, and kidnapping insurance were examples. Such proposals were hailed as new and innovative, which they were not.

Most of the ransom kidnappings during the year were classic in style: the offenders were motivated by a real or perceived need for instant wealth, and they preyed upon individuals thought to possess such wealth. Among the remaining cases, however, three other styles of ransom kidnapping developed: the reemergence of gangsters preying upon other gangsters, ransoming as a strategy of political terrorism, and the victimization of persons not wealthy in their own right but representing businesses and corporations which possessed wealth.

Two major ransomings were reported during the year before the Hearst case. Both took place in January, both occurred in

New York State, and both were of the classic style. The motivation of the offenders was strictly monetary, the offenders were white males, and the authorities made prompt arrests. The only distinguishing qualities of the cases were that in one of them the victim was killed and in the other the victim was black. Little national attention was attracted by either case, however.

The twenty-three cases reported in the *New York Times* after the Hearst kidnapping occurred at the rate of about two per month. Each, in turn, generated its share of national publicity and added to the accumulation of concern initiated by the Hearst case. Of the twenty-three cases, about half were ransomings in the classic vein. Reports of such cases came from Pennsylvania, Ohio, Texas, California, Florida, and Minnesota. Areas of the country popularly linked with concentrations of wealth were represented—Long Island, New York, and Palm Springs, California—and Florida was overrepresented with reports of ransomings from Miami, Miami Beach, Sanford, and Orlando. All the victims were perceived as wealthy in their own right, the motivation in all but perhaps one of the cases was easy money with ransom demands ranging from $1 million to $10,000, in only two of the cases did the kidnappers get away with the ransom, and only in one case were the victims harmed or killed.

Although a variety of occupations was represented among the victims, their spouses, or parents, in three of them the occupations involved banking. In and of itself, this commonality was not significant. The occupation of banking historically has been used by kidnappers as an indicator of their potential victim's ability to pay large ransoms. In the context of a new style of kidnapping that was to emerge during 1974, however, being a banker increased the risk of victimization.

Two weeks after the February kidnapping of Patricia Hearst, Reginald Murphy, an editor of the *Atlanta Constitution*, was ransomed. Initially the case was perceived as the work of a political terrorist group incited by the Symbionese Liberation Army's example in the Hearst kidnapping. It soon became evident, however, that the Murphy ransoming was, in the opinion of most observers, just another get-rich-quick scheme without special significance. In light of kidnapping developments later in the year, the case did have special significance. It was one of the first in the development of a new style of ransom kidnapping in which banks, as well as other corporate holders of wealth, played a key role. Once before in the history of ransom kidnapping in America, banks had played an important, but different, role. During the depression of the 1930s, ransom kidnapping had served as an alternative crime for Midwest bank robbery gangs. Now, forty years later, ransom kidnapping became a means for robbing banks and other corporate holders of wealth.

When Reg Murphy was kidnapped on February 22, the $700,000 ransom was demanded not from Murphy himself, but from his employer, the *Atlanta Constitution*. (Because of the initial reaction to the case as an act of political terrorism, details and reactions will be described in relation to the Hearst kidnapping.) Federal agents working with local authorities apprehended the kidnapper and recovered the ransom in short order. Demonstrating their ability to stay abreast of changing styles in crime, federal prosecutors invoked federal jurisdiction, not on the traditional ground of interstate transportation of the victim (none having been involved), but on the fact that the ransom had been extorted from an institution doing business in interstate commerce. On March 9, Atlanta again was in the news, this time as the site of the third ransom kidnapping in the last four months involving a K-Mart executive or his family.

In the next eight months, five more cases were reported in which abductors selected their victims not because of personal wealth but because of the wealth held by the business enterprises with which the victims were associated. In four of the cases banks were involved. The wife of a St. Paul, Minnesota, bank president was ransomed for $200,000 taken from her husband's bank. An assistant vice-president of a Fort Lauderdale, Florida, bank was kidnapped and $60,000 demanded from his employer. An undisclosed amount of money was collected from a rural Georgia bank in exchange for the wife of the bank's manager. Tragically, the victim, locked in the trunk of her car for more than a day and a half, was dead of carbon monoxide poisoning when found by authorities. A Grass Lake, Michigan, bank manager used $35,000 of the bank's holdings to ransom his wife and two children. In Deland, Florida, executives of a local radio station paid $10,000 ransom for the return of their program director, but to no avail; he had been slain by the ransomers.

The remainder of the ransom kidnappings reported in 1974, following the Hearst case, represented a revival of gangster/gangster ransomings which had been widespread in the late 1920s. The locations were familiar—New Jersey, New York City, and Detroit. The motives for the crimes also were familiar—the collection of gambling debts and a power struggle over gambling territory. In two of the cases, however, the victims and offenders were not familiar—they were black—and in one case, they were identified in the media as members of New York City's "Black Mafia." [16]

The Hearst Case and Its Aftermath

Most of the ransom kidnappings which followed the Hearst case were evaluated in the context of the Hearst kidnapping. Empirical evidence could not be found to support the widespread belief that the kidnapping of Patricia Hearst incited the other cases. Many, if not most, seemed to be merely a continuation of the resurgence of the crime well underway before the Hearst case. Nevertheless, the kidnapping of Patricia Hearst clearly was the nexus for societal reactions to kidnapping in general during 1974. The February 2 abduction riveted the attention of the nation on ransom kidnapping to a degree that rivaled the American experience of the 1930s.

The Hearst case provided a focal point for many frustrations about current crime conditions in American society. Initially the case generated reactions from prodeath penalty sectors of the population who saw in it the fruits of the *Furman* decision of 1972. More broadly, reactions came from sectors of the population frustrated by what they perceived as the hamstringing of the criminal justice system accomplished by a series of Supreme Court decisions and criminal justice reforms in recent years. When the political terrorist aspects of the case came to light, frustrations built up in many sectors of the society by political activists in the 1960s and early 1970s contributed to the reactions.

Local, state, and national figures felt the need to come forward and be heard on their interpretations of the case and its significance for crime and punishment in America. As in the 1930s, much-publicized directives flowed from the White House to the Department of Justice and the FBI. Sensational cases from the past were reviewed in feature articles in the press. Television commentators devoted air time to reviewing the history of ransom kidnapping in America, and a talk-show host made the crime the topic for an evening's show. Wealthy sectors of the population, as in the 1930s, again were in the market for kidnapping insurance, bodyguards were hired, and chauffeurs were sent to driving school to learn how to escape from pursuing kidnappers. A Harvard Law School professor received nationwide press for his "startling new" proposal that the payment of ransom be made a crime, and kidnapping gained more prominence in legislative efforts to reinstate the death penalty. Few people had noticed the steady resurgence of kidnapping for ransom in America that had begun in 1967–68; almost everyone was made aware of it now.

Less than a week before the kidnapping of Patricia Hearst, President Nixon took the occasion of his State of the Union Address to reaffirm to Congress and the American people his position that the death penalty should be restored for certain "especially heinous" crimes, such as a killing resulting from a kidnapping.[17] Probably uppermost in Nixon's mind, however, was not the domestic situation but rather the political terrorist kidnappings, bombings, and airplane hijackings occurring abroad. Indeed, earlier in the month, the State Department had begun distributing through United States embassies a pamphlet titled *General Security Tips for U.S. Businessmen Abroad.* According to the *Times,* "The pamphlet in effect . . . warns Americans abroad not to expect the United States Government to ransom them" (20 Jan. 1974, p. 13).

On the morning of February 6, front-page headlines across

America heralded the event which, in short order, would switch the focus of concern to the domestic scene. The *Times* headline read: "Granddaughter of Hearst Abducted by 3." Although the Berkeley, California, abduction of the victim and the beating of her fiance by a white woman and two black men was known to the media shortly after it occurred on the evening of February 4, media announcements had been withheld at the request of authorities. By February 6, speculation already existed in the Berkeley area about "possible connections between the abduction and other crimes here that radical groups have said they have committed for political motives" (p. 1). The Symbionese Liberation Army was mentioned by name in initial media reports as one such radical group.

The next day, speculation about the role of the Symbionese Liberation Army was confirmed when a local radio station received a letter containing a credit card belonging to Patricia Hearst, in which the SLA announced that it had perpetrated the abduction and warned that she would be executed if authorities attempted to rescue her. The front pages of newspapers across the country introduced the SLA to the American public on February 8, and heretofore diffuse concerns about ransom kidnapping in America became linked with concerns about political terrorism. Immediately on the scene, the FBI reaffirmed its historical strategy in ransom cases—nothing would be done which could threaten the safety of the victim. Never before would the bureau have to defend its strategy as it would in this case.

That ransom kidnapping had been adopted as a weapon of domestic political terrorism initially prompted reactions of disbelief on the part of some of the media. The "real" explanations for the Hearst kidnapping were sought out, such as the one expressed in a *Times* editorial titled "The Insane Ones." It stated, in part,

> Like airplane hijacking, terrorism is a worldwide phenomenon. By the standards of the Middle East or Northern Ireland, the incidence in the United States is slight. The atmosphere in this broadly prosperous and open society is not conducive to terrorism.

But any occurrence of it such as the kidnapping this week of Patricia Hearst in Berkeley, Calif., is shocking.

Terrorism is peculiarly repulsive because it usually has little or no relationship to the culpability of or authority of the particular victim. Like young Miss Hearst, the victim may bear a famous name or have a wealthy father but be no more responsible for adverse social conditions than her captors . . . .

Because of the lack of any proportion between the anguish and suffering inflicted upon the victim and the ostensible purposes of the terrorists, these episodes are in the true sense insane. Society has the urgent obligation to search out these insane ones in its midst and put them where they are beyond possibility of doing further harm (9 Feb. 1974, p. 28).

In the law enforcement sector, the initial reaction at the federal level was more of outrage than of disbelief. In a Washington news conference, U.S. Attorney General Saxbe expressed his impatience over the lack of immediate results by law enforcement agencies, particularly the FBI, and labeled the bureau's policy of taking no action that might endanger the safety of the victim as a "dereliction of duty" (15 Feb. 1974, p. 1). The attorney general's comments immediately prompted a retort from the victim's father who labeled Saxbe's remarks as "damn near irresponsible" (14 Feb. 1974, p. 1).

When the SLA demanded, as a symbol of Randolph Hearst's good faith to engage in subsequent ransom negotiations, that he finance a multimillion-dollar distribution of free food to the poor of California, Hearst said he would try, Saxbe spoke against it, and the FBI expressed their optimism that the program would lead to the release of Patricia Hearst. On February 20, the details of the program were announced. About $100,000 of the costs of the program would be defrayed by contributions received by the Hearst family from members of the public anxious to help them to ransom their daughter.

As the Hearst family, authorities, and the public awaited the SLA's response to Randolph Hearst's $2 million good faith offer, Reginald Murphy was kidnapped in Atlanta by a self-proclaimed member of the "American Revolutionary Army."

A voluntary news blackout on the case ended on February 22 with the front-page headline in the *Times:* "Atlanta Constitution Editor Kidnapped: 'Revolutionary Army' Seeks $700,000." For the first time in forty years, an entire page of the *New York Times* was devoted exclusively to the simultaneous coverage of ransom kidnappings.

About two hours after Murphy had been lured from his home on the night of February 20, the managing editor of the paper received a telephone call in which he was told that Murphy had been kidnapped by the revolutionary army and that further communications would be forthcoming. Similar calls also were placed to the victim's wife and to a local television station. When no further word had been received from the kidnappers by the next afternoon, the newspaper management issued a public appeal for the kidnappers to make contact. Shortly after the public appeal, a cassette arrived at the newspaper offices. In a taped message, the kidnappers described themselves as members of the American Revolutionary Army "who were displeased with what they described as the 'too leftist and too liberal' American news media." [18] They stated that their organization was strong all across the country, that they intended to engage in future guerrilla warfare, and demanded a ransom of $700,000 for Murphy's return. The victim himself spoke on the tape and related that his captors had told him that his abduction had been planned at the same time that the SLA had planned the Hearst kidnapping, but that the two groups were not working together. A spokesman for the paper stated that the ransom would be paid. Shortly after it was delivered and collected on February 22, the victim was released, unharmed.

The Murphy case, on top of the Hearst case, prompted another Washington press conference attended by the nation's two chief law enforcement officials. Attorney General Saxbe called for capital punishment for kidnapping. FBI Director Kelley reaffirmed the bureau's chief concern with the safe return of Patricia Hearst and, as to the Murphy affair, expressed his opinion that the "American Revolutionary Army" merely was a cover for an ordinary ransom kidnapping. A short time later, Kelley's suspicions were confirmed.

If the Murphy case was less than convincing to the FBI as a cause for alarm over terrorist kidnappings in America, it had quite a different impact on others, including the *New York Times*. The incredulity expressed in editorials generated by the Hearst case now gave way to the expression of more ominous concerns. Titled "Stealing People," an editorial concluded that underground political movements in the United States generally have avoided the crime of kidnapping—"Until now" (24 Feb. 1974, sec. 4, p. 1).

A large segment of the American public and officials was aligned with Saxbe's posture of indignation and frustration over the SLA's ability to hold at bay the entire law enforcement community. Their temper was rankled further when, on February 21, the SLA labeled Randolph Hearst's proposal for a $2 million food-giveaway program as "throwing a few crumbs to the people" [19] and demanded an additional $2 million for the project. When Patricia Hearst, herself, in one of a series of taped messages being received by the local media, chastised her father for claiming he was unable to raise the additional money, the ranks of the indignant and the outraged swelled.

Through the first week in April, there was little reason to doubt that Patricia Hearst remained the unwilling political captive of the SLA, and reactions were based upon this belief. Wealthy residents in the locale of the kidnapping shuttered their mansions and took expensive security measures. By the middle of March, American insurance companies were reporting a brisk business in kidnapping coverage in major cities across the country. According to one Detroit insurance executive: "We haven't even begun advertising and we've already had several inquiries." [20] From Boston, it was reported that kidnapping insurance was being sold not only to individuals but to corporations for the protection of key executives, the latter market created by the increasing victimization of bank, media, and chain store executives.

In the legislative sector, the Hearst case spurred congressional action on the Nixon administration's proposal to reinstate the death penalty for killings resulting from a kidnapping, among other crimes. The draft legislation had been languishing on Capitol Hill for almost a year. On February 27, the Senate Judiciary Committee, in a highly publicized move, approved the bill, declaring that capital punishment was "a valid and necessary remedy against certain dangerous types of criminal offenders." [21] Consistent with its abolitionist stance, a *Times* editorial criticized the members of the committee for succumbing to the administration's crime control program. The editorial cited social-behavioral science findings on the apparent inability of the death penalty to deter, reminded readers of the 1971 recommendation of the National Commission of Reform of Federal Criminal Laws that the death penalty be abolished, and reviewed the historical abolition trend in most Western countries. All of this evidence, wrote the editorialist, contradicted the president's "hunch" that: "Contrary to the view of some social theorists, I am convinced that the death penalty can be an effective deterrent against specific crimes" (5 Mar. 1974, p. 32). The writer concluded that efficient law enforcement and judicial action to increase certainty of apprehension and conviction is a better deterrent than severity of punishment.

As the other ransomings were reported from across the nation, the publicity increased public awareness of the crime and reinforced positions already formed in reaction to the Hearst case. On March 9, for example, in addition to a front-page report, all the news on an inside page of the *Times* was devoted to the Hearst, Murphy, and other cases. Detailed coverage was given to the federal arraignment of the suspects in the ransoming of a Long Island, New York, youth. Upon learning of the release of the victim in the case, President Nixon, from Key Biscayne, ordered Attorney General Saxbe to increase his efforts to get Congress to reinstate the death penalty and to study "What additional measures the Federal Government might take to deal with this problem of kidnapping" (9 Mar. 1974, p. 60).

The renewed pressures brought by the Nixon administration touched off heated debates in the Senate reminiscent of those that had preceded Senate approval of the death penalty amendment to the Lindbergh Law in 1934. Senator Harold E. Hughes stated that the restoration of the death penalty would be "a simplistic and illusory way to sidestep the real problems of deterrence and corrections." [22] Chief Democratic sponsor of the bill, Senator John L. McClellan, ended an emotional rejoinder by stating: "A society that refuses to protect the innocent invites repetition of the dastardly deed." [23]

On March 13, the U.S. Senate voted fifty-four to thirty-three to restore the federal death penalty, after twelve hours of debate. The measure then went to the House where, according to the *Times,* "support is strong but prospects are uncertain because the Judiciary Committee is involved with the impeachment investigation of President Nixon" (17 Mar. 1974, sec. 4, p. 2). A few weeks later, it became obvious that the House Judiciary Committee, now with half-a-dozen capital punishment bills before it, would not have time to act before adjournment in the fall. The legislation would die and the legislative process would have to be begun anew in 1975.

By April 1974, twenty-two states had reinstated the death penalty for specific crimes, including in some jurisdictions death resulting from a kidnapping, but there was no indication that the crime of kidnapping itself had displaced various forms of murder as the dominant concern of legislators. Among the general public, however, concern with legislative efforts to protect against ransom kidnapping clearly was mounting, and the Nixon administration's push for restoring a federal death penalty to deter it received support from readers of the *Times.*

As early as the middle of March, there had been growing speculation in the press and among officials and the public that perhaps Patricia Hearst was other than an unwilling captive of the SLA. The speculation began to be expressed more openly, as in a *Times* editorial comment, titled "Without Facts, Doubts Grow in the Hearst Case" (ibid., p. 3). On April 13, the matter came to a climax when, in a taped message received from the SLA, Patricia Hearst stated that she voluntarily had joined the SLA even though they had offered her her freedom. Widely publicized as a startling turnaround, this latest development intensified already existing cleavages of opinion about the affair.

At the federal level, tensions had continued to build between Attorney General Saxbe and FBI Director Kelley over the handling of the Hearst affair, tensions exacerbated by the Watergate investigation. In reaction to Patricia Hearst's apparent vow of allegiance to her captors, the official FBI opinion was that she had been coerced into the vow and the bureau's strategy in the case would remain unchanged. Attorney General Saxbe made it known that "now that the lid is off," he expected the FBI to "get results." [24]

Sensational developments in the Hearst case now became commonplace. On April 16, the FBI announced that Patricia Hearst had participated in the robbery of a San Francisco bank, and security camera photos confirmed her participation. According to a *Times* report, Attorney General Saxbe reacted characteristically by calling her a "fugitive" and a member of a group of "common criminals" (18 Apr. 1974, p. 1). In so doing, he incurred the wrath not only of the Hearst family but of a considerable segment of the mass media. Saxbe now was joined, however, by the California attorney general who "accused law enforcement officials of being timid in investigating the Hearst abduction and called for a broad re-examination of policies in kidnapping cases" (16 Apr. 1974, p. 1). Bureau Director Kelley consistently emphasized the possibility that the SLA had forced her to take part in the bank robbery. On May 20, however, the FBI classified Patricia Hearst as "an armed and dangerous fugitive," as the result of her alleged machine-gunning of a Los Angeles sporting goods store to cover the escape of two comrades from an abortive shoplifting.

With her change in status from kidnapping victim to political terrorist, at least in the minds of many, attention turned away from the Hearst case to the other ransomings that had been taking place. A *Times* front-page article, titled "Kidnapping Stirs Fear among Wealthy," was accompanied by pictures of the victims of four of the recent cases (14 Apr. 1974). The article stressed the widespread fear among wealthy potential victims and the precautions they were taking—hiring twenty-four-hour-a-day bodyguards, buying $2,500 attack dogs, installing sophisticated alarm systems in their homes, and employing armed chauffeurs to drive their children to school. Public and private security personnel expressed their opinions that the kidnapping wave may have just begun, that the wealthy were highly vulnerable to ransomers, and that it had dawned on the wealthy "that political extortions can quickly shift to criminal extortions" (ibid.).

Newspaper articles noted the apparent increase in the victimization of employees of business enterprises and the response of some companies of assigning guards to protect their high-level executives. An article in the business section of the *Times* focused on the K-Mart experience and wondered if a conspiracy was underway against the company. K-Mart spokesmen scoffed at the conspiracy idea but did admit that the company had developed its own program for counteracting kidnappings. Later in the year, another article in the business section of the *Times* described additional changes in the corporate way of life in response to the threat of kidnapping, including some companies imposing "a more secluded, even hidden life style" on their employees (29 Sept. 1974, sec. 3, p. 14).

On May 17, the Hearst case dramatically regained the kidnapping spotlight as a result of the televised shoot-out in Los Angeles between authorities and five members of the SLA. The immediate interest of the media was in whether Patricia Hearst was among the five persons burned beyond recognition in the fire that erupted during the gun battle. When it was determined that she was not among the casualties, media coverage of the Hearst case subsided for the remainder of the year as federal authorities pursued their frustrating and fruitless search for Patricia Hearst. It would be over a year before their efforts would be rewarded.

With the Hearst case having vaulted the crime to national prominence, other ransom kidnappings and reactions spawned by them kept the situation at an intense level. In May, a television network talk-show devoted an evening's program to the subject. In July, a nationally distributed Sunday newspaper supplement carried articles on ransom kidnapping and the precautions prominent persons were taking to protect themselves.

As ransomings continued to be reported throughout the summer, the national media kept the public abreast of the latest developments. State officials began to express greater impatience with the U.S. Supreme Court concerning its failure to hand down a definitive ruling on the constitutionality of the death penalty. For example, in reaction to a Florida kidnap-murder case, the state's attorney general stated: "I plead with the United States Supreme Court to move quickly during its fall session to have the arguments on the death penalty so that Florida may reassert its prerogative to remove those who commit such heinous and irrational crimes from our midst."[25]

Twenty-nine states had restored the death penalty by October, 147 persons had been condemned to die under the new legislation, and nine capital cases were pending before the Supreme Court. In a *New York Times* article of October 11, a Columbia law professor predicted that the Court soon would confront "the ultimate question of the government's right to kill" (p. 39). As to the outcome, he predicted that the Court would make it even more difficult to enact a constitutional death penalty than it had by the *Furman* decision. The *Gregg* decision of 1976 and the Gilmore execution of 1977 proved him wrong.

Summary

In the 1940s, the occasional ransom kidnapping that came to light generated little alarm. Even the posture of the federal government toward the crime had changed significantly. President Truman commuted a federal ransoming death sentence, and the Supreme Court refused to expand the definition of capital law beyond the narrow limits of classic ransom kidnapping. Two sensational ransom slayings of the children of prominent families in the 1950s demonstrated the capacity of the crime for generating societal reaction, but otherwise the crime remained dormant. If one had been counting the cases and comparing their incidence with earlier years, one would have noticed that in the 1960s ransom kidnappings began occurring more regularly, but only at the incidence of one case a year.

One also would have noticed the concentration of the cases in the West, particularly in California.

The main developments through the 1960s were legal in nature. Sentiment against capital punishment in America for all crimes grew significantly, particularly among law reform groups. Although capital ransom kidnapping laws proved to be highly resistant to change at the state level, a significant change at the federal level occurred in 1968 when the U.S. Supreme Court declared the death penalty provision of the amended Lindbergh Law unconstitutional. During its thirty-four-year existence, six ransom kidnappers had been put to death.

Beginning in 1968, the crime of ransom kidnapping began to emerge from its dormant state at an increasing rate. By the early 1970s, three to four major cases were being reported each year. While still not perceived as a cause for alarm in America, concern was growing over the use of ransom kidnapping as a weapon of political terrorism abroad. Political radicalism in America also was creating alarm although there was no reason to link it with ransom kidnapping. When the Supreme Court handed down its historic *Furman* decision in 1972, formalizing the de facto moratorium on executions in America that had existed since 1967, another source of frustration was created among some potential reactors. Ransom kidnapping became linked to the *Furman* decision only because of its prominent mention by President Nixon as a crime for which he believed the death penalty was needed as a deterrent.

In 1974, the Patricia Hearst case served as the nexus for several frustrations over the state of crime control in America. Ransom kidnapping once again was central to the alarm not only because of the Hearst case but because of the twenty-five other cases reported for 1974, the highest incidence in forty years and second only to the historic peak of 1933. By the end of 1974 (the most recent year covered in this work), it was clear to reactors in all sectors that ransom kidnapping had emerged from its dormant state. Once again, the crime demonstrated the unique ability to generate intense and pervasive societal reaction.

5

The Crime,

Societal Reaction, and

Law Creation

The historical data presented in the preceding chapters contain a number of insights into the causation of ransom kidnapping in America, strategic differences between victims and offenders of this crime and other capital crimes (particularly murder), and the continuing potential for outbreaks of ransom kidnapping in the society. In this concluding chapter, however, we concentrate on describing the reported incidence of the crime from 1874 through 1974 and the social identity of the victims. Against this background we analyze the societal reaction context in which ransom kidnapping laws were created.

The Crime

From 1874 through 1974, the *New York Times* reported 1,703 cases of kidnapping occurring entirely, or in part, in the United States. In 187 of the cases it could not be determined what type of kidnapping was involved because of insufficient information contained in the reports. Twenty-five other cases involved instances of child abandonment, lost children, runaways, and the like, which occurred too infrequently to warrant their

TABLE 1.

TYPOLOGY OF ALL KIDNAPPING CASES REPORTED IN
THE *New York Times:* 1874–1974

TYPE	REPORTED INCIDENCE	PERCENT
Child stealing	292	17
Classic kidnapping for ransom	236	14
Kidnapping for robbery	153	9
Kidnapping for murder or other nonsexual assault	149	9
Domestic relations kidnapping	137	8
Kidnapping as extortion threat	108	6
Romantic kidnapping	100	6
Skyjacking	92	5
Kidnapping for rape or other sexual assault	65	4
White slavery	59	3
Conspiracy, plot, or aborted ransom kidnapping	45	3
Ransom kidnapping hoax	27	2
Hostage situation	23	1
Developmental ransom kidnapping	5	1
Other and unclassifiable	212	12
TOTAL	1703	100

inclusion in a special category. The remaining 1,491 reported cases were classified as in Table 1.

Classic ransom kidnapping, with a reported incidence of 236 cases, constituted 14 percent of the total reported cases, ranking it only behind child stealing. A reported incidence of only 236 cases over a one-hundred-year period demonstrates that ransom kidnapping is a rare crime. In comparison to criminal homicide (the official incidence of which has not fallen below 7,000 cases annually for the last fifty years), for example, the contribution of ransom kidnapping to the historical crime situation in America has been modest.

The total reported incidence of 1,703 cases, undifferentiated as to type of kidnapping, is important from a societal reaction perspective. When most readers scan the headlines of news reports on "kidnappings," it is ransom kidnapping that comes to mind rather than any of the other thirteen forms which the crime can, and usually does, take. This tendency can create the impression that ransom kidnapping has been more prevalent than it actually has been. When ransom kidnappings are reported, if only sporadically, the impression is reinforced. The result is a perceptual reality of the prevalence of ransom kidnapping in America that departs significantly from the objective reality. Members of the social audience, however, have reacted to the crime as they perceived it to be.

The accompanying graph charts the total reported incidence of kidnapping and of ransom kidnapping for each year of the period 1874–1974. A comparison of the reported incidence trends shown in the graph for all types of kidnapping, with the trends for ransom kidnapping, confirms the importance of the distinction between the perceived and objective realities of crime. Although both indexes generally fluctuated in the same direction (as they must to the extent that the ransom index is part of the total index), in a number of periods the two indexes fluctuated independently. The graph shows the periods when it was child stealing, white slavery, or skyjacking that was responsible for marked increases in the reported incidence of kidnapping rather than ransom kidnapping. To the extent that potential reactors equated all types with ransom kidnapping, there was genuine cause for alarm during several periods from 1874 through 1974. Objectively, however, such alarm was justified only during the early 1930s and the early 1970s.

The geographical distribution of all reported kidnappings and ransom kidnappings from 1874 through 1974 contains a number of distinct patterns. Jurisdictions with the heaviest concentration of kidnappings of all types also experienced the heaviest concentration of ransom kidnappings—New York, New Jersey, Pennsylvania, Michigan, Illinois, Missouri, California, Georgia, and Florida. The concentration of cases reported from the Northeast is inflated to an unknown extent by the more intensive coverage by the *Times* of this region. However, the data suggest that the New York-New Jersey area, in particular, has experienced a significantly higher incidence of kidnappings

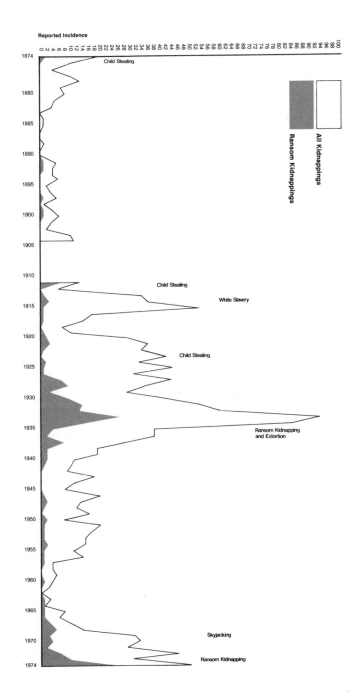

Reported incidence of total kidnappings and ransom kidnappings, 1874–1974.
New York Times Index *coverage was not available for 1905–10.*

of all types during the period studied. This certainly was the situation during the nineteenth century and early twentieth century when the region was far more heavily populated than any other. However, reports of child stealing and domestic relations kidnappings from as far away as Washington State and California did appear in the *Times* during the nineteenth century. Therefore, while the data source inflated the reported incidence of all kidnappings in some areas and deflated it in others, the index is not wholly a methodological artifact.

The following patterns characterized the geographical diffusion of reported ransom kidnappings. From 1874 through 1919, ransomings were concentrated in the New York-New Jersey-Pennsylvania area. From 1920 through 1932, two patterns emerged. First, there was a sharp increase in ransomings reported from the Midwest. The heaviest concentrations were in Illinois, followed by Michigan, Wisconsin, Minnesota, Missouri, and Iowa. Together, these states had a higher reported incidence than the northeastern states. The other pattern was the beginning of reports from California.

From 1933 through 1939, the reported incidence of ransom kidnapping reached its historic peak and then declined sharply. New York, Pennsylvania, and New Jersey again became the region of greatest concentration, while the reported incidence from the Midwest declined. The reported incidence from California remained basically unchanged. The reported incidence from the Southeast began to rise.

From 1940 through 1974, the most striking pattern was the clear concentration of cases in locations traditionally associated with wealth—Long Island, New York; Beverly Hills, Hollywood, and San Francisco, California; Dallas, Texas; Atlanta, Georgia; and several communities in Florida. The highest incidence was reported from California. The Chicago area reported the only significant concentration of ransomings in the Midwest. For the sharp rise in reported incidence during 1974, New York and Florida led the list. The most dramatic increase was in Florida: of the nine cases reported from the state for the entire hundred-year period, five occurred in 1974.

The Victims

From 1874 to 1974, the typical ransom kidnap victim was male (in 75 percent of the reported cases), eighteen years of age or older (62 percent), white (97 percent), and upper-class (56 percent).[1] The relative percentage of cases involving victims with these characteristics fluctuated across four chronological periods—1874–1919, 1920–32, 1933–39, and 1940–74. The preponderance of male victims in a given period ranged from 88 percent to 62 percent. The trend has been in the direction of an increase in the proportion of cases involving female victims since 1940. Child victims were involved in the majority of cases before 1920; since 1920, however, the percentage of cases involving victims eighteen years of age or older has ranged from 90 percent in the 1930s to 51 percent since 1940. The most consistent victim characteristic was race: only in 6 of the 201 cases were nonwhite victims involved, and 3 of these occurred in 1970 alone.

While reported cases involving upper-class victims have predominated in each period, middle-class victims have been involved in approximately one-third of the cases since 1920. In the most recent period, however, the relative percentage of cases involving upper-class victims has been increasing steadily. None of the reported cases involved lower-class victims for obvious reasons. Working-class individuals have been victimized only under such unique circumstances as the Black Hand ransomings at the beginning of the twentieth century.

Finding that even one-third of the reported cases for the one-hundred-year period involved middle-class victims indicates that ransom kidnapping has not been as exclusively an attack on the wealthy as popularly believed. However, since the relative percentage of cases involving wealthy victims has been increasing steadily since 1940, the crime appears to be moving in that direction. In addition, ransom kidnapping does appear to have victimized the wealthy more than other capital crimes, such as murder and rape. Of primary significance to us, however, is the manner in which societal reaction to ransomings varied with the social identity of the victims, a social identity in which wealth and prominence played a crucial role.

Reactions in the Sectors to Ransom Kidnappings

Although the legislative reactive sector is central to an analysis of law creation, reactions from members of the sector take many forms other than formal law-creating. In addition, reactions from members of the sector are influenced by, and influence, reactions from members of the other five sectors examined. Therefore, we first look at the broader reactive context which spawned ransom laws before narrowing our focus to law creating per se.

Of the 236 ransom kidnappings reported in the *Times* from 1874 through 1974, 48 were reported for the years 1933 through 1936, a period of perceived crime control crisis in America. Table 2 shows the percentage of reported cases which generated reactions from each of the reactive sectors for the period as a whole as compared to the crisis period.

Several factors were examined as possible determinants of the societal reaction to ransom kidnappings.[2] Among them, only those reflecting the social identity of the victim were found to bear a consistent relationship to the reactions generated: victim's sex, age (child or adult),[3] socioeconomic class (upper class or other),[4] fate of the victim (unharmed or harmed or killed),[5] and media identification of the victim (linked to the underworld by alleged membership in a criminal gang or by a known criminal record or portrayed as "respectable"). Of these characteristics, the upper-class status of victims emerged as the most critical determinant of societal reaction.

Mass media sector. For the hundred-year period as a whole, reactions from members of the mass media (beyond straight reporting of an event) were most likely to be elicited by ransomings in which the victims were female or children, were from respectable wealthy families, and were harmed or killed. In the crime control crisis period, when reactions in general were more intense, the wealth of victims appeared to become the

TABLE 2.

PERCENTAGE OF CASES GENERATING REACTIONS FROM REACTIVE SECTORS, 1874–1974 vs. 1933–36, AND PERCENT OF CHANGE

REACTIVE SECTORS	1874–1974	1933–36	CHANGE
Mass media	62%	94%	+32%
General public	58%	75%	+17%
Political	39%	81%	+42%
Law enforcement	53%	88%	+35%
Judicial	39%	81%	+42%
Legislative	51%	75%	+24%

dominant determinant of reactions from members of the sector. For example, in 1933 through 1936, ransomings involving wealthy adult males who were not harmed elicited more, and more intensive, reactions from the media sector than any other type of ransoming. The Boettcher, Hamm, Urschel, Bremer, and Luer ransomings are cases in point.

That the upper-class status of victims was a critical determinant of reactions from members of the mass media sector during the crisis period suggests the relevance of the radical contention that the mass media in America tend to reflect the interests of the economic elite. Our findings suggest that the influence of wealth and prominence on media reactions to ransom kidnapping for the period as a whole was less strong than implied by the radical position. During the 1933–36 period, however, the influence of upper-class status on reactions from the media increased markedly. The difference supports the radical claim that such influence, while ever present, is strongest during periods of perceived crisis in crime control.

General public sector. Members of the general public did not invariably follow the lead of the mass media either as to normative or actual reactions to ransom kidnappings. As noted in Table 2, members of this sector reacted to a smaller proportion of ransomings during the period as a whole (58 percent), and in 1933–36 (75 percent), than members of the media sector (62 percent and 94 percent, respectively). In addition, the increase in the proportion of cases eliciting reactions from the general public during the crisis period of 1933–36 was the smallest of any of the six sectors. Although apparently less reactive, or at least less visibly reactive, than other sectors, reactions from the general public did appear to be influenced by the social identity of ransom victims.

For 1874–1974, the ransomings most likely to elicit reactions from the general public sector were those involving child victims who were harmed or killed, male victims, and upper-class victims. In comparison with reactions from the mass media sector, only one difference stands out. Although in both sectors cases involving upper-class victims appeared to have been overrepresented, upper-class status seems to have been a weaker determinant of reactions from the general public sector than from the media sector. This pattern suggests that ransom kidnappings were condemned and reacted to by the general public on a basis other than uncritical acceptance of normative evaluations by the mass media. That the most important determinant of public reactions for the period as a whole seems to have been the fact that the victims were children suggests that the status of parent may have transcended class distinctions in the normative and actual reactions from this sector. The Ross, Conway, Verotta, Parker, Cash, and Crary cases, spanning 1874 through 1957, are examples. All involved middle or working-class victims, yet elicited intense reactions from the general public.

During 1933–36, public reaction to ransomings involving prominent businessmen who were not harmed appears to have increased. The reaction patterns for the general public sector, therefore, support the same conclusion as for the mass media sector. The difference is one merely of degree; reactions from the general public sector appear to have been less sensitive to the prominence of victims than media reactions, but sensitive nonetheless.

Political sector. For the one-hundred-year-period as a whole, ransomings which typically elicited reactions from members of this sector were those involving female or child victims, wealthy and prominent victims, and harmed or killed victims. Mayors, governors, and presidents appeared to offer normative evaluations of ransom kidnappings and kidnappers, to call for action, and to take a direct hand in the ransom situation, much to the same extent and in the same manner as members of the media and public sectors reacted in ways available to them.

During 1933–36, the changes that seemed to have occurred in reactions from the political sector provide still more support for a conclusion that the victimization of prominent businessmen, even though unharmed, constituted an important source of intense societal reaction to the crime. The types of victims most likely to elicit reactions from the sector changed from child to adult, from female to male, and from harmed to unharmed.

The historical data contain several illustratrations of the importance of upper-class status of victims as a determinant of intense reactions from the political sector: the proclamations issued by the mayor of Denver and the governor of Colorado urging citizens to cooperate in the rescue of Charles Boettcher II, millionaire broker, in 1933; the personal interest of President Hoover in the 1933 Atlanta ransoming of John King Ottley, whom the president had appointed to a national advisory commission two years earlier; the mobilization of state law enforcement and legislative machinery by New York Governor Lehman in reaction to the 1933 ransoming of John J. O'Connell, twenty-four-year-old son and nephew of the bosses of a county Democratic machine; the direct hand taken by President Franklin Delano Roosevelt in the 1933 ransoming of Charles F. Urschel, Oklahoma City oil millionaire; and the ordering by President Roosevelt of the FBI into the ransoming of St. Paul banker, Edward Bremer, whose father was a prominent Democrat and personal friend of the president.

Law enforcement sector. Ransomings most likely to elicit reactions from members of the law enforcement sector from 1874 through 1974 were those involving upper-class females, victims who were harmed or killed, and children. The most striking difference between reactions from this sector and those from the preceding ones appeared to be the prominence of the upper-class status of victims, whether male or female, as a determinant. Even more striking is the fact that the pattern characterized the entire hundred-year period. During 1933–36, the overrepresentation of cases involving upper-class victims appeared to have increased even further.

Like the findings for the media sector, these findings lend support to the radical position that wealth and prominence influence the administration of criminal justice in America. As to the role of law enforcement reactions in 1933–36, however, the findings suggest that only on the federal level was the influence of such factors particularly significant. Local law enforcers appeared to have continued to operate on the same low-key basis on which they had been operating since 1874. As an illustration, the friction that developed between local and federal authorities during 1933–36 frequently stemmed from differences in their respective "reactiveness" to suspected ransomings. Local enforcers typically desired to get on with an investigation of a suspected ransom kidnapping in much the same way as they investigated any other serious crime. Federal agents, however, typically preferred to stop everything until the ransom negotiations had been consummated and then begin a vigorous (and usually well-publicized) manhunt. The Urschel and Stoll ransomings are cases in point, as is the friction that developed between local and federal authorities in the handling of the Hearst case, forty years later.

Judicial sector. The judicial sector appeared to have been the most conservative in its normative and actual reactions to ransom kidnapping. Normative evaluations by jurists prior to judicial proceedings were infrequent. Even expressions of opinion after sentencing were limited in number and guarded in tone. Other members of the sector, such as law faculty members, law review writers and editors, and legal commentators, had more latitude to react, but their reactions, too, tended to be conservative. In addition, reactions from members of the sector appeared to have been influenced less by the social identity of ransom victims.

Cases involving children, males, victims who were harmed, and victims from the working or middle classes appeared to have been overrepresented. The overrepresentation of working-class and middle-class victims is attributable to reactions from the judiciary to the Black Hand cases during the early twentieth century. Because of the small number of total cases which elicited reactions from the sector, the effect of the reactions to the Black Hand cases is exaggerated for the period as a whole.

During 1933–36, jurists in particular became less conservative in their normative evaluations of ransomings and of ransomers. The normative reactions described for the McMath, O'Connell, and Urschel cases are illustrative. However, it appeared that the nature of the victims continued to have less effect on reactions from the judicial sector than from the others. The changes that did occur appeared to follow the same patterns found for the other sectors; namely, cases involving adult businessmen and cases in which the victims were unharmed became more prevalent. In sharp contrast to the other sectors, however, cases involving less affluent victims continued to be overrepresented among those reacted to by members of the sector. Even during periods of crime control crisis, members of the judicial sector appeared to have been less influenced by the wealth and prominence of victims.

Legislative sector. The distinguishing pattern for this sector is the consistency for the hundred-year period as a whole in the type of victim that was overrepresented in ransomings which elicited reactions from legislators: wealthy and prominent businessmen who were not harmed. Although reactions from members of the other sectors appeared to move toward this pattern for 1933–36, only reactions from the legislative sector were patterned in this manner for the entire period studied. During 1933–36, the overrepresentation of cases involving this type of victim became even more marked.

The findings for the legislative sector suggest that, historically, reactions from members of the sector have been particularly sensitive to the perceived threat to affluent businessmen represented by ransom kidnapping. The reactions of legislators to the Boettcher, Hamm, O'Connell, Luer, Urschel, and Bremer cases, which occurred during the period of crime control crisis of the 1930s, provide historical examples. Further documentation on this point is offered when we consider specifically the law-creating activities of members of the sector.

The Creation of the Ransom Laws

Three periods of particularly intense law-creating activity stand out: 1901, 1907–13, and the decade of the 1930s. In each period, the volume of law creating bore no simple, mechanistic relationship to the sheer incidence of ransom kidnapping. Instead, a variety of forces was involved in the creation of ransom laws during specific historical periods, forces championed by a variety of models of law creation. This finding suggests that, while a radical interpretation of the broader reactive context from which the laws emerged has general historical support, a radical interpretation specifically of the legislative reactions of members of the sector does not. In some periods, ruling-elite models of law creation of the type favored by radical thinkers clearly are applicable. In other periods, however, consensus models of the type favored by conservative thinkers are more appropriate.

Consensus models of law creation were found to be most applicable to the legislative activity of the nineteenth century. Normative reactions to the Charles Ross case of 1874 focused on the threat to society at large represented by ransom kidnapping. Editorials looked to the ransom experiences of European societies for an estimate. They concluded that it was only the wealthy who were victimized abroad, and it was the wealthy who were best able to protect their children from ransom kidnappers. The fact that the Ross family was middle-class, however, prompted speculation in the media that perhaps the American experience was going to be different in this respect.

With no progress made in the Ross case and with child stealing apparently on the rise, alarm spread among the general public. Reactions took the forms emphasized by consensus models of law creation. Kidnapping in general was evaluated as a serious threat to children; thus, parents of all socioeconomic classes had a common interest in calling for official action. The main action called for was increasing the severity of penalties threatened by existing kidnapping and child-stealing laws. In the relatively few jurisdictions which had laws directly applicable to the ransom kidnapping of children, the common-law maximum of seven year's imprisonment was the norm. The calls for action were based upon the combination of a belief in the deterrability of potential ransom kidnappers and a belief in retribution as a legitimate function of legal punishment.

Legislation was not forthcoming immediately. In 1881, when the New York legislature increased the maximum sentence for kidnapping from seven years to fifteen years, the reason for the action, the historical timing of the legislation, and the pace of the law-creation process supported consensus models of law creation. A few years earlier, another sharp rise in the stealing of children, predominantly from working-class and middle-class families, had been perceived as a kidnapping (child-stealing) epidemic. The crime was evaluated as a serious threat to all parents, and the matter was brought to the attention of the legislature, where it was debated thoroughly. The increased severity of the threatened punishment which resulted was believed by the legislators to be sufficient to deter potential ransomers or child stealers without being excessive. The remaining isolated instances of law creation during the nineteenth century reflected the operation of the same types of consensus forces.

The 1901 flurry of law creation. The law-creating activity in 1901, in contrast to the earlier activity, lends itself to a ruling-elite model interpretation. All of the legislative reactions are directly attributable to the successful ransom kidnapping of Edward Cudahy, of Omaha. The Cudahy case was preceded by neither an unusual amount of kidnapping in general nor an unusual amount of ransom kidnapping. The victim was a child, but he was fifteen years old, older than any of the child victims in earlier cases. He was not harmed and was held by his captors for a shorter period of time than in any of the earlier cases. The distinguishing feature of the case was that the victim was the son of a millionaire meat packer with considerable economic and political influence.

In reaction to the Cudahy case, there were calls from the

general public for a federal capital ransom law for the purpose of deterring potential ransomers and for societal protection. Legislators from several states announced their intentions to comply. Actual reactions took the form of the creation of the initial ransom laws, threatening life imprisonment as the maximum penalty, in South Dakota, Alabama, Indiana, and Oklahoma. The Iowa and Connecticut legislatures followed suit in 1902. The legislatures of Illinois, Missouri, Nebraska, and Delaware enacted their states' initial ransom legislation in 1901 and threatened death as the maximum penalty.

Also in 1901, the Congress of the United States created legislation aimed at protecting residents of the District of Columbia from being forcibly carried out of the district. More of an abduction law than a ransom kidnapping law, the federal statute carried a maximum penalty of seven year's imprisonment plus a fine, unless the victim was under sixteen years of age, in which case the maximum was twenty years plus a fine. Was it merely coincidental that the federal statute specified under sixteen years of age, and Edward Cudahy was fifteen?

While suggesting the relevance of a ruling-elite model, the Cudahy case also generated reactions which suggest the relevance of middle-class indignation models of law creation. Letters to the editor evidenced much indignation over the fact that by paying the $25,000 ransom and using his influence to hold law enforcers at bay until the victim was returned safely, Cudahy had endangered the children of all parents sufficiently affluent to pay even a modest ransom. It was the Cudahy case that initiated the enduring editorial theme in the *Times* concerning the moral dilemma facing the parents of kidnapped children—their parental duty to secure the safe return of their own children versus their duty as citizens to protect the children of other parents.

Legislative activity in 1907–13. Law creating in this period both supports and challenges ruling-elite models; in so doing, it testifies to the variety of forces involved in law creation even during a single historical period. In reaction to the 1907 ransoming of the son of a wealthy and prominent Delaware physician (the Marvin case), the Indiana legislature increased the term of years threatened for ransom kidnapping; the New Jersey legislature raised the maximum penalty to forty year's imprisonment, citing general deterrence as the sole rationale; and the Alabama legislature increased the penalty to death.

Two years later, the ransoming of Willie Whitla, son of a prominent Pennsylvania attorney, and nephew of a millionaire steel magnate, provided even stronger support for a ruling-elite model interpretation. The legislative activity generated by the Whitla case did not have the strong support of the national press. While supporting increases in the severity of threatened punishments for ransom kidnapping, short of capital punishment, the editorial position of the *Times*, for example, was that increased certainty of apprehension and punishment would serve as a more effective deterrent.

Support for the creation of capital legislation was voiced by members of other sectors, however. From the pulpit, a Pittsburgh clergyman told his congregation that although he opposed capital punishment for murder, he favored hanging or electrocuting the Whitla ransomers to make deterrent examples of them. A Chicago state's attorney expressed his dissatisfaction with the restriction of the Illinois law making the death penalty available only if the victim was harmed. He labeled the kidnapping of a child the worst offense that can be committed.

These types of normative reactions were followed by concrete legislative reactions. In Pennsylvania, a bill was introduced to make ransom kidnapping a felony carrying a mandatory penalty of hanging. The New York State legislature increased the penalty for ransom kidnapping to fifty year's imprisonment. In addition, the Whitla case spawned the first legislative attempt to make the ransom kidnapping of children a federal capital offense. The 1909 move was premature, however, because the use of the interstate transportation powers of the federal government to combat felonious crime had yet to come into fashion. The bill never made it out of committee; but a year later, the 1901 abduction law for the District of Columbia was amended to include ransom kidnapping in the district and in the territories. Each of these activities spawned by the Whitla case suggests the applicability of a ruling-elite model.

On the surface, the reactions of the New York State legislature to the Black Hand cases of this period appear to defy interpretation by ruling-elite models of law creation. The endeavors of the legislators in behalf of the victims of these ransomings suggest that laws also are created to protect the unique interests of the working class. New York lawmakers significantly increased the threatened penalties for Black Hand ransomings in 1909 and again in 1911. However, a good deal of local, state, federal, and even diplomatic pressure was brought to bear upon New York officials in behalf of such legislation. It must also be noted that the invisibility (or ignoring) of the plight of the Black Hand victims ceased only when the *Times* contrasted the reactions to the Whitla case with those to a Black Hand case in 1909. The legislative efforts in behalf of the Black Hand victims may have been, in part, a gratuitous spin-off of reactions to the Whitla case. To that extent, the situation does not render wholly inappropriate a ruling-elite model interpretation.

Law creation leading up to the activity in the 1930s. The decade of the 1920s witnessed a rash of brutal ransom slayings of children from wealthy and from working-class families. The feasibility of creating capital legislation to deter potential ransomers became a central focus of normative reactions in many sectors. The belief in the deterrent efficacy of such legislation, however, was far from consensual.

In response to the particularly cruel ransom disappearance of the Coughlin child from his middle-class home in Norristown, Pennsylvania, in 1920, and to the outrageous behavior of the offender, *Times* editorials directly addressed the issue of capital ransom laws for the first time. The argument of the writers against a death penalty was threefold: the threat of legal death would not deter potential ransom kidnappers because they lacked sufficient intelligence to appreciate the risks; some kidnappers were driven by distorted parental impulses, which negated their rationality; and juries would not be eager to convict in capital ransom cases. However, when Pascal, the offender in the Coughlin case, was sentenced to life imprisonment, the *Times* editorialists modified their stance. While adhering to their argument against the death penalty as a deterrent, they wrote that never did an offender better deserve the death penalty than Pascal, purely for the purpose of retribution. The sentiment was shared by reactors in other sectors. No concrete legislative activity was forthcoming, however.

The Verotta case in 1921 generated another modification in the capital punishment stance of the *Times*. This case involved the Black Hand ransoming of the young son of an Italian working-class family in New York City. The *Times* took an intense interest in the case when Verotta single-handedly captured one of the ransomers, in the face of threats to kill the boy and dispose of his body in a river. *Times* editorials hailed the father as an example of Roman fortitude and courage for putting his duties as a citizen to protect the children of others above his parental duties to his own son. When the slain body of the victim was found in a local river, a *Times* editorial stated that such fiends are to be deterred only by fear of death.

The Verotta case precipitated the second attempt to make ransom kidnapping a federal capital offense. However, U.S. Representative Siegel's bill to invoke interstate transportation powers against the ransom kidnappers of children died in the House Judiciary Committee. Although unsuccessful, this episode does seem to represent an attempt at law creation to protect the interests of the working class. Unlike the 1911 episode in New York State in response to Black Hand ransomings, Representative Siegel's actions cannot be attributed to the bringing to bear of political pressures. His actions do appear to have represented an attempt at law creation in the interests of the working class. The fact that his attempt was unsuccessful, however, suggests that the chances of law-creating efforts succeeding are facilitated if influential members or groups take an interest in them.

In the next few years, normative reactions from the sectors reflected growing consensus that ransom kidnapping indeed represented a threat to parents at all socioeconomic levels. The primary force in the diffusion of this act-focused evaluation was the belief (as would be emphasized in consensus models) that it was impossible for parents to protect their children from ransom kidnappers. Therefore, government intervention was necessary to provide such protection. Consensus also was growing in the actor-focused belief that potential ransomers were deterrable by severe legal punishment threats.

The Robert Franks case in 1924 resulted in a major challenge to the belief in the deterrability of potential ransom kidnappers. Leopold and Loeb were portrayed in the media as brilliant, knowledgeable, and frighteningly rational; however, they were also portrayed as conscienceless experimenters with human life. The nationwide cynicism reflected in reactions to their life sentences, despite the fact that Illinois provided a death penalty either for the kidnap murder or the murder, further eroded confidence in the belief that capital threats would deter potential ransomers. Even the editorial staff of the *Times*, which applauded the life sentences, admitted that the deterrent effect on the criminally disposed probably would not be as effective as hanging might have been. The Franks case and its aftermath were important forces in the failure of the case to result in the creation of ransom legislation.

The Daly case in New Jersey, two years later, provides additional support for the prominence of offender-focused beliefs in deterrability as a force in the creation of ransom laws. Noel, the ransom slayer of the Daly child, had a history of emotional problems and commitments to mental institutions. He was portrayed in the media as a wealthy, brilliant student whose college education had been cut short by his emotional problems. He admitted that he had studied the Franks case closely, and claimed that he had been incited by it. Noel's attorneys took the same line as had Clarence Darrow in defending Leopold and Loeb. These similarities combined to erode confidence in the belief that capital laws would deter potential ransomers, at least of the type represented by Leopold and Loeb and Noel. Indeed, a New Jersey appellate court overturned Noel's death sentence on the ground that to put a madman to death would have no deterrent effect on others. As in the Franks case, no legislative action resulted from the Daly case.

In 1927, the ransoming of the two-year-old daughter of a city commissioner of Chattanooga, Tennessee, contained several elements that should have released the frustration and cynicism created by the Franks and Daly cases, via a torrent of law creating. The victim in the Frazier case was the white, female child of a politically prominent father. The offender was black, and the victim had been drugged and released partially disrobed; neither of these factors escaped media coverage of the case. Reactions from several sectors were intense: talk of lynching was widespread; the city government offered a $5,000 reward for the capture of the offender, dead or alive. Bills were introduced in the Tennessee legislature to increase the maximum penalty of twenty years' imprisonment provided in the 1901 legislation (created in reaction to the Cudahy case) to death. The bills passed the senate, but died in the Tennessee house.

The lack of law creation in reaction to the Frazier case is significant, because it illustrates, for this period, the inapplicability of consensus models of law creation, the type of model the sociological literature suggests should have been most applicable, given these conditions. The case occurred in the aftermath of the frustration and cynicism generated by the Franks and Daly cases, during which the offense-focused belief in the heinousness of ransom kidnapping was widespread. Also widespread was the belief that the crime represented a severe threat to a most highly-valued, vulnerable possession, one that transcended class interests—children. Add the fact that the belief also was widespread that parents were helpless in the face of the threat, and we have a normative milieu which a consensus model would assess as highly conducive to law creation.

We submit that the inability of a consensus model to explain this historical situation lies in the fact that such models have focused exclusively on act-focused, normative evaluations of the heinousness of a crime. They have ignored actor-focused evaluations of the deterrability of potential offenders. Our findings suggest that the lack of widespread consensus on the latter point was primarily responsible for the lack of law creation in the 1920s.

Law creation in the 1930s. The historical version of ransom law-creating during the 1930s, popular among laymen and social scientists alike, is that the Lindbergh case was central. The worldwide outrage provoked by the crime initiated both the federal noncapital legislation and the federal capital legislation, and state legislatures merely followed suit. A consensus model of law creation clearly would seem to be the most applicable to the situation.

If the popular version were accurate, a consensus model interpretation would be the most appropriate. The popular version is not accurate, however. It is in error in several respects, not the least of which is that the Lindbergh case initiated neither the noncapital nor the capital federal legislation, despite the fact that the legislation came to be known as the Lindbergh Law. Although consensus forces were involved, the types of forces emphasized in interest-group models of law creation were much more influential in the creation of ransom legislation in the 1930s, particularly the federal laws.

Many of the inaccuracies in the popular historical version of the situation have resulted from confusing the 1932 noncapital legislation with the capital amendment in 1934. In analyzing the creation of the federal legislation, it is vital to distinguish between the two episodes. Although some of the same forces were involved in both, markedly different forces were involved in each.

The 1932 federal ransom legislation was initiated at least four months prior to the Lindbergh case. In addition, its initiation had nothing to do with the ransoming or ransom slaying of any child. In the fall of 1931, representatives of the St. Louis and Chicago chambers of commerce appealed to Congress for a federal death penalty for ransom kidnapping. Their motivation was to protect the interests of the members of the groups—their persons, the persons of members of their families, and their money.

Almost immediately, these interests came into conflict with the interests of other groups represented among the federal lawmakers: anticapital-punishment groups and political constituencies from abolitionist states; and states' rights advocates, fearing the potential of the proposed legislation for further centralization of power in the federal government. Other groups feared that the proposed legislation would subvert criminal justice by making juries hesitant to convict in capital ransom cases; criminal justice reformers argued that not only would the death penalty not deter, but that it would constitute a risk to the lives of ransom victims. Groups from within the federal judiciary, having witnessed the inundation of the courts by Prohibition violators, were not anxious to see a repetition of the experience. Fiscal conservatives in the Hoover administration argued that the federal government simply could not afford to finance the enforcement of such legislation. Finally, students of totalitarianism abroad feared the implications of the proposed legislation for the creation of a national police force. When the Lindbergh case transpired in March 1932, the battle of interests already was well developed.

The situation lends itself to an interest-group model interpretation. However, such models must be expanded beyond the heavy emphasis which they place on economic interests, in order to encompass the full range of conflicting interests actually involved in the creation of the 1932 federal legislation. In addition, the explanatory power of such models is enhanced by distinguishing between act-focused evaluations of the threat represented by the crime, and actor-focused evaluations of the deterrability of potential ransomers. The normative and actual reactions of the groups involved in the law creation process manifested both types of evaluations.

In the months preceding the Lindbergh case, the interest groups courted the support of the general public as to both the threat represented by the crime and the deterrability of potential ransomers. Their activity points to a weakness of ruling-elite models of law creation and a corresponding strength of interest-group models.

Particularly in the Marxist type of ruling-elite model favored by Richard Quinney, [6] the energy required of groups to create at least the impression of consensual support for their position is not fully appreciated. Quinney does emphasize the control of the ruling elite over the media to create a public reality of crime favorable to the elite's cause. However, he gives the impression that once the awesome powers of the ruling elite are mobilized, the winning of the public to the elite's version of reality is rather automatic. Our findings suggest that treating the creation of consensual support among the public as more problematic, as do interest-group models, is helpful in interpreting the creation of the federal ransom law of 1932.

Although ransom kidnapping did not become a federal capital crime until 1934, a federal death penalty was the goal of the midwestern business interests in the fall of 1931. By this time, consensus already was widespread that ransom kidnapping was a heinous crime. However, there was less consensus on two other points that were vital for attaining the consensual base needed to support the creation of the federal ransom law. The first point concerned what groups actually were threatened by the crime; the second point concerned the deterrability of potential ransom kidnappers. Proponents of federal capital legislation concentrated their efforts on both fronts.

In the months preceding the Lindbergh case, the representatives of the St. Louis and Chicago chambers of commerce, supported by business organizations and midwestern law enforcers, concentrated almost exclusively on the threat which the crime represented to the American way of life. While they might have been convinced that a threat to business represented a threat to everyone, the general public was not convinced that the threat was broad enough to warrant the federal legislative action being proposed, especially in light of the vocal resistance which had developed.

Only after the Lindbergh kidnapping in March 1932 did the proponents of federal capital legislation call up the American experience with the ransom slayings of children in the 1920s to support their cause. Senator Patterson, one of the sponsors of the proposed legislation, argued that President Hoover had acted without legislative authority in ordering federal forces into the Lindbergh case. The passage of his bill, however, would ensure that every kidnapped child got this kind of attention from the federal government, not just the children of prominent families. Representative Sumners likewise argued to his House colleagues that the prominence of the victim should not matter, and that if passed, the capital legislation would protect the poor as well as the rich.

Although the proponents of the legislation expended considerable energy toward disseminating their evaluation of the threat posed by the crime, they expended even more energy toward convincing the public that potential ransomers were deterrable. Effort on this front proceeded on the assumption that organized criminal gangs and racketeers were the main offender group responsible. The assumption was manifested in the normative reactions of the proponents of the capital law prior to the Lindbergh case, and after the case, it was manifested in the widespread opinion that the Lindbergh child had been stolen by members of the underworld. In testimony before congressional committees and in statements to the press, proponents hit hard at the point that ransom kidnapping committed by such offenders was patently deliberate and rational. A favorite contention was that the gangs were counseled by brilliant, but unscrupulous, attorneys on ways to exploit interstate transportation of the victim to avoid capture. When the press took up the cause, their normative evaluations also reflected efforts to convince the public that a federal death penalty would be an effective general deterrent. Federal lawmakers supported the deterrent efficacy argument on the floors of Congress. Representative Dyer of Missouri stated that the objective of the legislation was purely to deter kidnapping. Representative Cochran argued that if enacted, the death penalty legislation would cause future kidnappers to think deeply before repeating anything like the Lindbergh tragedy. When the bill came to the floor of the House for full debate, opponents centered their efforts primarily on the issue of deterrability of ransom kidnappers. The implications of the legislation for creating a federal police force received secondary attention. With the aid of the specter of a death penalty encouraging ransomers to kill their victims, the opposition won out, temporarily. Warning their colleagues that without a death penalty a federal ransom law would not curtail the ransoming epidemic, proponents of the provision eventually were forced to capitulate. President Hoover signed the noncapital Lindbergh Law on 22 June 1932.

As to the specific role of the Lindbergh case in the creation of the 1932 legislation, clearly the law was not initiated as part of a consensual, emotional, outburst in reaction to the case. Such reactions were important in overcoming most of the opposition to making ransom kidnapping a federal crime; however, neither the case nor the reactions to it were sufficent to overcome opposition to making ransom kidnapping a federal capital crime. The case did influence the creation of the legislation, but primarily the pace and historical timing of it. Even the nature of this type of influence, however, contradicts the popular historical version.

The Lindbergh case may have actually retarded the pace of the law-creation process, not only on the federal level, but in certain states as well. For example, in response to the personal request of Colonel Lindbergh, the New Jersey legislature agreed to postpone imminent action on the creation of a capital ransom law until the return of the child. The Judiciary Committee of the United States Senate acquiesced to a similar appeal. Apart from correcting the popular historical record, these findings also point to the influence which prominent members of the society can have on the pace of law creation, aside from their influence on the fact of law creation.

In addition to being qualitatively different from the popular historical version, the influence of the Lindbergh case on the creation of capital ransom laws by the states was more modest than popularly portrayed. Only seven of the forty-eight states had capital ransom laws at the time of the Lindbergh case. Add the seven jurisdictions in which the death penalty for all crimes had been abolished, and thirty-four states remain which could have created capital ransom laws in reaction to the case. Of this number, death penalty legislation was introduced only in five states, and became law only in one, as a direct reaction to the Lindbergh case. The most common legislative reaction was increasing the threatened punishment for ransom kidnapping, but to a level short of death.

The 1934 capital amendment of the federal law involved a different constellation of law-creation forces and calls for the application of different law-creation models. In addition, it, too, had little to do with the Lindbergh case. To the extent that the capital amendment was a direct response to any specific cases, it was to the ransoming and entombment in the Arizona desert of the Robles child in April 1934 and the ransom harming of wealthy California businessman, William F. Gettle, in May 1934. Both cases were cited prominently on the floor of Congress in support of the legislation.

The findings suggest that even the Robles and Gettle cases merely hastened the pace of the capital amendment. The more important forces were the Roosevelt administration's federal war on kidnapping and racketeering and, as a vital component of this crime control effort, the bureaucratic needs of the FBI. That ransom kidnapping spawned the Federal Bureau of Investigation as we know it today is itself of significant interest; but the role played by the Department of Justice in the creation of the capital ransom law is even more significant for the sociological study of law creation.

The peak incidence of twenty-seven reported cases in 1933 went far toward validating the claim of the supporters of a federal death penalty in 1932—without threatening potential ransomers with death, federal ransom legislation would prove ineffective. The sensational nature of some of the cases and their aftermath, such as the Brooke Hart case in San Jose, served to overcome further any opposition to a federal capital law. Combined with the growing frustration over lack of progress in the Lindbergh case and the appearance in the media of the label "kidnapping epidemic," a sufficient consensual threshold was created to support radical law-creation efforts.

The consensus that developed also embraced the belief that simply threatening potential ransomers with death was not enough. Deterrent examples would have to be made of those offenders who were not deterred, and to accomplish this goal, a federal enforcement and prosecution capability had to be facilitated by lawmakers. Federal officials did a good deal to strengthen consensus on this point. The attorney general asked for public support for the federal crime war in a national radio broadcast. Other members of the Roosevelt administration appeared before assemblages of law enforcement officials and state executives on the same mission. The Department of Justice missed few opportunities to point out how burdensome it was for the department to have to send federal prosecutors to assist in state capital prosecutions. The lack of sufficient enforcement powers and resources for the special division created in 1933 within the Department of Justice, specifically to combat ransom kidnapping, also was cited widely in support of additional federal ransom legislation. The receptiveness of the social audience to such pleas indicated the extent to which consensual support for federal legislative action now existed.

A consensual threshold of this type had been lacking in 1932. Even if it had been present, it is doubtful that the Hoover administration was aggressive enough to have exploited it. This was not the case when the Roosevelt administration took over in 1933. As stated by two historians of the depression: "[T]he day of the demagogue and primitive panacea had arrived." [7] This observation was made of the economic situation of the period, but it had equal applicability to the crime control situation.

In the creation of the federal ransom legislation in 1932, the death penalty provision had been the center of a highly publicized controversy. The law-creation process which spawned the death penalty amendment in 1934 differed in several respects. The death penalty bill did not come to public attention until relatively late in the legislative process, and then it was all but lost among the host of bills comprising the crime-war legislation. A crucial difference was that the death penalty amendment was initiated by the Department of Justice and had the full backing of the president. Congressional supporters merely had to contend with the remnants of the 1932 opposition. Debate on the death penalty bill was modest compared to the 1932 situation, and what there was received scant coverage in the national press.

The consensus model and interest-group model forces described above tell us something about the creation of the death penalty amendment in 1934, but the forces outlined in Austin Turk's model of legalization,[8] in which the bureaucratic interests of law enforcement agencies are emphasized, tell us more. From the examples he provides, Turk gives the impression that he did not intend his model for the interpretation of capital law creation. The fact that our findings suggest such an application increases the interpretive scope of his model.

Turk proposed that although law creation can occur independently of the empire-building desires of law enforcement bureaucracies, such desires can be a major force in law creation. More importantly, the creation of criminal laws can legitimate, after the fact, the agency's investment of resources and energies to control a threatening behavior prior to direct legislative authority. Turk proposed that escalation in the investment of such resources proceeds through several distinct levels prior to formal law creation: giving new meanings to existing legal powers in order to extend their application to the behavior; developing working norms among enforcers toward the same end; reorganizing and reallocating resources within the agency; creating written procedural rules defining how existing laws are to be interpreted and implemented toward controlling the behavior; and mobilizing budget, manpower, and materiel for detecting and sanctioning violators.

Several actions on the part of federal enforcers toward controlling ransom kidnapping, prior to the 1934 legislation, are documented in the historical data. A common practice was the use of the 1932 enforcement powers to apprehend ransomers suspected of transporting their victims across state lines, to charge them with violation of federal postal laws, and then to hold the charges in abeyance if the chances looked good for a conviction in a state capital trial. Sending federal prosecutors to assist in such state prosecutions is another example; the creation of a special prosecution staff in the Department of Justice to render such assistance indicates a major investment of resources. The speed with which Division of Investigation agents entered ransom cases, despite the seven-day waiting period required by the 1932 legislation, suggests the development of the type of working norms among enforcers mentioned in Turk's model.

On a grander scale, the need for the 1934 legislation to legitimate the major investment of federal resources in controlling ransom kidnapping is indicated in press reports of the period. Dated 21 July 1933 and headlined "Roosevelt Orders

War on Kidnapping by Federal Forces: Cummings is Instructed to Increase Agents and Push Fight on Racketeers: 'Super-Police' in Wind," a front-page story in the *Times* quoted Attorney General Cummings as follows: "We intend to spend as much money as needed and when needed to fight kidnapping and punish criminals." The story went on to report Cummings's plans for expanding the Bureau of Investigation, for diverting some of the manpower of the Prohibition Bureau to the Bureau of Investigation, and the attorney general's assurance that the enlarged force "will devote itself chiefly to interstate crime such as kidnapping." *Nine days later*, it was announced that a new division in the Department of Justice, under the directorship of J. Edgar Hoover, would include the present Bureaus of Investigation, Identification, and Prohibition, and would "conduct the nation-wide warfare against racketeers, kidnappers and other criminals." [9]

That the FBI had vested bureaucratic interests in the creation of the 1934 kidnapping legislation is clear. That the interests focused on such bureaucratic goals as taking over the functions of other agencies, acquiring new functions, and justifying increased budgets is also clear. The satisfaction of such bureaucratic needs was not tied directly to the creation of the death penalty amendment. However, the fact that the amendment was created as a vital component of the federal war legislation, to which the satisfaction of the needs was tied, supports an indirect, yet no less important, link between bureaucratic needs and the creation of a capital law.

The creation of ransom laws on the state level during the period involved more than merely following the lead of federal legislators. In addition, consensus model forces, rather than interest-group and bureaucratic forces, appeared to have played the dominant role. State legislators reacted much more directly and quickly to the widespread belief that the 1932 federal legislation was not effective in deterring ransom kidnappers and to the perception that the country was experiencing a ransom kidnapping epidemic.

A good deal of law creation in the states preceded the 1934 federal legislation by several months. In 1933, legislators in twenty-three states were considering, debating, or passing laws to strengthen existing penalties for ransom kidnapping. The belief in the deterrent efficacy of such punishment threats was extensive. Thus primed, ransomings of prominent citizens in the state, in the region, or if prominent enough, thousands of miles distant, were sufficient to trigger the creation of ransom laws. Although the still-unsolved Lindbergh case was a force in priming the legislators, it took other cases to trigger law creation. This pattern followed from the Boettcher case in Denver, which prompted the creation of ransom laws in Colorado, Montana, and Utah. The pattern was repeated by other cases in triggering the creation of ransom laws in New York, California, Ohio, and Texas.

Several state legislatures did create ransom laws after the federal capital amendment in 1934, but in these instances, too, the process cannot be explained as a reflex response to the federal action. The pattern continued to be the triggering of law creation by specific ransomings other than the Lindbergh case. The law-creation activity in 1937, in reaction to the Mattson case of Tacoma, Washington, is illustrative. This episode more than any other most closely approximates the consensus model of Sutherland (1950), which emphasizes the role of irrationality and panic in the creation and diffusion of criminal laws. Several months prior to the Mattson case, federal officials had assured the general public that the federal crime war had vanquished ransom kidnapping in America. The absence of ransomings in the interim before the Mattson case validated the assurances. When the ransom slaying of the Mattson child took place, it severely rattled the confidence of the social audience in such assurances, and raised the specter of another ransom epidemic. The legislative activity of 1937 was the direct result.

Conclusion

The creation of criminal law in America has been a complicated social process. Viewing the process from a societal reaction perspective, combined with a sociohistorical method, highlights the complexity. The forces involved in the creation of just the

single type of criminal law studied here varied among jurisdictions, historically, and even within relatively concise historical periods. In certain episodes, consensus-based models of law
creation are more applicable. In other episodes, conflict-
oriented models more accurately portray the empirical reality.
These findings support the position that the creation of criminal
laws in America has involved a mixture of consensus and conflict forces. The findings call into question a practice prevalent
among sociologists both of radical and of conservative persuasions—that of championing a particular type of model as applicable to the creation of criminal law in general in American
society.

The lack of attention by radical scholars to the creation of
laws in which consensus forces should be found to predominate
has weakened the radical position. Our findings demonstrate
that the creation of ransom kidnapping laws at both the state
and federal levels consistently involved some conflict-model
forces, and in some crucial instances involved a predominance
of such forces—the influence of the Midwest business interests
on the creation of the 1932 federal legislation, the influence
of the bureaucratic needs of the FBI on the creation of the
1934 legislation, and the effect of the upper-class status of
victims as a determinant of reactions from the legislative sector
throughout the hundred years studied. Such findings surely are
as persuasive as those which document the influence of interest-
group, bureaucratic-need, and ruling-elite forces on the creation
of drug, gambling, alcohol, and prostitution laws.

Notes

Index

Notes

Preface

1. Hugo Adam Bedau, ed., *The Death Penalty in America: An Anthology,* rev. ed. (Chicago: Aldine Publishing Co., 1968), pp. 57–58.

2. Hank Messick and Burt Goldblatt, *Kidnapping: The Illustrated History* (New York: Dial Press, 1974), p. v.

3. Bedau, *The Death Penalty,* p. 57.

4. In recent years, the *Times* has updated the *Index* for some of the years in the latter period.

5. In the early 1950s, law enforcement authorities requested the press to delay news of ransom kidnappings until after the fate of the victim had been determined. Later in the decade, legislation was introduced in some states to make it a misdemeanor for newspapers or broadcasters to give detailed accounts of ransom notes. Such efforts were unsuccessful for the most part, but the media tended to comply voluntarily. As a result, in all but the most sensational cases, the amount of highly detailed information about ransom kidnapping cases declined after this period.

6. In 1972, the Bell and Howell Corporation began publication of an index covering several major American newspapers. For studies of crime and criminal justice, however, the index has limited value. Toward minimizing the negative effect which newspaper publicity can have on the chance of ex-offenders' becoming reintegrated into society, and to guard against infringement of due process, newspaper reports of criminal proceedings are indexed only under certain conditions. The accused must be a prominent individual, such as a politician or government official, whose alleged offense is related to his official duties, and the nature of the offense attracts national publicity. Toward the same ends, the victims of crimes are not indexed, unless the victim is killed or the victim and the crime are both significant.

7. Sidney H. Aronson, "Obstacles to a Reapproachment between

History and Sociology: A Sociologist's View," in *Interdisciplinary Relationships in the Social Sciences,* ed. Muzafer Sherif and Carolyn W. Sherif (Chicago: Aldine Publishing Co., 1969), p. 296.

8. See Rita Bachmuth, S. M. Miller, and Linda Rosen, "Juvenile Delinquency in the Daily Press," *Alpha Kappa Delta* 30 (Spring 1960): 47–51; Herbert M. Danzger, "Civil Rights Conflict and Community Power Structure," (Ph.D diss., Columbia University, 1968); Danzger, "Validating Conflict Data," *American Sociological Review* 40 (October 1975): 570–84; Gaye Tuchman, "The News Manufacture of Sociological Data (Comment on Danzger, *ASR,* October 1975)," *American Sociological Review* 41 (December 1976): 1065–67; Danzger, "Reply to Tuchman," *American Sociological Review* 41 (December 1976): 1067–70.

9. Danzger, "Reply to Tuchman," p. 1070.

10. The format for abstracting the data on each case is as follows:

I. FACTS OF CASE

    a. Name of victim(s)
    b. Name of offender(s)
    c. Date of offense
    d. Place of offense
    e. Description of offense covering elements of planning, taking of victim, transporting of victim, sequestering of victim, demanding of ransom, retrieval of ransom, disposition of victim, escape of offender.

II. SOCIOECONOMIC AND BIOGRAPHICAL INFORMATION ON ACTORS

    a. Age of victim
    b. Sex of victim
    c. Race of victim
    d. Fate of victim (unharmed, harmed, killed)
    e. Prior criminal record, if any
    f. Social-political prominence of victim and/or victim's family (With the exception of fate, and the addition of whether the offender was a member of an organized crime gang, the same information was abstracted on the offender.)

III. CRIMINAL JUSTICE PROCESS INFORMATION

    a. Date of arrest
    b. Place of arrest
    c. Arresting officials (local, state, federal) and description of involvement of each level
    d. Nature of charges and jurisdiction under which charges brought (state and/or federal)
    e. Date, place, and nature of preliminary legal actions, e.g., arraignments, preliminary hearings, grand jury action
    f. Date, place, and nature of trial
    g. Outcome of trial(s) (verdict)
    h. Date, place, and nature of sentencing
    i. Date, place, and nature of imprisonment and/or execution
    j. Date, place, and nature of appeals, if any

IV. REACTIVE SECTOR INFORMATION *(full descriptions including exact wording of statements and documents)*

    a. Mass media sector
    b. General public sector
    c. Legislative sector
    d. Law enforcement sector
    e. Judicial sector
    f. Political sector
    g. Other sectors (e.g., religious, scientific, etc.)

For cases in which data provided by the *New York Times* were insufficient to provide the information called for, a search was made of available microfilmed files of other newspapers located closer to the scene of the incident. Concerning the reaction sector questions, however, attempts were made to go beyond the *New York Times* only to get more details about reactions reported in the *Times*. This procedure was followed in order to keep the data on reactions as constant as possible throughout the period studied.

Introduction: A Sociological and Historical Perspective

1. Jack P. Gibbs, *Social Control,* Warner Module Publications, Module 1 (1972), p. 3.

2. Ian Taylor, Paul Walton, and Jock Young, *New Criminology,* p. 140.

3. "A Rationale of the Law of Kidnapping," *Columbia Law Review* 53 (1953): 540.

4. *American Jurisprudence 2d State and Federal,* 2:161.

5. Sutherland and Cressey cited kidnapping as "a legal entity which is not a sociologically homogeneous unit" and identified ten "sociologically significant types": kidnapping as a basis for the slave trade; impressing of men into formal naval service; shanghaiing of men onto ships; kidnapping of women for commercial prostitution (White Slavery); ransom kidnapping of underworld leaders by other members of the underworld; kidnapping of wealthy members of the upperworld by members of the underworld for purposes of ransom; kidnapping related to a hostage situation, as in bank robbery; kidnapping of children by persons wanting a child of their own; and also illegal arrest and the child custody situation. See Edwin H. Sutherland and Donald R. Cressey, *Principles of Criminology,* 7th ed. (Philadelphia: J. B. Lippincott Co., 1966), pp. 298–99.

6. Gibbs, "Social Control," pp. 3–4.

7. Franklin E. Zimring and Gordon J. Hawkins, *Deterrence: The Legal Threat in Crime Control* (Chicago: University of Chicago Press, 1973), p. 1.

8. Taylor, Walton, and Young, *New Criminology,* pp. 168–69.

9. See Ralph Milliband, *The State in Capitalist Society* (New York: Basic Books, 1969); William J. Chambliss, *Crime and the Legal Process* (New York: McGraw-Hill, 1968); Austin T. Turk, *Legal Sanctioning and Social Control,* Monograph Series, National Institute of Mental Health, Center for Studies of Crime and Delinquency (Washington, D.C.: U.S. Government Printing Office, 1972); Gibbs, "Social Control."

10. Richard Quinney, *The Social Reality of Crime* (Boston: Little, Brown and Co., 1970), p. 285.

11. Gregg v. Georgia, 19 Cr. L. 3310 (U.S., 30 June 1976).

12. Taylor, Walton, and Young, *New Criminology,* p. 273.

13. James A. Inciardi, "Vocational Crime," in *Handbook of Criminology,* ed. Daniel Glaser (Chicago: Rand McNally Publishing Co., 1974), p. 353; Marshall B. Clinard and Richard Quinney, *Criminal Behavior Systems: A Typology* (New York: Holt, Rinehart and Winston, 1967), p. 20.

14. Hank Messick and Burt Goldblatt, *Kidnapping: The Illustrated History* (New York: Dial Press, 1974).

15. Rex A. Collings, "Offenses of Violence against the Person," *Annals of the American Academy of Political and Social Science* 339 (January 1962): 42–56.

16. Ibid., p. 53.

17. Inciardi, "Vocational Crime," p. 53.

18. "Rationale of the Law of Kidnapping," *Columbia Law Review.*

19. Collings, "Offenses of Violence," p. 52.

20. Harry Elmer Barnes and Negley K. Teeters, *New Horizons in Criminology,* 3d ed. (Englewood Cliffs, N. J.: Prentice-Hall, 1959), p. 71.

21. Collings, "Offenses of Violence," p. 53.

22. Inciardi, "Vocational Crime," p. 353.

23. Hugo Adam Bedau, ed., *The Death Penalty in America: An Anthology,* rev. ed. (Chicago: Aldine Publishing Co., 1968), pp. 13–14.

24. Jerome Hall, *Theft, Law and Society,* rev. ed. (Indianapolis: Bobbs-Merrill Co., 1952).

25. Edwin H. Sutherland, "The Diffusion of Sexual Psychopath Laws," *American Journal of Sociology* 56 (September 1950): 142–48.

26. Clarence Ray Jeffery, "The Development of Crime in Early English Society," *Journal of Criminal Law, Criminology and Police Science* 47 (March–April 1957): 647–66.

27. Alfred R. Lindesmith, "Federal Law and Drug Addiction," *Social Problems* 7 (Summer 1959): 48–57.

28. Edwin M. Schur, "Drug Addiction in America and England," *Commentary* 30 (September 1960): 241–48; Troy Duster, *The Legislation of Morality: Laws, Drugs, and Moral Judgement* (New York: Free Press, 1970).

29. William J. Chambliss, "A Sociological Analysis of the Law of Vagrancy," *Social Problems* 11 (Summer 1964): 67–77.

30. Kai T. Erikson, *Wayward Puritans* (New York: John Wiley & Sons, 1966).

31. Joseph Gusfield, *Symbolic Crusade: Status Politics and the American Temperance Movement* (Urbana: University of Illinois Press, 1963); Donald T. Dickson, "Bureaucracy and Morality: An Organizational Perspective on a Moral Crusade," *Social Problems* 16 (Fall 1968): 143–56; Andrew Sinclair, "The Law of Prohibition," in *Crime and Justice in Society,* ed. Richard Quinney (Boston: Little, Brown & Co., 1969), pp. 69–87.

32. Anthony Platt, *The Child-Savers: The Invention of Delinquency* (Chicago: University of Chicago Press, 1969); Edwin M. Lemert, *Social Action and Legal Change: Revolution within the Juvenile Court* (Chicago: Aldine Publishing Co., 1970).

33. Pamela Roby, "Politics and Criminal Law: Revision of the New York State Penal Law on Prostitution," *Social Problems* 17 (Summer 1969): 83–109.

34. W. G. Carson, "The Sociology of Crime and the Emergence of Criminal Laws: A Review of Some Excursions into the Sociology of Law," in *Deviance and Social Control,* ed. Paul Rock and Mary McIntosh (London: Tavistock Publications, 1974), p. 71.

35. William J. Chambliss, ed., *Criminal Law in Action* (Santa Barbara: Hamilton Publishing Company, 1975), p. 5.

36. Ronald L. Akers and Richard Hawkins, eds., *Law and Control in Society* (Englewood Cliffs, N.J.: Prentice-Hall, 1975), p. 45.

37. Chambliss, *Criminal Law in Action,* p. 6; William Graham Sumner, *Folkways* (Boston: Ginn, 1906); Jerome Hall, *General Principles of Criminal Law* (Indianapolis: Bobbs-Merrill Co., 1947), p. 1, as cited by Chambliss, *Criminal Law in Action,* p. 5; Talcott Parsons, "The Law and Social Control," in *Law and Sociology, Exploratory Essays,* ed. William M. Evan (New York: Free Press of Glencoe, 1962).

38. Wolfgang Friedmann, *Law in a Changing Society* (Berkeley: University of California Press, 1959), p. 165, quoted in Richard Quinney, *Criminal Justice in Society* (Boston: Little, Brown & Co., 1969), p. 23.

39. Sutherland, "Sexual Psychopath Laws."

40. Peter H. Rossi et al., "The Seriousness of Crimes: Normative Structure and Individual Differences," *American Sociological Review* 39 (April 1974): 224–37.

41. Svend Ranulf, *Moral Indignation and Middle Class Psychology* (New York: Schocken, 1964); Kai T. Erikson, *Wayward Puritans: A Study in the Sociology of Deviance* (New York: John Wiley & Sons, 1966).

42. Erikson, *Wayward Puritans.*

43. Gusfield, *Symbolic Crusade.*

44. Becker, *Outsiders;* Lindesmith, "Federal Law and Drug Addiction"; Duster, *Legislation of Morality.*

45. Edwin M. Schur, *Crimes without Victims* (Englewood Cliffs, N.J.: Prentice-Hall, 1965).

46. Chambliss, *Criminal Law in Action,* pp. 5–6.

47. Turk, *Legal Sanctioning.*

48. Ibid.

49. Lindesmith, "Federal Law and Drug Addiction."

50. Quinney, *Crime and Justice in Society; Social Reality of Crime;* William J. Chambliss and Robert B. Seidman, "Poverty and the Criminal Process," in *Problems of Industrial Society,* ed. William J. Chambliss (Reading, Mass.: Addison-Wesley Publishing Co., 1973).

51. Quinney, *Social Reality of Crime,* pp. 43–44.

52. Georg Rusche and Otto Kirchheimer, *Punishment and Social Structure* (New York: Russell and Russell, 1939); Taylor, Walton, and Young, *New Criminology;* Richard Quinney, "Crime Control in Capitalist Society: A Critical Philosophy of Legal Order," *Issues in Criminology* 8 (Spring 1973); "There's a Lot of Folks Grateful to the Lone Ranger," *Insurgent Sociologist* 4 (Fall 1973); *Critique of Legal Order: Crime Control in Capitalist Society* (Boston: Little, Brown & Co., 1973).

53. Akers and Hawkins, *Law and Control,* p. 48.

54. Quinney, *Critique of Legal Order,* pp. 15–16.

55. Ibid., p. vi.

56. Ibid., pp. 86–87.

57. Jerome Hall, "Theft, Law and Society: The Carrier's Case," in Chambliss, *Crime and the Law in Action.*

58. "The Law of Vagrancy," in Chambliss, *Criminal Law in Action.*

59. Ibid., p. 34.

Chapter 1: Ransom Kidnapping in the Nineteenth and Early Twentieth Centuries: 1874–1919

1. *New York Times,* 17 August 1897, p. 1.

2. Ibid., 21 December 1900, p. 1.

3. Ibid., 26 December 1900, p. 1.

4. Ibid.
5. Ibid., 24 March 1909, p. 1.
6. Ibid., 3 April 1907, p. 1.
7. Ibid., 19 March 1909, p. 1.
8. Ibid., 22 March 1909, p. 2.
9. Ibid., 25 March 1909, p. 2.
10. Ibid., 24 March 1909, p. 2.
11. Ibid., 6 April 1909, p. 18.
12. Ibid., 31 August 1911, p. 2.
13. Ibid.
14. Ibid., 12 June 1917, p. 5.

Chapter 2: Slain Children and Unharmed Businessmen: 1920–32

1. *New York Times,* 9 June 1920, p. 9.
2. Ibid., 4 August 1920, p. 8.
3. Ibid., 21 November 1920, sec. 2, p. 1.
4. Ibid., 4 June 1921, p. 1.
5. Ibid., 21 October 1923, sec. 2, p. 4.
6. Ibid., 1 June 1924, p. 1.
7. Ibid.
8. Ibid., 2 June 1924, pp. 1, 3.
9. Ibid., 11 September 1924, p. 1.
10. Ibid., 16 September 1924, p. 8.
11. Ibid.
12. Ibid., 11 September 1924, p. 2.
13. Ibid.
14. Ibid., 12 September 1924, p. 19.
15. Ibid., 11 September 1924, p. 2.
16. Ibid.
17. Ibid., 29 March 1927, p. 1.
18. Ibid., 19 December 1927, p. 4.
19. Ibid., 23 December 1927, p. 4.
20. Ibid.
21. Ibid., 29 December 1927, p. 4.

22. Ibid., 24 September 1928, p. 1.

23. Ibid., 17 March 1928, p. 1.

24. Ibid., 9 April 1928, p. 23.

25. *St. Louis Post-Dispatch,* 26 February 1930, sec A, p. 3.

26. Ibid., 11 November 1931, p. 32.

27. Ibid., 3 January 1932, p. 3.

28. Ibid., 5 February 1932, p. 42.

29. *Kidnapping Hearings on H.R. 5657 before House Judiciary Committee,* 72d Cong., 1st Sess., at p. 1 (26 February 1932).

30. Ibid., p. 6.

31. Ibid., p. 7.

32. Ibid.

33. Ibid., pp. 7–8.

34. Ibid., p. 12.

35. Ibid., p. 13.

36. Ibid., p. 14.

37. *New York Times,* 26 February 1932, p. 20.

38. The data on kidnapping for ransom legislation was compiled from two sources: the *Congressional Record* (House), 72d Cong., 1st Sess. (75 *Cong. Rec.* 13285-86 [daily ed. 17 June 1932]); and an Associated Press summary which appeared in the *New York Times,* 4 March 1932, p. 8. The latter source contained several errors.

39. *New York Times,* 2 March 1932, p. 1.

40. Ibid.

41. Ibid.

42. Ibid.

43. Ibid.

44. Ibid., 4 March 1932, p. 10.

45. 75 *Cong. Rec.* 5267–68 (1932).

46. 75 *Cong. Rec.* 5385–86 (1932).

47. Ibid., 14 May 1932, p. 2.

48. Ibid., p. 1.

49. Ibid., 19 May 1932, p. 4.

50. S. Rep. No. 765, 72d Cong., 1st Sess., 1–2 (1932).

51. 75 *Cong. Rec.* 12399 (1932).

52. Ibid.

53. *New York Times,* 1 July 1932, p. 3.

Chapter 3: The Federal War on Ransom Kidnapping: 1933-39

1. *New York Times,* 14 February 1933, p. 3.
2. Ibid., 27 July 1933, p. 4.
3. *New York Times,* 1 August 1933, p. 2. Other legislation recommended by the governor would make it a felony to refuse to divulge to the proper authorities any information concerning the crime or the whereabouts of the kidnapper or victim; would prohibit the use of the right against self-incrimination to avoid giving testimony, with the understanding that no prosecution would follow on the basis of such testimony; would require prosecutors to bring an indicted kidnapper to a speedy trial and shorten the time within which an appeal must be brought; and would amend the penalty for kidnapping for ransom to provide an optional death sentence if the victim had not been returned alive before the beginning of the trial.
4. Ibid.
5. Ibid., 3 August 1933, p. 4.
6. Ibid., 12 July 1933, p. 3.
7. Ibid., 14 July 1933, p. 3.
8. Ibid., 21 July 1933, p. 8.
9. Ibid., 7 August 1933, p. 1.
10. Ibid., 20 July 1933, p. 1.
11. Ibid., 15 August 1933, p. 3.
12. Ibid., 12 September 1933, p. 3.
13. Ibid., 9 August 1933, p. 9.
14. Ibid., 12 August 1933, p. 26.
15. Ibid., 9 August 1933, p. 9.
16. Ibid., 15 August 1933, p. 3.
17. Ibid., 17 November 1933, p. 3.
18. Ibid., 17 December 1933, p. 12.
19. 78 *Cong. Rec.* 448-49 (1934).
20. Ibid., pp. 455-56.
21. Ibid., p. 454.
22. *New York Times,* 19 January 1934, p. 1.
23. Ibid., 20 January 1934, p. 3.
24. Ibid., 21 January 1934, p. 3.
25. Ibid., 23 January 1934, p. 3.

26. Ibid., 4 February 1934, p. 3.

27. Ibid., 4 May 1934, p. 1.

28. H. R. Rep. No. 1457, 73d Cong., 2d Sess. (1934).

29. *New York Times,* 16 May 1934, p. 5.

30. A number of arrests were made by federal agents during the remainder of 1934 and into 1935, but all suspects were released, even those against whom federal indictments had been obtained. When one of the suspects was arrested in November 1934, J. Edgar Hoover expressed relief that he could mark the case closed. A federal grand jury, however, eventually dismissed the charges against the suspect. The case continued until December 1936 when a grand jury closed the federal investigation of the case by finding that the government did not have sufficient evidence to convict anyone. The response of the Department of Justice was to strike the case from its records, thus preserving its batting average against kidnappers.

31. The other bills signed into law by the president made it a federal offense to use the telephone, telegraphy, oral message, and the like, in kidnapping cases; to cross state lines to avoid prosecutions; and to assault a federal officer.

32. *New York Times,* 13 February 1935, p. 1.

33. Ibid., 9 January 1935, p. 42.

34. Ibid., 16 January 1935, p. 1.

35. Cabell Phillips, *New York Times Chronicle of American Life: From the Crash to the Blitz 1929–1939* (New York: The New York Times Co., 1969), p. 325.

36. Gooch v. United States, 297 U.S. 124, 56 S. Ct. 395 (1936).

37. *New York Times,* 13 January 1937, p. 4.

Chapter 4: Decline, Dormancy, and Resurgence: 1940–74

1. *New York Times,* 3 January 1946, p. 24.

2. Ibid., 12 July 1956, p. 51.

3. H. R. Rep. No. 2763, 84th Cong., 2d Sess. 2–3 (1956).

4. *New York Times,* 5 October 1969, p. 50.

5. Ibid., 13 January 1967, p. 1.

6. On the evening of January 16, two black males in their early twenties embarked upon a series of bizarre kidnappings, the motiva-

tion for which was variously described as a black power attempt to exchange the politically prominent victims for Angela Davis, under indictment for murder in California (*New York Times,* 30 January 1971, p. 25) or to ransom several of the wealthiest residents of the little tobacco town of Bennettsville, South Carolina (*New York Times,* 19 January 1971, p. 19). Beginning with the abduction from their home of a local barber, his wife, and four children and driving away with them in the family's van, the abductors drove to the home of a state senator. The senator was not at home, but his wife was abducted and forced into the van. The next stop was the home of a state representative at which no member of the family could be located. One of the abductors then forced his way into the home of a neighbor, a former state representative; the neighbor got his gun and during the scuffle, the abductor was mortally wounded. His accomplice, waiting outside in the van with the hostages, fled but was arrested by local authorities the next day. The offender, wounded during the escapade, died a short time later, and his accomplice was prosecuted by South Carolina.

7. National Commission on Reform of Federal Criminal Laws, "Final Report to the President and Congress" (Washington, D.C.: U.S. Government Printing Office, 1971).

8. *New York Times,* 8 January 1971, p. 1.

9. Furman v. Georgia, 11 Cr. L. 3231 (U.S., 29 June 1972).

10. Ibid., p. 3257.

11. *New York Times,* 30 June 1972, p. 1.

12. *Washington Post,* 25 February 1973, sec. A, p. 18.

13. *New York Times,* 9 December 1973, p. 92.

14. Ibid.

15. Ibid.

16. Ibid., 25 September 1974, p. 34.

17. Ibid., 31 January 1974, p. 21.

18. Ibid., 22 February 1974, p. 1.

19. Ibid., 22 February 1974, p. 1.

20. Ibid., 16 March 1974, p. 42.

21. Ibid., 28 February 1974, p. 16.

22. Ibid., 13 March 1974, p. 29.

23. Ibid.

24. Ibid., 10 April 1974, p. 82.

25. *Miami Herald,* 19 July 1974, sec. B, p. 4.

Chapter 5: The Crime, Societal Reaction, and Law Creation

1. Of the 236 cases reported in the *Times* from 1874 through 1974, it was possible to ascertain the sex of the victim and whether the victim was eighteen years of age or older, in every case; race in 85 percent of the cases; and socioeconomic class in 85 percent.

The reported occupation of the victim was used to determine socioeconomic class. In those cases in which the victims were children residing at home or were spouses, the socioeconomic class assigned was that of the head of the household. A four-category index of socioeconomic class was used: upper class—victims reported in the press as wealthy or as owners or top executives of large business enterprises; middle class—victims identified as small business owners, middle level managers, white-collar employees, or members of the professions not reported as wealthy; working class—victims identified as tradesmen, employed in lower-level supervisory or white-collar jobs, or as skilled blue-collar workers; and lower class—victims identified as day laborers or as impoverished, chronically unemployed, drifters, or itinerants. The same classification was applied to the socioeconomic position of offenders.

2. In addition to the victim characteristics, the novelty of the crime, the sheer volume of the crime, and the social identity of the offenders were examined as possible determinants of societal reaction. For the offenders, data were gathered on the following characteristics: sex, age, race, socioeconomic class, known previous criminal record, gang membership, and expressed motivation. On each characteristic, the offender data were less complete than comparable data on victims.

3. Victims under eighteen years of age were categorized as children.

4. There were no lower-class victims involved in the reported cases. In relation to the reactions generated by cases, the critical differences were between upper-class victims as compared either with middle-class or working-class victims.

5. The critical distinction as to reactions was between harmed, and harmed or killed. In cases that did generate reactions, those in which the victims were killed consistently were over-represented to a larger extent than those in which the victims were harmed but not killed.

6. Richard Quinney, *Critique of Legal Order: Crime Control in Capitalist Society* (Boston: Little, Brown & Co., 1973).

7. Daniel Aaron and Robert Bendiner, eds., *The Strenuous Decade: A Social and Intellectual Record of the Nineteen-Thirties* (Garden City, N.Y.: Anchor Books, 1970), p. 137.

8. Austin T. Turk, *Legal Sanctioning and Social Control*, Monograph Series, National Institute of Mental Health, Center for Studies of Crime and Delinquency (Washington, D.C.: U.S. Government Printing Office, 1972).

9. *New York Times*, 30 July 1933, p. 2.

Index

Abduction: legal definition, xvi; early reports, 3

Adkins, Orville: offender in Seder case, 120, execution of, 121

Alabama: ransom laws, 19, 26, 180, 181

Alcorn, Gordon: offender in Boettcher case, 80, 101; mentioned 79

Anderson, Bella: offender in Clarke case, 14, 15

Arizona: ransomings, 61, 102, 128, 191; ransom laws, 105; mentioned, 103

Arnold, Keith: ransom slaying of, 149

Ashurst, Henry F.: in federal ransom laws, 88

Bailey, Harvey: offender in Urschel case, 84, 91; mentioned, 83, 101

Barker, Arthur: offender in Bremer case, 102, arrest of, 111; mentioned, 110

Barker, Fred: slain, 111; mentioned, 102, 110

Barker, Ma: slain, 111; mentioned, 79, 82, 100

Barrow, Addie: offender in Clarke case, 14, 15

Barrow, George: offender in Clarke case, 14, 15

Bates, Albert: offender in Urschel case, 84, 91; mentioned, 101

Black Hand: suspected in Whitla case, 26–27; ransomings, 30–34, 36, 37, 39, 40–43; New York laws on, 31, 182; and judicial sector, 177; mentioned, 171, 183

Blumer, Fred: ransoming of, 57–58

Boettcher, Charles II: ransoming of, 79–81; federal efforts in case, 82,

101; mass media sector, 173; political sector, 175; legislative sector, 177, 195; mentioned, 101

Bohn, Haskell: ransoming of, 76; arrests in, 101

Booth, Arnett: offender in Seder case, 120; execution of, 121

Bower, Benjamin: ransoming of, 60

Boyle, Helen: offender in Whitla case, 30

Boyle, James: offender in Whitla case, 30

Bremer, Edward: ransoming of, 100–101, 102, 103, arrests in 111, 116, mass media sector, 173, political sector, 175; legislative sector, 177; mentioned, 110, 116

Brownell, Herbert, Jr.: in federal kidnapping war, 129

Burger, Warren E.: in *Furman* decision, 146

California: ransomings, 3, 51, 54, 56, 85, 94, 104, 125–42 passim, 149, 152, 156, 165, 168, 170, 191; ransom laws, 50, 55, 87, 95, 105, 135–36, 144, 195; support for death penalty, 136, 144, 147; mentioned, 97, 162

Campbell, Harry: offender in Bremer case, 116; mentioned, 111

Cash, James Bailey: ransom slaying of, 121–22, public relations, 174; mentioned, 124

Celler, Emanuel: reaction to Franks case, 47; opposition to federal capital ransom law, 73–74

Centralization of power: as argument against federal ransom law, 62, 65, 67, 69, 70, 186

Chicago Association of Commerce: in creation of federal ransom law,

323362
11 0183
NOV 15 '84
MAY 3 0 1985
NOV 2 0 1985
MAR 2 0 1986
APR 1 4 1988
APR 2 3 1990
JUN 2 0 1990
AUG 1 6 200
DEC 0 2 2010
OCT 2 4 2012
MAR 0 6 2013

WITHDRAWN